Autism
Preparing for Adulthood

Patricia Howlin

London and New York

First published 1997
by Routledge
11 New Fetter Lane, London EC4P 4EE

Simultaneously published in the USA and Canada
by Routledge
29 West 35th Street, New York, NY 10001

Reprinted 1998, 2000

Routledge is an imprint of the Taylor & Francis Group

© 1997 Patricia Howlin

Typeset in Times by J&L Composition Ltd, Filey, North Yorkshire
Printed and bound in Great Britain by
TJ International Ltd, Padstow, Cornwall

British Library Cataloguing in Publication Data
A catalogue record for this book is available from the British
Library

Library of Congress Cataloging in Publication Data
A catalog record for this book is available from the Library of
Congress

ISBN 0–415–11531–0 (hbk)
ISBN 0–415–11532–9 (pbk)

Dedication

To Rosemary, with whom it all began, and to Ros and all those like her whose stories fill this book.

Contents

List of figures

List of tables

Acknowledgements

The author and publishers wish to thank Peter Gaboney for his permission to reproduce Figure 3.1.

Every effort has been made to contact all copyright holders. However, if anyone has not been contacted they should contact the publisher in the first instance.

1 Introduction

What this book is about

Autism is a life-long, often devastating, disorder that profoundly affects almost every aspect of an individual's functioning. Impairments in communication limit the ability to understand what is happening or why, and make it almost impossible effectively to control events, people or the environment. Difficulties in social understanding mean that even the simplest interactions are fraught with problems. Inability to cope with change, and the need to adhere to fixed routines and patterns of behaviour can make every-day life threatening and disturbing.

It is not surprising, therefore, that many people with autism are described as having behaviours that are challenging or disruptive.

There is no chapter in this book on Challenging Behaviour!

Instead, the problems faced by people with autism and their carers are set firmly within the context of their social, communication and obsessional impairments. Only if the profundity of these deficits is fully accepted can the behaviours of someone with autism be understood. If such behaviours are adequately understood then maybe these will be viewed, not as maladaptive or challenging, but as the individual's only effective means of making sense of or controlling a world that is unpredictable, confusing and rejecting.

The aim of this book is to foster understanding of the fundamental deficits of autism, and the impact these can have on the lives of those living with the disorder. With understanding, much can be done to help those who are affected, either directly or indirectly. Thus, whilst each chapter begins with a description of impairments and difficulties, each ends with a discussion of the strategies that can be used to help overcome or minimise these.

WHO THIS BOOK IS ABOUT

This book tells a tale of people with autism and their families. It encompasses individuals with a wide range of skills and disabilities and the examples of problems faced, and strategies implemented are all taken from real life.[1] The central focus is, however, on adults with autism rather than children, and on those of higher ability rather than those who are more severely disabled.

WHY A FOCUS ON ADULTS?

Since Kanner's initial descriptions of autism in the 1940's there has been a constant outpouring of literature on the topic. Understanding of the causes of autism, particularly the genetic links, has made significant strides (Bolton *et al*, 1994); diagnostic criteria have been greatly improved (Lord, Rutter and Le Couteur, 1994); knowledge about specific areas of deficit, especially those related to social dysfunction, has been enhanced by the work of Uta Frith and colleagues (Frith,, 1989; Happé, 1994; Baron Cohen, 1995) and there are vast numbers of books and papers on issues related to education and intervention.

The majority of this work, however, focuses on children. Relatively little has been written about the needs of adults with autism, or their families, on what can be expected in adulthood, or how the quality of life for adults with autism can be enhanced.

WHY A FOCUS ON THE MORE ABLE?

With some notable exceptions, such as the work by Eric Schopler and his colleagues, (see Schopler and Mesibov, 1983, 1992; Taylor, 1990), discussion of the issues related to autism in adult life have tended to concentrate on individuals who are less able. Intervention programmes generally focus on the challenging needs or behaviours of those who also have severe learning disabilities (Clements, 1987); most accounts of residential provision relate to those requiring high levels of support and care; even successful occupational programmes have tended to emphasise the needs of individuals who are more severely handicapped (Smith, 1990). Morgan (1996) addresses many of the problems faced by adults with autism who continue to need substantial support as they grow older and his book offers much-needed advice and guidance for carers.

Very little has been written on the needs of those who are more able, yet their difficulties in communication and social interaction, and with obsessional and ritualistic behaviours continue to persist throughout adulthood. Although many make good progress as they grow older, the impact of these deficits remains profound. Moreover, since specialist provision or training is often lacking or inappropriate for their needs, the help and support they continue to need is rarely available. They may be unable to find jobs, make friends or form close relationships. All too often they are well aware that they are 'different' and fully recognise their own limitations but they can do little to alter the fundamental deficits. There is the additional frustration of knowing that although they have skills, and sometimes very special gifts, they are unable to make use of these. Yet, apart from their families they often have no-one to whom they can turn for comfort or guidance.

The emotional distress that such awareness, frustration, and sense of failure brings is almost impossible to imagine. Often the only people who can truly empathise are parents, who because they recognise the continuing need for protection are then dismissed as 'overprotective' or 'neurotic'. Many parents, indeed, will admit to being both but they know, too, the disasters that lie in wait should they cease to provide this security.

Society's perceptions of individuals who appear to be only mildly disabled also tend to be much less sympathetic. The demands made on someone who is clearly very disabled, has little or no speech, and withdraws from social contact into a life of solitary routine, are unlikely to be excessive. But, for someone who appears 'nearly normal', who has had the benefits of a 'good' education, and who possesses considerable ability, at least in certain areas, expectations are often unrealistically high. When the adolescent or adult with autism is unable to meet these expectations they may well be faced with criticism and rejection, which in turn do little to improve their feelings of failure and low esteem.

It is for these reasons, therefore, that the central focus of this book is on those who are more able. However, because the range of ability in autism is so wide, attention is also given to the problems faced by those whose cognitive, social and linguistic abilities are more limited.

WHAT ABOUT 'ASPERGER SYNDROME'?

At much the same time that Kanner was writing about children with autism (Kanner, 1943) Asperger was describing the group of children who eventually came to be named after him (Asperger, 1944). With an ocean and a world war between them, collaboration at the time was hardly to be expected. However, as the years have gone by, the striking similarities in the two accounts have come to be widely recognised (Frith, 1991; Wing, 1981). Although there continues to be some debate about whether the two conditions are quantitatively or qualitatively different (Lord and Rutter, 1994) most well-designed research studies suggest that 'there are no substantive, qualitative differences' in either early history or outcome between children with Asperger syndrome and high-functioning children with autism (Szatmari, Bartolucci and Bremner, 1989). Asperger syndrome is generally viewed as a 'milder' form of autism and Wing, writing over 15 years ago, noted that 'Until the aetiologies of [the two] conditions are known, the term is helpful when explaining the problems of children and adults who have autistic features, but who talk grammatically and who are not socially aloof' (Wing, 1981). Aetiology still remains unclear, but formal diagnostic criteria for Asperger syndrome note that the obsessional and social-communication deficits have the same characteristics as in autism (World Health Organization, 1992). The two main distinguishing features are the presence of relatively normal cognitive skills and the lack of early language delays (see Table 1.1).

Despite earlier suggestions that motor clumsiness is another distinguishing feature of Asperger syndrome, recent research has tended to query this (Ghaziuddin *et al.* 1994). A study by Margot Prior and colleagues (Manjiviona and Prior, 1995) showed that 50 per cent of children diagnosed as having Asperger syndrome and 67 per cent of those with high-functioning autism were clumsy and they conclude that there is little evidence to differentiate the groups on this basis.

ICD-10 Research Criteria for Asperger Syndrome

A
No clinically significant general delay in language or cognitive development.
Single words present by 2 years; phrases by 3 years.
Self-help/adaptive behaviours/curiosity about environment in first 3 years normal.
Motor development may be delayed, with clumsiness evident later.

B
Qualitative abnormalities in reciprocal social interaction. **Criteria as for autism**.

C
Intense, circumscribed interests or restricted, repetitive and stereotyped patterns of behaviour, interests and activities. **Criteria as for autism** although less usual for motor mannerisms/preoccupations with parts of objects etc. to occur.

Table 1.1 ICD-10 research criteria for Asperger syndrome

When describing case examples in the present book, the terms 'high-functioning' and 'more able' have been used to describe individuals whose *current* language and cognitive functioning is relatively intact. This is because, in many cases, early diagnostic information is insufficient to make the distinction between autism and Asperger syndrome. In the case of accounts by other authors relating to Asperger syndrome, it is not always clear that diagnostic criteria are fully met, but the original terminology has been retained in reporting these studies.

APPROACHES TO INTERVENTION

Parents of children with autism are faced by a bewildering and often conflicting number of claims about the merits of different interventions. Amongst the treatments said to cure, or have a dramatic impact on outcome are holding therapy (Welch, 1988), scotopic sensitivity training (Irlen, 1995), sensory integration (Ayres, 1979), auditory integration (Stehli, 1992), drug and vitamin treatments (Rimland, 1994), music therapy (Alvin and Warwick, 1991) and facilitated communication (Biklen, 1990). Even intensive behavioural programmes have claimed to be able to cure individuals with autism (Lovaas, 1987; McEachin, Smith and Lovaas, 1993). The very titles of much of the writing (e.g. '*A Miracle to Believe in*', Kaufman, 1981; '*The Sound of a Miracle: A Child's Triumph over Autism*', Stehli, 1992) proclaim the hopes that are offered to parents, whilst promises such as the following abound:

Facilitated communication
Successful even for those 'previously presumed to be amongst the lowest intellectually functioning . . . Able to carry on high level conversations, discuss abstract thoughts and feelings and even tell jokes' (Biklen, 1990).

Holding therapy
'*All these results much better than generally claimed for other therapies . . . children lost their autistic symptoms . . . became entirely normal' (Richer and Zapella, 1989).*

Intensive behavioural treatments
Many children 'indistinguishable from their normal peers' (Lovaas, 1987).

Unfortunately, on the whole, the more extravagant the promises the more limited are the data on which they are based.

Facilitated Communication, for example, has been the focus of many recent claims. The technique involves a Facilitator supporting the client's hand, wrist or arm whilst he or she uses a keyboard, or letter board, to spell out words, phrases or sentences. Its use with people with autism is based on the theory that many of their difficulties result from a movement disorder, rather than social or communication deficits. The Facilitator should presume that the client possesses unrecognised literacy skills, and the provision of physical support can then lead to 'Communication unbound' (Biklen, 1990).

However, in a review of the literature from 1990 to 1994 (Howlin, 1994b), in which 40 control trials of facilitated communication were identified, involving over 300 subjects, there seemed little evidence to support any such statements. The studies assessed the numbers of correct responses made by subjects *when Facilitators were unaware of the pictures or objects that were presented.* As Table 1.2 indicates, independent communication was confirmed in *under one per cent of subjects* (i.e. in over 99 per cent of cases the responses were found to come from the Facilitators, not the clients!). Even in these cases, responses were often only partially correct, and generally consisted of minimal, one-word answers. In many of the studies the proportion of correct responses was lower than might have been expected on a chance basis alone.

So far there is no evidence of any cures for autism, any more than there is for other chromosomal or genetically determined conditions, such as Fragile X or Down's syndrome. The fact that children may be

Table 1.2 Controlled trials of Facilitated Communication, 1990–94

Total studies	40
Independent communication confirmed [a]	8
No evidence of independent communication	32
Total subjects	327
Autistic/pervasive developmental disorders	238
Learning disabled (moderate to profound)	79
Other (head injury; unknown)	10
Independent communication confirmed [a]	13
No evidence of independent communication	314

Note: [a] In all cases 'confirmed' indicates minimal naming responses – usually single words; partially correct responses are also included.

able to attend normal school, or later find jobs or get married, does not mean that they are cured, nor that the treatment advocated has been responsible for their progress. Many able children do well despite totally inadequate provision, and to a great extent eventual outcome is dependent on innate cognitive, linguistic and social abilities. There is little good evidence to suggest that *long-term outcome* can be dramatically improved following the implementation of any particular intervention programme (Howlin and Rutter, 1987). That is not to suggest that appropriate treatment has no positive effects. It can make all the difference in helping to minimise or avoid secondary behavioural problems, and can have a significant impact on ensuring that children develop their existing skills to the full. The individuals will continue to be autistic, but the extent to which their social, communication and obsessional difficulties impinge on other areas of functioning, or on family life in general, can be greatly modified.

The following chapters describe the problems that adolescents and adults with autism may experience in these areas, and the sorts of strategies that may be useful in dealing with them. Problems and some solutions related to educational and occupational attainments are also discussed, as are ways of coping with psychiatric and other difficulties, and fostering independence in later life.

No magic answers are proposed; indeed many of the techniques suggested are remarkably simple. The crucial issue is that, in dealing with problems, the fundamental difficulties associated with autism need to be fully understood. Intervention can then be adapted to meet the *individual* needs of people with autism and those caring for, living or working with them. The focus is not on 'cures' or 'miracles' but on the improvement in the quality of life for all concerned.

NOTES

1 Individual characteristics and circumstances have been transposed for the sake of anonymity.

2 What becomes of adults with autism?

Until relatively recently, the vast majority of literature on autism has focused on children. There are numerous books exploring the causes of autism, the implications for families, therapeutic interventions, and training and educational programmes. In contrast, there is remarkably little written about outcome in adulthood. Moreover, when autism in adults is described, the picture is often far from reassuring. Accounts of individuals with autism are frequently found in books or reports dealing with 'challenging behaviours', leaving many families to fear that all that may be expected in adulthood is the development of aggressive, self-injurious or disruptive behaviours. On the other hand, there are impressive personal narratives, such as those by Donna Williams (1992, 1994) and Temple Grandin (Grandin and Scariano, 1986), documenting how, often against tremendous odds, individuals have fought against, and to a considerable extent overcome, their early handicaps. Occasionally, too, reports appear in the media of young people who, although remaining generally disabled, may show remarkable skill in isolated areas, such as art, music or calculations (Wiltshire, 1987; O'Connor and Hermelin, 1988).

Most individuals with autism, however, will fall into none of these categories and few families know what to expect as their children grow older. Many parents dread the onset of adolescence, fearing that this is certain to bring increased difficulties. Furthermore, reports of possible links with 'schizoid' disturbances (Wolff and Barlow, 1979; Wolff, 1991; Wolff and McGuire, 1995) may conjure up the spectre of a schizophrenic illness waiting in the wings. Almost all parents will worry about the degree of independence that can ever be attained, or the ability of their son or daughter to cope when they are no longer there to care for them.

To make matters worse, the anxieties and uncertainties of caring for a young adult with autism are frequently faced with little or no support. For, even if families did have access to appropriate resources when their child was younger, once late adolescence is reached paediatric, psychiatric or psychological services are often summarily withdrawn. The valuable informal support systems available via school teachers and other parents also tend to evaporate. There may be no-one to whom families can turn at times of stress; no-one who knows their son or daughter well; no-one to offer information or advice.

Nevertheless, information does exist which may help to allay at least some of these anxieties, and which can enable families to plan more effectively for the future. Much of this comes from studies that have followed up children with autism as they reach adolescence or adulthood. Because of the cost of long-term research, investigations of this kind are relatively few, often involve small numbers of cases and, because they tend to ask rather different questions, may produce somewhat variable findings. Despite these caveats, the findings do provide important data on the lives of adults with autism, as well as indicating ways in which outcome might be improved in future years.

THE FIRST DESCRIPTIVE STUDIES

In the mid-to-late 1950's there began to appear a number of studies reporting on the outcome for children with 'childhood psychosis' or other autistic types of disorder. It is clear that many of the subjects involved in these reports did show the characteristics of autism, but the heterogeneity of the groups, in terms of age, intellectual level, diagnosis and aetiology, meant that few conclusions could be drawn about long-term prognosis. Victor Lotter, for example, in 1978, reviewed a total of twenty-five follow-up studies of 'psychotic children', but because the majority of these suffered from serious flaws, such as inadequate diagnostic criteria, subjective reporting or very mixed subject groups, findings were difficult to interpret.

One of the earliest reports focusing on children who clearly met diagnostic criteria for autism was that of Leon Eisenberg (1956), a colleague of Leo Kanner, and one of the first writers to describe the condition in detail. Although the account is largely anecdotal, with many cases still in their early teens when assessed, Eisenberg, like many subsequent authors, illustrated the wide variety of possible outcomes. Most of the individuals described remained very dependent but about one-third were found to have made 'at least a moderate social adjustment', despite the lack of any specialist provision or treatment available at that time. A minority had managed to achieve good independence, although even amongst this group social impairments remained apparent, as in the case of the young man who, called upon to speak as a student leader at a football rally, announced (with absolute accuracy) that his team was going to lose.

In a slightly later report from Britain, Mildred Creak (1963), describes a hundred cases of 'childhood psychosis' (the term then often used for autism). Again the information is very anecdotal, and includes both adults and children, so that the longer-term outcome is unclear. Although 43 were placed in institutional care, 40 remained at home, attending school or day centres, and 17 were coping with mainstream schooling or employment.

Among the most fascinating and detailed accounts of this period, however, are those of Kanner himself. Kanner, who first described autism in detail in 1943, kept meticulous records of what happened to the children and followed up many of them into their twenties or beyond. He, too, noted the great variability in outcome, and, like Eisenberg, stressed the importance of well-developed communication skills and intellectual ability for a good prognosis. Individuals who remained mute had the least favourable outcome. Most of these remained highly dependent as they grew older, living with their parents, in sheltered communities, in state institutions for people with learning disabilities, or, in a few cases, in psychiatric hospitals. Amongst cases with better communication skills outcome was rather more positive. Just over half of this group were functioning relatively well, at home or in the community, although with varying degrees of support (Kanner and Eisenberg, 1955).

Some of the most interesting cases are those described in Kanner's account of 96 individuals, first seen before 1953, and in their twenties and thirties when followed up. Eleven of these were reported to have done remarkably well as they grew older, and were said to be 'mingling, working and maintaining themselves in society'. Kanner also notes that in the majority of these cases 'a remarkable change took place' around their mid-teens. 'Unlike most other autistic children they became uneasily aware of their peculiarities and began to make a conscious effort to do something about them.' In particular they tried to improve their interactions with their peers, often using their obsessional preoccupations or special skills 'to open a door for contact'. As adults,

> They have not completely shed the fundamental personality structure of early infantile autism but, with increasing self-assessment in their middle to late teens, they expended considerable effort to

fit themselves . . . to what they came to perceive as commonly expected obligations. They made the compromise of being, yet not appearing alone and discovered means of interaction by joining groups in which they could make use of their preoccupations . . . as shared 'hobbies' in the company of others. In the club to which they 'belonged' they received – and enjoyed – the recognition earned by the detailed knowledge they had stored up in years of obsessive rumination of specific topics (music, mathematics, history, chemistry, astronomy, wildlife, foreign languages, etc.). Rewards came to them also from their employers who remarked on their meticulousness and trustworthiness. Life among people thus lost its former menacing aspects. Nobody has shoved them forcibly through a gate which others had tried to unlock for them; it was *they* who, at first timidly and then more resolutely, paved their way to it and walked through.

(Kanner, 1973).

The following vignettes illustrate what, for some, lay on the other side of this gate.

Kanner's 'success stories'

Thomas G Found recognition by teaching astronomy and playing the piano; he also joined the Boy Scouts and swimming and athletic clubs. Despite developing grand-mal epilepsy (and neglecting to take his medication) he had a series of jobs, eventually working for a charitable organisation. Owned his own house and car, but was not interested in girls 'because they cost too much money'.

George W Interested in languages, played the violin, and was in charge of mailing books in a library. He lived with his mother but had no friends and 'girls are not interested in him'.

Fred G At university; gifted in mathematics and earned the respect of his peers through his academic ability. Drove his own car, living partly at home and partly at college.

Sally S Utilised her good memory to achieve highly at school and college. Although she failed in her attempt to become a nurse (she would stick rigidly to rules, and for example, having been told that 20 minutes was the usual time it took for breast feeding, would remove babies from their mother's breasts if they exceeded this), she later succeeded as a lab technician in a hospital. She belonged to a church singing club and lived alone. She had a 6-month relationship with a man but was 'frightened by any intimacies' and at school noted 'I don't have the same interest in boys that most girls of my age have'.

Edward F   Obtained a BA degree in history, despite initially attending a class for 'retarded children'. Had an active social life involving hiking clubs, and was much admired for his knowledge of plants and wildlife. Had his own apartment and car and had begun to date girls. Worked 'in blue-collar capacity' in horticultural research station, but was disappointed at not having a higher-level post, preferring to associate with 'educated people'.

Clarence B   Obtained a Master's degree in economics, but failed when employed in a supervisory capacity. Worked as an accountant and had his own apartment and car. His main hobby was collecting train timetables. He felt he ought to get married but 'can't waste money on a girl who isn't serious'. Remained socially awkward 'but can make superficial adjustments'.

Henry C   Enlisted in the army, and despite 'an uncontrollable urge to gamble' had several well-paying jobs, mostly as a general office worker. He lived alone 'with no desire to get tied down for a long time'.

Walter P   Worked in a restaurant as dish washer, doing well there despite his communication difficulties. He lived with his mother and was helpful at home but had no voluntary conversation.

Bernard S   Had continuing difficulties at school and junior college and eventually helped to fill shelves in his father's store. His chief interest was the streetcar museum, where he would lay tracks, paint cars and go on trips; his other main interest was politics.

Donald T   Worked as bank teller, no ambitions for promotion; had trophies for golf, and was described as a 'fair' bridge player, though lacking in initiative. Was a member of several clubs and secretary to a local church group.

Frederick W   Interested in music and bowling. Worked in an office on the photocopying machine. A letter from his Acting Director noted: 'He is an outstanding employee by any standard. Outstanding to me means dependability, reliability, thoroughness, and thoughtfulness toward fellow workers.'

Robert F (described in the earlier paper by Kanner and Eisenberg, 1955) Worked as a meteorologist in the Navy, and was married with a young son. He studied musical composition, and had works performed by chamber orchestras.

Two other cases are also noted. One, formerly attending college, could no longer be traced, and a 'gifted student of mathematics' had been killed in an accident.

Noting that 11 to 12 per cent of his original sample had done well in the absence of any specialist intervention or support, Kanner speculated that the outcome for people with autism might well improve in future years as recognition of the disorder and knowledge about appropriate educational and therapeutic facilities progressed.

Asperger's accounts

Writing at much the same time as Kanner, Hans Asperger also noted the very variable outcome amongst the individuals he studied. The least favourable outcome was for those with learning disabilities in addition to their autism, and Asperger commented that 'the fate of the latter cases is often very sad'. For those more able individuals who did make progress, it was, again, often their special skills or interests that eventually led to social integration. Asperger quotes examples of many individuals who had done remarkably well in later life, including a professor of astronomy, mathematicians, technologists, chemists, high-ranking civil servants, and an expert in heraldry. Indeed he suggests that

able autistic individuals can rise to eminent positions and perform with such outstanding success that one may even conclude that *only* such people are capable of certain achievements. It is as if they had compensatory abilities to counterbalance their deficiencies. Their unswerving determination and penetrating intellectual powers . . . their narrowness and single mindedness . . . can be immensely valuable and lead to outstanding achievements in their chosen areas.

(For an annotated translation of Asperger's
initial paper, see Frith, 1991)

Although Asperger also notes that 'in the majority of cases the positive aspects of autism do not outweigh the negative ones' his somewhat romanticised views of the benefits of autism need to be treated with some scepticism. As Uta Frith wisely comments 'There is no getting round the fact that autism is a handicap . . . It would be tragic if romantic notions of genius and unworldliness were to deprive bright autistic people of the understanding and help they need' (Frith, 1991).

There is no doubt that amongst adults of high intellectual ability, especially if this is accompanied by specialist skills or interests, many do manage to function well. Nevertheless, even if they are able to find ways of coping with their disabilities, few are successful in entirely overcoming these and virtually all individuals will remain affected to some degree throughout their lives.

AUTOBIOGRAPHICAL WRITINGS

Personal accounts offer great insight into the daily struggles faced by individuals with autism. Although they provide evidence of the successes of which individuals are capable, they also make clear the extent of the difficulties with which they have to contend. Donna Williams, now married and making an independent living though her writings, writes movingly of her journey from *Nobody Nowhere* (1992) to *Somebody Somewhere* (1994). Misunderstood, often mistreated as a child and adolescent by her teachers, her family and her peers, in adulthood her great strength and determination, the eventual support of an understanding psychologist and her contacts with individuals similarly affected have resulted in considerable personal and professional success. Her latest book concludes with the clarion call

I CAN CONTROL AUTISM . . . I WILL CONTROL IT . . .
IT WILL NOT CONTROL ME.

Yet the penultimate sentences indicate that life remains a continuing battle:

Autism tries to stop me from being free to be myself. Autism tries to rob me of a life, of friendship, of caring, of sharing, of showing interest, of using my intelligence, of being affected . . . it tries to bury me alive.

Temple Grandin, a woman in her mid-forties, has carved out for herself a successful career as an animal psychologist (see Grandin, 1995; Sacks, 1993). She travels throughout the United States, Europe,

Canada and Australia, designing livestock-handling facilities for farms and meat-packing plants. Many of her designs have been developed from the 'squeeze machines' that she first began to construct while she was at school. Although she continues to have difficulties in understanding ordinary social relationships and feelings, describing herself, in many ways, like 'an anthropologist on Mars' (Sacks, 1993) she has clearly come a long way from her confused, withdrawn, non-communicating early childhood.

There are many other, although less extensive, accounts of the personal experience of autism, such as those written by David Miedzianik (1994) and Therese Jolliffe (Jolliffe, Lansdown and Robinson, 1992). Newsletters produced by self-help or support groups also contain many first-hand accounts of the difficulties, tribulations and achievements experienced by people with autism and Asperger syndrome. These include the National Autistic Society's publication *Communication*, and newsletters produced by Asperger United and Autism Network International.

Edited writings, too, allow some access into the world of the person with autism. Jim Sinclair, a psychology graduate, was first written about by Cesaroni and Garber in 1991, but has since published his own accounts of his experiences (1992). Bemporad (1979) writes of the experiences of Jerry, a 31-year-old man originally diagnosed by Kanner, and the tale of 'Tony W', retold by Volkmar and Cohen (1985), graphically illustrates the many problems that individuals with autism may have to face throughout their lives.

Autobiographical writings by people with autism are of course fascinating, partly because they are so unusual, and partly because of what they reveal about the ways in which people with autism think and feel and understand. Nevertheless, although providing us with a rich source of information, these accounts give little indication of what happens to most people with autism as they grow older. In order to investigate this, larger-scale and long-term follow-up studies are required.

EARLY FOLLOW-UP STUDIES

Initial reports of the outcome for children with autism were, as noted above, largely anecdotal and unsystematic (Lotter, 1978). However, towards the end of the 1960's Michael Rutter and his colleagues carried out a detailed assessment of 63 individuals, initially diagnosed as autistic at the Maudsley Hospital in London in the 1950's and early 1960's. At follow-up, 38 of the group were aged 16 years or over. Of these, 2 were still at school, but of the remainder only 3 had paid jobs. Over half were placed in long-stay hospitals, 7 were still living with their parents, with no outside occupation; 3 were living in special communities and 4 attended day centres. Rutter notes that at least some of the individuals living at home or in a special community could have been capable of employment 'at least in a sheltered setting, had adequate training facilities been available'. General outcome for the adult cases in this study is not differentiated from that for the under-16s, but overall only 14 per cent of the group was said to have made a good social adjustment. Nevertheless, most individuals tended to improve with age, and although there were a number of cases who showed a worsening in certain aspects of behaviour over time 'it was rare to see marked remissions and relapses as in adult psychotic illnesses'. No significant sex differences were found, although girls were somewhat less likely to fall within the 'good' or 'very poor' outcome groups. (For details see Lockyer and Rutter, 1969, 1970; Rutter and Lockyer, 1967; Rutter, Greenfield and Lockyer, 1967.)

Although a number of other follow-up studies were conducted around this time (Mittler, Gillies and Jukes, 1966; DeMyer *et al.*, 1973) most of the individuals involved were still in their early teens, so the studies contain little information on later employment or living conditions. The first study to look specifically at outcome in an older age group was that of Victor Lotter (Lotter, 1974 a, b). Twenty-nine young people between the ages of 16 and 18 years, who had been diagnosed as autistic when younger, were assessed. In general, the findings were similar to those of Rutter and his colleagues. However, many more of the children (24 per cent) were still at school, perhaps reflecting the substantial improvements in educational provision that had occurred over the previous decade: less than half of the children seen by Rutter had received as much as two years' schooling and many had never attended school at all. Nevertheless, amongst the 22 individuals who had left school only 1 had a job, 14 were in long-stay hospitals, 2 were living at home and 5 were attending day training centres. In terms of overall social adjustment, again 14 per cent were described as having done well, although the majority were described as having a 'poor' or 'very poor' outcome. Overall, girls did less well, with none being rated as attaining either a 'good' or 'fair' outcome.

In all these early follow-up studies three particular factors were consistently related to later prognosis. The first, noted initially by

Eisenberg, was the importance of early language development. For individuals who had developed some useful speech by the age of around 5 years outcome tended to be much more favourable. Only a tiny minority of children who remained without speech after this age made significant improvements.

The degree of intellectual impairment was another crucial factor. Children who were either untestable, or who had non-verbal IQ scores below the range of 55–60, almost invariably remained highly dependent.

The third major factor was that of education. Kanner (1973) noted that admission into hospital care, rather than a school placement, was 'tantamount to a death sentence' and subsequent studies, particularly those of Rutter and Lotter, also noted the association between years of schooling and later outcome. However, since educational placement is directly affected by factors such as language and IQ, the influence of schooling, per se, on long-term functioning remains somewhat unclear.

The impact of other factors, such as the severity of autistic symptomatology, early behavioural difficulties, family factors, or the sex of the child also remains uncertain. Rutter and colleagues found no significant association between individual symptoms (apart from lack of speech) and later outcome, although there was a significant relationship with the total number of major symptoms rated. Thus, hardly surprisingly, the more severe the social and behavioural problems, the worse the ultimate outcome.

The relationship with gender is also confused. Rutter found that girls fell in neither the very good nor very poor categories, although Lotter reported that the outcome for girls was generally worse than for boys. Again the impact of intellectual level needs to be taken into account here, since there is some indication, from the studies of Catherine Lord and colleagues, that females with autism may tend to have a lower IQ than males (Lord and Schopler, 1985).

As far as family factors are concerned, whilst socio-economic factors and ratings of family adequacy may be *correlated* with outcome (DeMyer *et al.*; Lotter, 1974a), there is little evidence of a direct causal relationship between an impoverished or disruptive family background and later outcome, although, as with any other condition, disruption at home is unlikely to be beneficial.

LATER FOLLOW-UP STUDIES

Although the 1980's and 1990's witnessed a steady stream of new follow-up reports, many of these have involved subjects who were still relatively young, or have focused more specifically on high-functioning individuals, with the result that the implications for older people within the *wider* autistic spectrum remain unclear.

Chung, Luk and Lee (1990), for example, followed up 66 children attending a psychiatric clinic in Hong Kong in the decade from 1976. As in other studies, the best outcome was found for cases who had developed speech before the age of 5, and who scored more highly on tests of intellectual and social functioning. However, as only 9 cases were above 12 years old, there is no information about longer-term outcome.

Gillberg and Steffenberg (1987) report on a group of 23 individuals aged 16 or over, living in Sweden. Only one person was found to be fully self-supporting at the time of follow-up, although the authors suggest that the numbers may increase with time (only one-third of the group was then aged above 20). Of the remainder, almost half were described as functioning fairly well, but 11 individuals had a 'poor' or 'very poor' outcome. As in other studies, an IQ above 50 at initial diagnosis, and the presence of communicative speech before the age of 6 were the most important prognostic indicators. In some, but not all cases, the development of epilepsy around puberty seemed to result in a worse outcome. Again, women tended to have a 'very poor' outcome more frequently than men.

A much larger study of young adults with autism (170 male, 31 female), aged between 18 and 33, was conducted by Kobayashi and colleagues (1992) in Japan. Outcome was assessed by means of postal questionnaires to parents. The average follow-up period was fifteen years, during which time 4 cases, all male, had died (from encephalopathy, age 6; head injury from severe self-injury, age 16; nephrotic syndrome, age 20; and asthma, age 22). Almost half the group were reported as having good or very good communication skills, and over a quarter were described as having a good or very good outcome (i.e. able to live independently or semi-independently and succeeding at work or college). Women tended to have better language outcomes than men but there were no significant differences in social functioning between the sexes.

Forty-three individuals were employed, with a further 11 still attending school or college. Jobs were mostly in food and service industries, but several individuals were described as having realised 'their childhood dreams' of being a bus-conductor, car mechanic or cook. The highest level of jobs obtained were by a physiotherapist, a civil servant, a printer and 2 office workers. All but 3 of those with jobs still lived with their parents, 1 was in a group home and 2 had their own apartments; none was married.

Approximately one-fifth of the sample had developed epilepsy (usually in their early teens) but this was well controlled in all but three cases. Seventy-three families reported a marked improvement occurring in their children between the ages of around 10 to 15 years, the period when Kanner, too, had remarked on significant change. However, in 47 cases, deterioration in behaviour (such as destructiveness, aggression, self-injury, obsessionality, overactivity, etc.) was noted, and these changes also tended to occur at around early adolescence. As in earlier studies it was found that outcome in adulthood was significantly correlated with early language abilities and intellectual functioning in males. However, there was no significant correlation with early language in females, and the correlation with IQ was also small. Generally the outcome for females was less good than for males.

Although, by virtue of its size, this remains a very informative study in many ways, reliance on questionnaire data, with little or no direct contact with the autistic individuals themselves, clearly raises problems. Parents' ratings of how well their children are functioning may not always accurately reflect their true status. Moreover, diagnostic assessment of autism in the past has not always been entirely satisfactory, and hence some current confirmation of diagnosis is also required.

In a more recent study carried out at the Maudsley Hospital in London (Goode, Rutter and Howlin in preparation) parents and individuals were all interviewed independently, diagnostic criteria were reconfirmed, and detailed assessments were carried out of language, cognitive, social and academic functioning. Seventy-five individuals aged 21 or older were involved in total (62 male and 13 female), the average age being 29 years. Eight individuals were living independently, or semi-independently, but a third were still with their parents, and 40 per cent lived in sheltered communities, mostly specifically for people with autism. Ten individuals were in long-stay hospital care. Despite the fact that one-fifth had obtained some formal qualifications before leaving school (7 had attended college or university) employment levels, too, were generally disappointing. Only 7 individuals were in regular, paid employment and 1 was self-employed; 4 others worked in a voluntary capacity and a few (15 per cent) were in some form of sheltered occupation. Two-thirds attended day or residential centres, where there was little scope for the development of competitive work skills.

In terms of social functioning, a quarter of the group were described as having some friends, with 14 individuals showing evidence of shared enjoyment or closer intimacy. One individual was married, although he later divorced, and another has married more recently. However, almost two-thirds had no friends at all.

A composite rating of outcome, based on social interactions, level of independence and occupational status, indicated that 15 individuals could be described as having a 'good' or 'very good' outcome. Most of these had some friends and either had a job or were undergoing training. Even if they still lived at home they had a relatively high level of independence, being largely responsible for their own finances, buying their own clothes or taking independent holidays. Eighteen remained moderately dependent on their families or other carers for support, and few in this group had any close friendships. Thirty-one people were in special residential units, which by their very nature (most were geographically very isolated) severely limited individual independence, and outcome in all these individuals was considered 'poor'. The 10 individuals in long-term hospital care were all rated as having a 'very poor' outcome.

FOLLOW-UP STUDIES OF MORE ABLE PEOPLE WITH AUTISM

In addition to the more general follow-up studies, some recent investigations have focused more specifically on individuals with autism or Asperger syndrome who are of higher intellectual ability.

Rumsey and his colleagues (Rumsey, Rapoport and Sceery, 1985), in a very detailed study involving a five-day inpatient assessment, followed up 14 young men aged between 18 and 39 years of age, all of whom fulfilled DSM-III (American Psychiatric Association, 1980) criteria for autism, and several of whom had initially been diagnosed by Kanner himself. Nine were described as 'high-functioning', with verbal IQs well within the normal range. In the 'lower-functioning' group, 3 were of normal non-verbal IQ but had continuing language impairments; 2 were also mildly intellectually impaired.

Socially, all the group continued to have marked difficulties. Most were described as 'loners'. None was married or was thought to have contemplated this; only one had friends, mostly through his church (although he was described as 'underinhibited') and a number, even amongst the intellectually more able group, were said still to show socially inappropriate behaviours. Half the group, including those who were high-functioning, showed peculiar use of language, such as stereotyped and repetitive speech or talking to themselves.

Academically, those in the 'lower-functioning' group had needed specialist education into late adolescence, but all had developed basic reading, writing and mathematical skills commensurate with their intellectual levels. In the higher-ability group, only 1 had remained in specialist educational provision, 5 had completed high school and 2 had attended junior college; several showed good ability in maths and 2 in foreign languages.

Nevertheless, assessment of social outcomes, as measured by the Vineland Social Maturity Scale, indicated that their scores here were often 'strikingly' low in relation to IQ. Problems amongst the more able group were generally related to deficits in the areas of self-direction, socialisation and occupational achievements. Similar difficulties were found in those who were less able but they also had additional impairments in communication and independence of travel.

In terms of independent living, 6 individuals in the more able group still lived with their parents and 2 were in supervised apartments; only 1 lived entirely alone. In the less able group none was living independently; 3 lived with their families; 1 was in a group home and 1 in a state hospital. With the exception of one person who was unemployed, all the 'lower-ability' group were attending a sheltered workshop or special job programme. Amongst the others, 4 were in employment (a janitor, a cab driver, a library assistant, and a key punch operator); of the remainder, 3 were in special training or college courses, 1 was in a sheltered workshop and 1 was unemployed. Even amongst those who had jobs, only 2 had found these independently and generally 'parents played a major role in finding employers willing to give their sons a chance'.

Szatmari and his colleagues (1989b) working in Toronto, studied a group of 12 males and 5 females aged 17 or over, with an average IQ of above 90. Educationally, half the group had received special schooling but the other half had attended college or university, with 6 obtaining a degree or equivalent qualification. Two were unemployed and 4 were in sheltered workshop schemes; 3 were still studying; 1 worked in the family business and 6 were in regular, full-time employment. Of the latter, 1 was a librarian, another a physics tutor, 2 were salesmen with semi-managerial positions, 1 worked in a factory and 1 was a library technician.

In terms of independent functioning, 10 of the 16 cases still lived at home and 1 was in a group home but 5 lived independently and a further 3 individuals living at home were said by their parents to be completely independent. Only one individual was felt to need constant supervision at home, 1 required moderate care and 6 required some minimal supervision. Socially, 9 individuals had never had a sexual relationship with anyone of the opposite sex but a quarter of the group had dated regularly or had long-term relationships; 1 was married.

In contrast with some other studies, little or no relationship was found between early measures of language or social behaviour and later functioning (early IQ data were not available). However, there was a high and significant correlation between current IQ and social functioning as measured by the Vineland.

The authors are open about the problems related to the study, including the small sample size (compounded by a high refusal rate), and, because of the group's high IQ, a lack of representativeness for autistic individuals as a whole. Nevertheless they note that outcome is not necessarily as gloomy as many earlier studies had indicated. They conclude: 'A small percentage of non-retarded autistic children . . . can be expected to recover to a substantial degree. It may take years to occur, and the recovery may not always be complete, but substantial improvement does occur.'

Another Canadian-based study (Venter, Lord and Schopler, 1992) has also assessed later functioning in more able children. Fifty-eight children (35 males and 23 females) with an average full scale IQ of 79, were given a detailed battery of tests and assessments. The results focus predominantly on intellectual and academic attainments rather than overall functioning and the authors note a marked improvement in children's academic attainments compared with the earlier follow-up studies carried out by Rutter and Bartak in the mid-1970's (Rutter and Bartak, 1973; Bartak and Rutter, 1976). Thus, even amongst the lower-functioning group, over half could read and do simple arithmetic, compared to about one-fifth in the studies conducted 20 years ago.

Twenty-two individuals in the study were aged 18 or over; of these 6 were competitively employed and 13 were in sheltered employment or special training programmes. Only 3 had no occupation. Nevertheless, again, all those who were employed were in relatively low-level jobs and all but 1 had required special assistance in finding employment. Of the 3 individuals not involved in any adult programme 2 were female, and all of the competitively employed people were male. No individual was married, and only 2 lived alone, 1 of these with considerable support from his mother. Four people lived in apartments with minimal supervision.

In a further study based at the Maudsley Hospital, London (Rutter, Mawhood and Howlin, 1992), the outcome for 19 young men was studied in great detail, as part of a comparative follow-up study of individuals with autism and developmental language disorders. Individuals had initially been seen between the ages of 4 and 9 years and all had a non-verbal IQ within the normal range. At follow-up the average performance IQ of the group remained well within the normal range and 5 individuals had attended college or university. Despite this they showed continuing problems in social relationships, and most remained very dependent. Only 3 individuals were living independently, 1 of these in sheltered accommodation; 3 had jobs (2 of these under special arrangements); none had married and only 3 were described as having close friendships. Almost half the group were said never to have had any friends, and about one-third had 'acquaintances' only. Fifteen subjects had never had either a close friendship or a sexual relationship. Thirteen were still described as having moderate to severe behavioural difficulties, associated with obsessional or ritualistic tendencies. A composite rating of outcome, based on communication skills, friendships, levels of independence and behavioural difficulties indicated that, overall, only 3 subjects were considered to have a good outcome, 2 remained moderately impaired and 14 continued to show substantial impairments.

Tantam (1991) describes outcome in 46 individuals with Asperger syndrome, with an average age of 24 years. Despite being of normal intellectual ability, only 2 had had any education after school, and only 4 were in jobs. One individual was married but most continued to live with their parents or in residential care.

A somewhat similar group of 93 young adults was described by Newson and her colleagues in 1982. Unfortunately, formal diagnostic and IQ data are lacking, but overall more subjects than in Tantam's study had received further education, 22 per cent were in jobs and 7 per cent lived independently. Of this group, 15 per cent were said to have had heterosexual relationships, although only 1 was married. Nevertheless, at an average age of 23 almost three-quarters still lived with their parents.

A list of the principal follow-up studies to date is given in Table 2.1; a summary of the main findings from these studies is presented in Figure 2.1. The results of studies over the last two decades (1980s and 1990s) are compared with those appearing in the 1950s to 1970s in

Table 2.1 Studies of autism in adult life: 1956 to 1995

Study	Date	No. of cases	Mean IQ (range)	Mean age (range)
1 Eisenberg	1956	63	No details	15.0 (9–25)
2 Creak	1963	100	No details	(9–28)
3 Mittler et al.	1966	26	49.7 (24–111)	15.2 (7–27)
4 Rutter et al.	1967	63	72.0	15.7
5 Kanner	1973	96	No details	(22–39)
6 DeMyer et al.	1973	126	53.5 6% 85+; 55% <50	12.0
7 Lotter	1974a	30	71.0 (55–90); 66% <55	(16–18)
8 Newson et al.	1982	93	No details	23.0
9 Rumsey et al.	1985	14	98.0 (55–129)	28.0 (18–39)
10 Tantam	1991	46	92.2 verbal IQ; 86.7 performance IQ	24.4
11 Gillberg and Steffenberg	1987	23	26% 70+; 35% 51–70; 39% <51	19.8 (16–23)
12 Szatmari et al.	1989b	16	92.4 (68–110)	26.1 (17–34)
13 Chung et al.	1990	66	24% 70+; 56% 35–69; 11% <34	Only 13% >12yrs
14 Venter et al.	1992	58	83.3; all >60	14.69
15 Kobayashi et al.	1992	201	24% 70+; 61% 35–69; 16% <34	21.5 (18–33)
16 Goode et al.	in prep	75	75.0	29.8 All 18+
17 Mawhood	1995	19	82.8 (67–117)	23.9 (21–26)

Note: IQ data are generally based on performance IQ scores

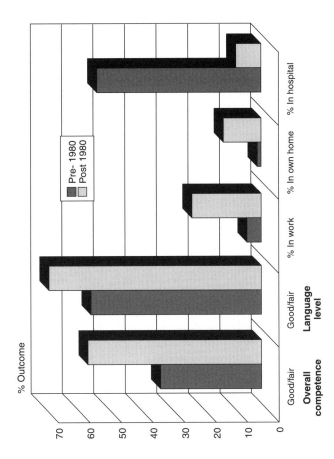

Figure 2.1 Changes in outcome between samples studied pre- and post-1980: a summary of findings from follow-up studies of autism

terms of general outcome, language competence and independent living.

WHAT CAN FOLLOW-UP STUDIES TELL US?

Factors related to outcome

As already noted, there are a number of factors related to early development that appear to be significantly associated with later outcome. The presence of at least simple communicative language by the age of 5 or 6 years is one of the most important prognostic indicators, as is the ability to score within the mildly retarded range or above on non-verbal tests of ability. There is also some indication from the work of Lynn Mawhood and colleagues (1995) that social development in childhood is related to measures of later social competence. It would seem crucial, therefore, that in the early years children are offered every opportunity to foster their social, cognitive and linguistic abilities.

However, the presence of relatively good cognitive and communication skills alone does not necessarily guarantee a successful outcome. This is far more readily achieved if individuals possess *additional* skills or interests (such as specialised knowledge in particular areas or competence in mathematics, music or computing) which allow them to find their own special 'niche' in life, and which enable them to be more easily integrated into society. Eccentric or unusual behaviours are much more likely to be accepted in individuals who are able to demonstrate exceptional skills in certain areas, than they are in those who have no such redeeming features. Thus, as Kanner, Eisenberg and Rutter all proposed many years ago, adequate educational opportunities, and encouragement to develop skills that may lead to later acceptance, are crucial. Moreover, particularly for those who are more able, it would seem more profitable in the long term for educational programmes to concentrate on those areas in which the person with autism already demonstrates potential competence, rather than focusing on areas of deficit.

Patterns of change over time

In some ways the summary in Figure 2.1 would seem to bear out Kanner's earlier hope that, over the years, there would be a gradual improvement in the treatment and outcome for people with autism. Comparisons between studies must, of course, be treated with caution for a number of reasons. Firstly, the data from the later studies are much more systematic and objective than those from earlier ones, and hence it is possible that certain important findings may have been omitted from these. Secondly, several of the later studies have concentrated on individuals of higher ability, and therefore a more favourable outcome would be expected. Nevertheless, there were many individuals in the earlier reports who were of relatively high intellectual ability, and indeed the average non-verbal IQ of subjects in the Rutter and Lotter studies fell *just* within the normal range (i.e. above 70). Similarly there were many subjects in the later investigations who were well below average intelligence. Thirdly, overall judgements of whether outcome is 'good', 'moderate' or 'poor' tend to be somewhat subjective, even if attempts are made to quantify what is meant by these terms. Finally, no doubt because of factors related to the variability in subject selection and assessment, there continue to be quite marked differences between studies in outcome results. Thus, although most of the later studies indicate that around 20–30 per cent of subjects have attained a good outcome, only 4 per cent of individuals in the Swedish study reached this level. As the author, Christopher Gillberg, notes, this may well be due to their relative youth, and indeed a new follow-up of these subjects is currently under way.

Language outcomes, too, are variable, with good or near-normal language being reported in over 70 per cent of subjects in the Rumsey study, but in only 21 per cent of the subjects studied by Mawhood and colleagues, who were of similar intelligence. This, again, is probably due to the fact that only verbal IQ data were available for the first group, whilst data on the second group are based on a variety of different measures, including grammatical and pragmatic functions. It is quite possible for able people with autism, even if their conversational skills are limited, to achieve high scores on verbal intelligence scales, as these tend to be based on skills related to general knowledge or memory, tasks on which this group tends to perform particularly well.

Even if data from the Gillberg study are excluded because so few subjects had reached adulthood, the proportions in work or living independently remain very variable. The best outcome was reported in the Canadian study of Szatmari and his co-workers, and although this may be partly understood because of the high ability of the subjects involved, it does not explain why the findings should be considerably better than for the British subjects in the Mawhood study, who were of very similar intellectual levels. It may well be that cultural factors play an important role here, since schemes involving supported employment or semi-sheltered living are generally much better established in Canada and the USA than in Britain. The very small number of subjects living independently in the Japanese study is also likely to be related to cultural factors.

Despite these qualifications, improvements do appear to be taking place. In particular, it is clear that rates of institutionalisation have fallen dramatically over the last two decades. Thus, while over half of all cases studied before 1980 were placed in long-stay hospital provision, post-1980 the figure has been only a little over 7 per cent. Similarly, the average numbers in work had risen from around 5 per cent in the earlier period to over 20 per cent later, and these figures would be even higher if those in sheltered workshops were also included. Very few individuals had no work or training provision of any kind; indeed in several states in the USA the provision of adequate day provision is now mandatory for anyone living in a residential home. There has been a substantial increase, too, in the numbers of those living in their own homes or apartments, either independently or with some minimal supervision. Apart from the individuals described by Kanner in his follow-up, none of the earlier studies mentions subjects living independently. However, in the post-1980 studies an average of around 12 per cent had their own homes. This may not be a particularly high figure but is certainly a great improvement compared with earlier years.

Although the quality of relationships has generally not been studied in great detail, in the few investigations to have looked at this crucial aspect of adult life it appears that some individuals are capable of making close relationships. It is true that very few people with autism marry, but both Goode and Mawhood found that around 15–20 per cent of subjects were described as having friendships that involved both selectivity and shared enjoyment. A quarter of the subjects studied by Szatmari also had close relationships, and over 40 per cent had had some relationships with members of the opposite sex. Heterosexual relationships were also reported by 15 per cent of subjects studied by Newson and her colleagues.

Would Kanner have considered that these findings fulfil the 'better expectations' he was hoping for, as therapeutic and educational provision for individuals with autism improved? We shall never know. Yet it is clear that at least a minority, although continuing to be affected by their autism, can find work, may live independently, and may even develop close relationships with others. These achievements do not come easily, however. Jobs are often found only with the support of families; opportunities to live independently seem to depend heavily on local provision; and friendships are often forged through special interests and skills, rather than via spontaneous contacts. Nevertheless, as admissions to hospital care have fallen, and expectations about the future for people with disabilities generally have risen over the years, the outlook does seem far less bleak than was once assumed. At least for those individuals who are of relatively high intelligence, and who develop effective communication skills, appropriate education is able to offer them a chance of being accepted, if never quite completely integrated, into society. In particular, those who view their autism as a challenge to be overcome seem to make most progress, although the extent to which they can succeed is likely to depend heavily on the assistance offered by families, teachers and other support systems.

The difficulties faced by people with autism as they enter adulthood, particularly those related to the fundamental impairments in communication, social understanding and ritualistic behaviours, are discussed in the following chapters, as are strategies for coping with these. The implications of such problems for education, work and general independence are also considered, and possible ways of enhancing the lives of individuals with autism, and those who live with them, are explored.

3 Problems of communication

As follow-up studies have consistently indicated, the development of language is a factor of crucial importance for later outcome in autism. Unless some useful speech is acquired by around the age of 6 years, future development is likely to be severely limited. Very few individuals who fail to achieve spoken language by this age later develop complex speech, although there are, of course, occasional exceptions to this. Cases have been reported of individuals who did not begin to speak until their teens, and Jim Sinclair (1992), for example, notes that he did not learn to use speech to communicate until the age of 12. On the whole, however, the level of language acquired after this stage is almost always very limited. Overall, approximately 30 per cent of individuals with autism remain without useful speech but, even amongst those who do learn to talk, significant impairments may continue throughout adulthood.

These difficulties are not confined to individuals of lower intellectual ability. Thus, Szatmari and his colleagues (1989b) found almost two-thirds of their sample of young adults continued to have problems related to verbal inflection or over-formal language; one-third had impoverished speech and had difficulties in making sense of conversations. Rumsey *et al.* (1985) reported that 50 per cent of their cases continued to demonstrate 'peculiar' language usage and the same proportion showed perseverative and repetitive speech patterns. Over 40 per cent still had little spontaneous speech, and abnormal intonation was also common. Mawhood (1995) also found that only a fifth of her sample of 19 young adults could be regarded as having good communication skills ('good' was defined as having good comprehension, using mature grammatical structures and being able to take part in reciprocal conversations). Almost two-thirds were rated as having 'poor' or 'very poor' verbal ability: that is, they had immature grammar, were unable to take part in even simple conversations, and had very limited comprehension of speech.

These difficulties are brought to life even more vividly in the personal accounts of people with autism. Therese Jolliffe, now studying for a PhD, wrote:

> It was ages before I realised that people speaking might be demanding my attention. But I sometimes got annoyed when I realised that I was expected to attend . . . because my quietness was being disturbed . . . Speaking for me is still often difficult and sometimes impossible . . . I sometimes know in my head what the words are but they do not always come out . . . sometimes when they do come out they are incorrect. Sometimes when I really need to speak and I just cannot, the frustration is terrible. I want to kick out at people and objects, throw things . . . scream. People's names are difficult to remember . . . and I still get the names of similar objects confused (e.g. knives and forks, dresses and skirts) . . . It is hard to understand words that are similar in sound . . . You do not seem to be aware that words can be put across using all different kinds of voices and that there are alternative ways of saying things. It was only from my academic work that I picked up the fact that there is more than one way of saying things . . . Sometimes I used to repeat the same words over again as this made me feel safer . . . when I first started repeating back phrases exactly as I had heard them. I think I did this as I was only able to come out with one or two words for myself.
>
> (Jolliffe *et al.*, 1992)

In the following sections some of the most common problems associated with the use and understanding of speech by young people with autism are discussed.

COMPREHENSION DIFFICULTIES

Discrepancies between the use and understanding of language

For the majority of individuals with language impairments, the comprehension of language is generally at a higher level than their expressive abilities. In autism this is frequently not the case. Superficially, spoken language can seem well developed, with many individuals possessing good vocabulary and syntax. However, there may be profound comprehension difficulties, particularly within a social context. Problems are further compounded by the fact that on formal tests of language many individuals may perform relatively well, as their understanding of *individual words* may be better developed than the ability to decode more complex instructions or concepts. Because of this very uneven profile of linguistic functioning, it is often difficult for other people to appreciate the true extent of the language impairment. In consequence, the failure of someone with autism to respond appropriately to instructions may be variously misinterpreted as uncooperative, rude, or mere 'stupidity'. Paradoxically, problems of this nature may actually increase with age, as expectations of their competence increase. Thus, although it is widely recognised that children with autism have comprehension difficulties, as they grow older, often showing marked improvements in spoken language, deficits in understanding may be less in evidence. Tamsin was a 15-year-old girl who had initially shown marked delays in language development. However, from the age of 5 she had made rapid progress and by the time she started secondary school her spoken vocabulary far outstripped that of many of her peers, and sometimes even her teachers. Nevertheless, although she had few problems coping with strictly factual information, more abstract concepts continued to cause problems and frustration, for both herself and others. A simple question from her mother on her return from school, such as 'had a nice day?' could provoke a lengthy discussion on what exactly was meant by this remark: *who* was supposed to have had a nice day and *what exactly* nice meant, until her mother swore to herself she would never make such a remark again!

Colin, a young man with mild learning difficulties, had not been diagnosed as having autism until he was over 18. Relationships within the family were greatly strained because 'he never did anything he was told'. For example, if asked to take a towel (clearly meant for the bathroom) upstairs, he would infuriate the family by simply leaving it on the top stair; if told to get something from the kitchen he would go and find it, but then fail to return to the person needing it; if sent to ask his mother if she wanted a cup of tea he would deliver the message but not the answer; on one occasion, when asked to post a letter to a family friend, he spent all day travelling across London to take the letter to the friend's house. Whilst his mother was much distressed by what seemed to be deliberate provocation, his father openly ridiculed him for his 'stupidity' and 'ignorance', and finally threw him out of the house.

Literalness

A further difficulty associated with poor comprehension, and one that continues to cause problems well into adulthood, is the tendency to interpret what is said very literally. Chris, a young man who had just started college, became so distressed when one of the other students, obviously joking, threatened to 'kill him' after a slight argument, that he refused to return. David, who was on a work experience placement was warned by his exasperated boss: 'You do that once again . . . !' and promptly repeated his action. Another young woman, attending a special class in art at her local college was asked not to come back, after allegedly deliberately destroying a flower-display. Knowing that she was usually an extremely careful and reliable individual her key worker explored this accusation further. It appeared that the tutor had instructed the class to paint the flowers on display, and the young woman had done exactly that! Another young man, attending a long-awaited interview for a residential placement, was clearly unhappy with the seating arrangements. When the principal suggested 'you can have my chair if you like', he sat down in it immediately, although the occupant had not yet had time to move. In Chapter 6 the example is also given of a young teenager who got into serious trouble at school for refusing to co-operate in maths lessons. In particular, he had become very upset at being asked to measure the area of tarmac in the playground. His reason for not doing so was that tarmac could only be measured by its *volume*. Lorna Wing recounts the tale of her daughter who was told that, on their next holiday to France, she would be 'going to *sleep on* the train'. Thinking that she would be delighted by such a novel experience her parents could not understand her distress at this news. It was only when they re-phrased the explanation to 'going to *bed in* the train' that they realised their original message had been totally misinterpreted.

This literal response to language can also make individuals sound very abrupt or even rude at times. Eric, when asked what year his birthday was by his new tutor looked at her with incomprehension and replied with scorn 'Well, every year of course!'

PROBLEMS IN SPOKEN LANGUAGE

Although many aspects of spoken language improve as individuals grow older, especially in the case of those of higher intellectual ability, other, more subtle, deficits tend to persist and continue to pervade many aspects of linguistic functioning.

Intonation and delivery

In many cases the very stilted, mechanical, almost robotic quality of speech that characterises the delivery of younger children, diminishes somewhat with time. However, there is considerable variation here, and some people continue to have poorly modulated speech, which can be difficult to understand or interpret. Neville is a 40-year-old man, living in semi-sheltered accommodation who, because of staffing problems, has taken on considerable responsibility in the organisation of the house where he lives. Many of his views on how the other residents can make their lives more comfortable, or how they can get a better deal from the Housing Association involved, have proved very constructive. The problem is that his tone of voice is unremittingly querulous and somewhat aggressive. This frequently leads to resentment amongst both residents and careworkers, and the rejection of his often sensible proposals.

A 'flat', poorly modulated voice can also give other people a mistaken impression of an individual's general level of competence. Peter, for example, is a young man of normal intellectual ability, who has obtained a number of GCSE qualifications over the years. Through his attendance at a part-time art-history course he also has interesting and informative views on art and drawing. However, the slowness of his delivery, and the time he takes to find the 'right' words to express himself, tends to make him *sound* both unintelligent and boring, although in fact he is neither.

Even the accents acquired by people with autism can lead to difficulties. Many never seem to recognise the importance of 'fitting in' with their peer group, and may continue to speak in the same style and accent as their parents, regardless of the social environment. This can be a particular problem for adolescents, who fail to appreciate that speaking in a different accent or style from their peers is very likely to result in bullying, teasing or rejection.

Semantic problems

Although the vocabulary of some people with autism continues to remain limited, many do show considerable improvements in their expressive skills over time. Nevertheless they may continue to experience problems in finding the correct form of words to express their ideas so that what is said can appear slightly 'odd' or out of place. Jenny, for example, had once been told by a teacher that she should try to avoid repetition and should use more variety in her written work. She then adapted this to her spoken language, and would never use a simple word if a more unusual one existed. Events would be described as 'melancholy', rather than 'sad'; people as 'amicable', rather than 'friendly'; places as 'repellent', rather than 'nasty'. Although the words were not incorrect, they made her speech sound slightly absurd and certainly far too formal. Johnny, whose use of English had also been corrected at school, began to correct others in the same way, becoming extremely agitated if anyone used 'me' instead of 'I' or 'should' instead of 'would' etc., and would continually interrupt conversations with his corrections.

The way in which words are used may also be out of keeping with an individual's age, social group, or family background. Giles was frequently taunted by his brothers and peers for his use of terms such as 'spiffing' or 'jolly good show'. He appeared to have picked these up from boys' comics produced in the 1950's and early 1960's, but he had no awareness of the fact that they now belonged to a totally different era. Similarly, Asperger (see Frith, 1991) describes one individual as sounding like 'a caricature of a degenerative aristocrat' because of his over-formal and pedantic style of speech and his 'high, slightly nasal, and drawn-out' voice. Such problems are not necessarily restricted to those of higher ability. Gareth, a young man of 17, with mild to moderate learning difficulties, was asked what he did with his small amount of weekly pocket money. Somewhat disconcertingly he replied solemnly: 'I spend all my allowance on confectionery or comestibles'.

Whilst having a superior vocabulary might, on the surface, appear to be an advantage rather than a handicap, for individuals who already have difficulties in 'fitting in' or being accepted, any unusual aspects to the way in which they speak can easily exacerbate existing problems. Josh, a young teenager who had moved into a new comprehensive school, was so bullied and teased by his peers for his 'posh voice and big words' that teachers actually became anxious for his physical safety. Moreover, whilst an unusual vocabulary is often a sign of superior intelligence in the general population, in autism this is not necessarily the case, and may again give a deceptive impression of an individual's true level of understanding.

Echolalic speech

Echolalia, both immediate and delayed, is a common characteristic of the language of people with autism. Although often viewed as inappropriate and non-communicative, studies by Barry Prizant and his co-workers (Rydell and Prizant, 1995; Rydell and Mirenda, 1994; Prizant and Schuler, 1987) have been influential in illustrating the functional nature of much echolalia. They have shown that echoing, particularly in older and less cognitively impaired individuals, frequently serves identifiable and important functions. Thus, it may be used to indicate a lack of comprehension, for self-regulation and rehearsal, or as a direct but simplified form of communication. Echolalia is also more likely to occur when individuals are stressed, anxious, or in highly constraining situations. In many cases, too, echolalia is an important precursor to more creative and rule-governed language. As with any other 'autistic' behaviour, therefore, it is crucial to assess the role that the echolalia plays for the individual concerned before any attempts are made to modify it.

A particular problem associated with echolalia is that speech copied from other people may lead to serious overestimates of an individual's true level of competence. Although some adults may continue to echo at a very simple level, others develop much more complex and in many ways contextually appropriate forms of repetitive speech. Micky, for example, who had left school some months earlier, was asked by a visitor if he had heard anything of his ex-headmaster. There then ensued a lengthy monologue, which the questioner eventually recognised as the repetition of a radio interview in which the headmaster had been speaking about the problems of children with autism. The interviewer's questions and the head's replies were all faithfully reproduced. Micky had certainly replied to the question, but not in quite the way expected, nor in the most efficient manner. Sarah, when asked if she had any problems making contact with the people she met socially (she was an avid swimmer and received professional coaching at her local pool), said this was no problem for her. As a teenager her parents had deliberately coached her in the most appropriate ways to engage visitors in conversation, and since the family entertained a great deal she received considerable practice in this. However, difficulties arose when the early stages of the conversation had passed and she was then expected to develop, or expand on, more socially complex themes, for which rote learning was of little use. Adrian, who was seen by an occupational psychologist for a job skills assessment, so impressed her by his sophisticated use of language, that she became convinced that earlier reports of his social and learning difficulties must be mistaken. Despite warnings from his school teachers of the problems that could occur if his abilities were overestimated, he was sent on a work experience placement that demanded far greater social and intellectual competence than he was capable of.

Repetitive use of language

Repetitive language may occur for a variety of reasons: it may be the individual's only effective way of making contact with others; it may be deliberately attention-seeking; it may be caused by anxiety or insecurity; it may be linked to an individual's obsessions and routines; or it may be associated with a combination of these factors. Whatever the underlying origins, however, speech of this kind can lead to considerable problems either because it tends to disrupt ordinary social exchanges or because of the annoyance it causes to others.

Dominic, a young man attending a day centre, had very limited phrase speech, but nevertheless caused considerable disruption there by repeating certain phrases to other clients or members of staff. None of these was particularly offensive; he might say one client's name in a certain way; repeat the title of a TV serial to another; accuse another of liking John Major (the prime minister of the time); or tell another that they would be having semolina for lunch. The use of these phrases, no matter how innocuous they may have appeared to outsiders, was clearly deliberately calculated to irritate the individuals concerned. Even staff admitted to 'getting very wound up' by this and several of the clients had actually hit him, but the attention he received was more than enough to ensure that the behaviour persisted.

Other people with autism, especially those whose language skills are poor, show high levels of repetitive speech in situations in which they are unsure or anxious. Any potential changes, or the occurrence of situations that they do not like, can provoke persistent questions, repetitions or even self-admonishments: 'Not going to go swimming on Thursday?', 'Not going to kick grandma', 'Going to see mummy and daddy?' are typical of the types of utterances that may be repeated over and over again, and which, although harmless in themselves, can be very wearing for people living or working with them. Lydia constantly asked everyone she met throughout the day if she could go in the mini-van to fetch petrol on Friday. If the answer were 'No' or 'Don't know' she would become very distressed. If it were 'Yes' she would continuously ask *when* she could go. Persistent questioning about birthdays, makes of cars, or bus and train routes, can also become very tedious, as can constant seeking for reassurance. Carol had been on numerous work experience placements, all of which had broken down because of her need for continuous guidance. A simple task, such as licking envelopes, would require repeated assurances that she had done it correctly and even the most sympathetic of supervisors rapidly became exasperated.

Even if direct questioning is not involved, constant repetition of the same phrases can prove very irritating for listeners. Maria, a young woman in her mid-twenties, goes through phases of using particular utterances which are said to 'drive her family mad'; the current one, for some reason, being 'unsecured floating-rate loan stock'.

Repetitive speech can also disrupt attempts to foster more normal conversation. Chris, a young man with a history of placement break-downs, proved very difficult to help because his conversation was entirely dominated by complaints about the wrong done to him during the previous placement, interspersed with questions about the relative sizes of London hospitals.

Even if the topic of interest seems to be rather more socially 'promising' it usually still proves difficult to develop the conversation much further. Owen, for example, was a young man who appeared to know everything possible about Welsh rugby teams. He knew all the important players, past and present; the positions they played; and the scores of previous matches. However, if asked a simple question about which teams would be playing the next weekend he was often quite unable to answer and insisted instead on talking about games gone by.

As they grow older some individuals are able to learn to control this constant repetition or questioning, particularly if they realise that it is likely to reduce their chances of making friends, or that it can lead to teasing or bullying. Nineteen-year-old Sally had had an obsession with the singer Edith Piaf since she was very young but had gradually learned to talk less and less about her. She knew the topic tended to irritate other students at college and although she admitted that she 'still really wanted to talk about her all the time' had learned to suppress her obsession as far as possible. Nevertheless, certain triggers continued to set her off, despite her good intentions. In particular, any mention of the number 49 (the age at which Piaf died) would result in an explosion of questions again, often to indi-viduals who had never even heard of the singer.

Neologisms

Idiosyncratic or made-up words generally seem to be less in evidence in adulthood than they are in younger children. As they grow older many people come to recognise the 'silliness' of these words or phrases, and may become quite embarrassed if other people mention them. If neologisms are maintained these are often kept as a sort of 'family joke' and tend to be rarely used in public. Maria, mentioned above, now jokes about the time when she used the phrase 'little glacien jars' to describe anything made from glass. The utterance had originally arisen from a little glass jar in which she kept a small piece of her toy tiger's tail! As a child she used numerous convoluted utterances of this kind, but now the only one remaining is 'flappy' which is used to describe the pieces of paper or cardboard that she continues to hoard.

'Bluntness'

A major problem for many people with autism as they grow older results not so much from the actual words they use, as from the ways in which they use them. This is closely interwoven with their lack of appreciation of social rules and their failure to understand the impact of what they say on others. For people with a knowledge of autism such remarks are unlikely to give offence. However, for strangers, particularly if the individual concerned possesses a good vocabulary and has no obvious learning difficulties, such remarks can appear at the very least insensitive, and at worst extremely offensive. A few examples here should suffice to illustrate these problems.

In the course of my own clinical work, patients often remark on my somewhat small size. Indeed, one young woman always refers to me simply as 'Little Doctor'. Another individual, who had grown considerably since I had last seen him, announced: 'I think your desk has shrunk since I was last here . . . and I think you may have too'. Another young woman said nothing about my size during my interview with her, although I knew she was particularly interested in people's weights and heights. As she left she remarked loudly, 'I think I must have grown taller today' and then announced proudly to her key worker 'There, I didn't say anything about how little she is!'.

Similar comments in other circumstances may be viewed with less affection. Notions of 'political correctness', in particular, are often difficult for people with autism to grasp. Damien, attending an employment preparation course, was soon under threat of suspension because of comments about his supervisor. Having previously been taught by men he was obviously surprised that his new supervisor was a young Asian woman. He was constantly remarking on her colour, race and gender, and although this was not done in any negative way, his remarks were considered totally unacceptable. Jason, a young man in his late teens, alienated all his sister's friends after one of them had a baby by an Afro-Caribbean man, to whom she was not married. Jason was fascinated by the skin colouring of the baby and repeatedly questioned its mother about whether or not she had realised that she would have 'a half-white baby' as well as lecturing her on the perils of single motherhood and what the likely impact on her offspring would be. Jonas, another young man who was usually very well-mannered, horrified his mother at a large social gathering by approaching a very small, elderly, white-haired woman with protruding teeth and asking politely 'Excuse me, but are you a rabbit?'.

DEALING WITH ABSTRACT CONCEPTS

Talking about the future

Abstract or hypothetical concepts are frequently a source of particular difficulty for people with autism. Even vague or uncertain responses to questions, such as 'Soon', 'Perhaps', or 'I'll think about it' can give rise to immense anxiety, since the individual has no real information on whether, or when something will happen. Irony, too, can to give rise to major problems and will almost certainly result in confusion and misunderstandings.

The ability to cope with events that are due to happen in the future is also a source of difficulty. Even if the individual seems to understand the explanations given, or appears to comply with plans for his or her future, a real understanding of what is to happen may be woefully lacking. David, a young man with autism and severe learning difficulties, was to be transferred to a new group home in the community. Great efforts had been made by his key worker to explain what would be happening; he had been involved in the plans for decorating his new bedroom and he had visited the house on a number of occasions, spending increasing periods of time there. However, when the day of the move came it was clear that he still had little understanding that this was to be his permanent home, After several hours he re-packed his case and attempted to leave, becoming terribly distressed when prevented from doing so.

Talking about feelings or emotions

This failure to cope with abstract concepts also affects the ability to talk about feelings or emotions, or even physical pain. A number of cases have been reported of individuals with autism who have become seriously ill with tooth abscesses, infections, even appendicitis, without being able to indicate that they were in pain. This inability to explain how they are feeling, coupled with a possible lowered sensitivity to pain (Biersdorff, 1994), can have serious implications. The problem is obviously most marked in individuals who have severe learning difficulties and little or no speech. For example, in a study by Gunsett and colleagues (1989), 9 out of 12 residents living in an institution, who had developed severe behavioural problems in adulthood, were found to have undiagnosed medical conditions, including fractures, urinary tract infections and toxic levels of anti-convulsants.

Emotional or psychiatric disturbance may be even more difficult to convey and the ways in which language difficulties can disrupt normal diagnostic processes or lead to a failure to obtain appropriate help are described in further detail in Chapter 9.

Humour

Perhaps surprisingly, given their concrete language and thought processes, humour is something that can be enjoyed by many people with autism. Admittedly, their sense of humour tends to be somewhat unsubtle, and appreciation of comedy is often restricted to the slapstick, but jokes, puns and riddles may all be enjoyed, and are often used to entertain families, carers and friends (Ricks and Wing, 1975). Van Bourgondien and Mesibov (1987) specifically studied the humorous responses of adults with autism and found a high rate of riddles and simple jokes, which clearly resulted in considerable enjoyment for all concerned. Indeed, a 'joke time' is now incorporated into the TEACCH social skills programme (Mesibov, 1986) and is considered to play an important role in encouraging positive social interactions. Autistic humour may give rise to difficulties, however, if jokes are socially inappropriate or so repetitive that they become a source of irritation to others.

LACK OF RECIPROCITY

Although people with autism may exhibit many of the problems noted above to a greater or lesser degree, the over-riding problem, for almost everyone, and at whatever linguistic level they function, is the lack of reciprocity in their language: their failure to engage in normal conversations, to listen to other people's points of view, or to 'chat' simply for the pleasure of doing so. This does not mean that they do not wish to take part in conversations. On the contrary, as they grow older, many people with autism become almost desperately keen to interact with others and to be accepted by them. However, they are not able to engage in the often inconsequential 'chit-chat' that is so important in normal social interactions; they often have little or no interest in the other person's views and may be quite unaware of cues indicating that they are becoming boring, disrupting ongoing discussions, or dominating the conversation in an unacceptable way. This lack of reciprocity, and the failure to appreciate the 'two-way' nature of conversation, is often most evident in more intellectually handicapped individuals who may tend to bombard almost any one they meet with stereotyped questions or phrases, frequently regardless of the answers they receive. However, the problems can be equally disruptive in individuals who are verbally and intellectually much more able. Stephen, a young man with superficially good language skills, would launch into lengthy diatribes on the potential dangers of the Channel Tunnel whenever the opportunity arose, often disrupting family gatherings or outings because of this. Fred, a 20-year-old whose family entertained a lot, prided himself on his conversational skills and claimed that he had no problems meeting people or making friends. His parents had tried to stop him from 'barging into conversations' by persuading him not to speak until someone introduced a topic relevant to his over-riding interest in computers. This helped to make his comments rather more relevant, but even so, he would often misinterpret what had been said. Someone's innocent comment about fish and chips, for example, could launch him into intricate descriptions about the internal workings of the latest computers. Even if the ongoing discussion were related to computers he would then completely dominate the conversation, until people moved off in boredom or embarrassment. However, because he did manage to talk to lots of different people in this way, and because no-one wanted to be directly rude to him, he remained convinced of his excellent conversational skills.

WHAT CAN BE DONE TO HELP?

As is apparent from the follow-up studies reviewed in the previous chapter, difficulties related to speech and understanding generally persist throughout adulthood, even in the most able of individuals. Other research also indicates that impairments in communication are both central and fundamental to the disorder. Hence, any approaches to intervention in this area are likely to have their limitations. Nevertheless, there are many different strategies that can be used to enhance communicative functioning in adulthood, even in individuals who have little or no spoken language, and intervention can be crucial in helping them to develop more effective ways of expressing their needs or better to understand what is happening around them (Howlin, 1989).

Increasing understanding and decreasing inappropriate speech

As with any successful intervention programme, the development of appropriate strategies relies on understanding the underlying reasons for the behaviours involved and recognition of the functions that they may serve for the individual concerned. Thus, many of the communication problems described above, such as apparent lack of co-operation or repetitive and stereotyped questioning, may result from the failure to understand what is required, or because of misinterpretation, or anxieties about what is likely to happen.

Helping to improve **others'** *communication skills*

In many instances co-operation can be significantly improved if the individual is given greater help to understand what is required. However, this may well require a change of focus to the ways in which *others* communicate, rather than on the person with autism. The situation between Colin and his father, described above, was greatly helped, firstly by the family's realisation that his understanding was much more limited than had been previously thought, and secondly, by his father being given help to make his own speech much more specific, and in particular to avoid complex, abstract or ambiguous instructions. For example, it was often necessary to split apparently simple commands into separate components. Thus, asking him to 'Take the towel upstairs *and* put it in the bathroom' avoided Colin simply dumping the towel on the top stair. Telling him to 'Ask your mother if she wants a cup of tea *and then* come and tell me what she said' improved his ability to take messages. Instructions such as: 'Go to the kitchen, look for a knife in the drawer and then bring it back here to me' significantly increased the chances of family members obtaining the items they needed.

Similarly, if anger or distress occur when new activities or events are suggested, then it may well be that the intended message is being misinterpreted in some way, and will need to be conveyed in a different form. Sometimes this can be relatively easy, and may simply require a restructuring of what has been said. Explaining to someone that they are to go 'to bed in the train' rather than 'sleep on the train' may remove any number of unknown and frightening images. Many unforeseen problems can arise over the literal interpretation of what is said, and hence care needs to be taken to establish what the source of the confusion is, and then to remedy this. Peter's mother began to have great trouble with him when they were out in the car, as he would attack her whenever they stopped. Eventually it was realised that the problems occurred because if she said 'We're going to see Auntie Jean' he would expect to go straight there and became very angry if they had to stop en route for traffic lights, pedestrians or other drivers. The problem was dealt with by helping him first to tolerate *brief and predictable stops* and later with more frequent and unpredictable ones. Thus, she began by saying, *before* they set off: 'We are going to Auntie Jean's, but we will stop at the traffic lights on the way' (usually the lights were against them but she would stop there even if they were not). Peter accepted this without difficulty and his mother then began to predict more stops (e.g. at the corner by the pub or opposite the paper shop), which again were readily tolerated. The next stage was to tell him, before they left, that they would stop *somewhere* on the way, but that she would not tell him where. He would then have to try and guess where this would be. Turning the trips into a guessing game in this way, and at the same time making it clear that a specified trip would require additional stops, quickly reduced his 'aggressive' behaviour.

Removing uncertainty

As noted above, lack of understanding may be a primary cause of obsessional speech. Asking questions is a natural way to gain information but if the answers supplied are not understood then the questioning will tend to continue. Sometimes re-phrasing the reply may be enough but more often information may need to be supplied in an alternative and non-verbal form. Visual information is often far more powerful than verbal messages alone. Thus, photographs of places that are to be visited, people who are to be met, activities that are to be followed, can prove much more effective than words alone (Mac-Duff, Krantz and McClannahan, 1993). In many instances, once the information is understood, repetitive questioning will be greatly reduced. Moreover, if an individual continues to seek reassurance in this way, he or she can be guided to look at the pictures (or written instructions etc.) for information, rather than remaining dependent on direct, verbal assurance.

Again, although particularly important when dealing with less able or non-verbal individuals, such aids can prove surprisingly effective in helping those of higher ability to deal with complex or abstract situations. Patrick became very anxious when he started a college placement and was constantly asking his parents, the college staff, other students, or whoever happened to be close by, where he should be at every hour of the day. This behaviour was a source of considerable irritation and Patrick's anxiety was not lessened by the answers he received, as he then worried that his informant 'could have got it wrong'. Eventually he was supplied with a Filofax diary, and with the help of the special needs tutor this was filled in on an hourly basis, with each entry indicating where he should be at any time of the day. He was reminded to look in his diary every time the anxious questioning began and eventually his reliance on the written information reduced his need for verbal reassurance and guidance.

Reducing attention for inappropriate speech

Although repetitive and obsessional speech is frequently used to gain attention, and although traditional behavioural techniques, such as time-out or extinction, are usually effective in reducing attention-seeking behaviours, this is often not the case with verbal routines. Ignoring someone who is spinning a piece of cloth, lining up bricks, or making long trails of coins around the house is *relatively* simple and, if carried out consistently, can prove remarkably effective. However, with verbal obsessions it is all too easy for other people to become part of the repetitive pattern, without their even realising that this is happening.

Richard's principal obsession was with quiz games and, with quite remarkable skill, he could turn around almost any question one asked of him into a response related to quiz games. A remark about his new jumper would elicit a reply about the similarity to one worn by a recent quiz contestant; a comment on the weather would be immediately associated with a question he had been able to answer the previous week; even if he were told off for doing something unacceptable at home he would begin to talk of the 'rules' of various programmes, and how contestants sometimes flouted these, too. His obsession was thus being constantly and unwittingly reinforced by others, despite their attempts to try to ignore or reduce it.

Even if family members are able to avoid responding to obsessional

themes themselves, visitors may well act differently and the intermittent reinforcement of behaviours in this way is a particularly
powerful way of maintaining them. Jeff, for example, had a passion
for politics and in brief interactions could actually be very interesting
and informative. Constant exposure to political debate, however,
became increasingly irritating for his family and eventually they
decided that the only way to cope was to ignore his political comments totally. Although this resulted in a reduction of the behaviour
at home, whenever visitors came, or when he met people outside, his
favourite topic of conversation would be unwittingly reinforced once
more.

In another case, Jerry's mother had managed to reduce his swearing
at home to a reasonably low level by ensuring that she, her husband,
and his sister ignore it. Although this had proved very difficult for
them initially, over the years they had become quite expert and had
established good control over the problem. However, whenever his
grandmother came to the house the swearing would instantly increase
once more. She refused to tolerate this behaviour, gave him lengthy
lectures whenever it occurred, scolded her son and daughter-in-law
for allowing it, and generally afforded Jerry great satisfaction. The
only other situation in which the problem was just as difficult to
control was on the bus, whenever he sat in ear-shot of other elderly
women!

Setting rules

A more effective approach, but one which needs to be established
from the earliest years, is to lay down explicit 'rules' as to *when,
where, how often* or *with whom* such speech can be used. If children
can be taught, from an early age, that obsessional talk is only
allowed with certain people, in certain situations, at a certain time
of day, or for a specified period, it is much easier to minimise the
disruption that it can cause. At the same time, knowledge that such
talk will be allowed, at least at certain times or in particular situations, reduces the anxiety that tends to erupt if the behaviours are
banned altogether. Although it is possible to impose such limitations
on older people, if the habit has been well established for many
years it will be much more difficult to deal with than if appropriate
steps had been taken in childhood. However, this requires that
parents be given early help, by the relevant professionals, to identify
the stage at which behaviours may be becoming a problem and,

most importantly, that they be provided with adequate support to enable them to intervene effectively.

It is also necessary to be aware that communication patterns that are acceptable in childhood may become less acceptable as the individual grows older. Repetitive questioning about Thomas the Tank Engine, for example, may not seem too inappropriate for a 5-year-old, but would certainly be considered very abnormal for someone in their late adolescence. Similarly, whilst informing complete strangers all about one's private life, or asking them intimate personal questions, can seem quite amusing in a 3-year-old, in a 13-year-old it may sound impertinent and in a 30-year-old quite threatening. Thus, intervention may be needed *even before* the behaviour becomes a problem – a balance that, without adequate support, may be very difficult for families to achieve.

Moreover, although the need to establish consistent rules regarding appropriate and inappropriate topics of conversation cannot be over-emphasised, rules of this kind can also have their drawbacks. Normal social communication is regulated by highly subtle, complex and ill-defined influences and attempts to apply concrete (and hence often inflexible) guidelines, although helpful in certain situations, may backfire in others. Ronnie's parents decided, as he grew older, that they must stop him from approaching strangers and asking them questions (usually about distances or directions). He was told firmly that he must never talk to people whom he did not know in the street and, on the whole, this rule proved very effective. As he grew more independent, however, he began to travel about on his own and on one occasion failed to return after a train journey. When he finally arrived home, late at night and obviously very distressed, it emerged that he had accidentally got off at the wrong stop and had become hopelessly lost. When his parents asked why he had not asked anyone the way he replied 'Because you told me not to!'.

Rules can also backfire for other reasons. Laurie was a young man working in a voluntary capacity for a large charity. He was a calendrical calculator, able to work out accurately, within seconds on what day of the year any date would fall (see O'Connor and Hermelin, 1984 ; Young and Nettlebeck, 1994). His favourite pastime was to ask people when their birthday was and then to tell them what day of the week it fell on. Although amusing initially, his constant questioning soon became a source of irritation for the people at work and it was agreed that he should restrict his questions about birthdays to one per day. Usually he would ask the first person he met in the morning when their birthday was, but on one day, when the charity's royal patron was visiting, Laurie was unusually silent. Finally the royal visitor arrived and Laurie had been chosen as one of the people to greet her. After politely shaking her hand he immediately asked his daily question!'

Recognising the importance of obsessional speech

Whatever strategies are implemented, it should always be recognised that repetitive or obsessional speech may be one of the few resources that someone with autism may have to occupy his or her time, to fill in the many hours of solitude, to reduce anxiety or deal with potentially troubling situations; it may, too, be the individual's only way of making verbal contact with other people. To deny them the opportunity of talking about these topics at all, unless they can somehow be replaced with alternative and more socially effective conversational skills, is not acceptable. Indeed, attempts to do so may well prove counter-productive, leading to an upsurge in anxiety and, in turn, even higher levels of obsessional or repetitive speech. As with other obsessional behaviours, therefore, the aim should be to modify it to the extent to which it is no longer disruptive, whilst at the same time retaining any potential benefits.

Teaching alternative skills

One of the particular advantages of ritualistic or stereotyped forms of speech is that they avoid the need to develop different ways of greeting people and, in turn, others' responses will be much more predictable. Asking someone about the make of car they drive, for example, results in a much more restricted set of responses than more general questions about their health, their job or their family. Stereotyped questions of this nature can reduce uncertainty and the risk of being questioned about unfamiliar topics. Thus, whilst offering the opportunity to indulge in obsessional interests, they also allow the individual to maintain much greater control over social interactions.

If the obsessional or inappropriate conversational routines are to be reduced, the autistic person will need additional help to develop more effective strategies. Role play, social skills groups, drama classes can all be helpful in teaching more appropriate conversational skills, and research indicates that such interventions can be helpful for people of very different levels of ability (Mesibov, 1986). For the more handicapped, learning how to shake someone's hand, to say hello, and to introduce themselves by name may have a great impact on how they are perceived by others. Teaching at higher levels of ability is obviously much more complex, since attention needs to be directed towards so many different social issues (Mesibov, 1992). Once the early stages of introduction are over, the scope for conversational development becomes so wide that it can be very difficult to offer detailed guidelines on how to proceed. However, helping individuals to develop better listening skills and the ability to pick up obvious signs of interest or boredom in others, helping them to develop conversational strategies around the news, films, TV programmes, sport, music, etc., can all be valuable. The TEACCH programme of Gary Mesibov and his colleagues offers helpful advice in this area and there are a number of other social skills programmes available that can be used to guide teaching (Spence, 1991). However, as the latter are not specifically designed for individuals with autism they will generally need some modifications. In particular, instruction needs to be very basic, concrete and highly specific. Role-play techniques can prove very effective, and feedback from audio or video recordings can help to improve conversational exchanges generally or more specific behaviours, such as tone of voice or speed of delivery (Howlin and Yates, 1995).

The appropriate generalisation of newly taught skills, however, may give rise to problems. Ina van Berckelaer-Onnes (1994), who conducts social skills training in Holland, recounts how she had been encouraging one of her students to use compliments when talking to other people. Learning how to comment on the colour or style of people's clothes or hair were skills much practised. Finally, one student reported excitedly that he had met a girl at a dance and had put his skills to good use. 'What did you say to her?', asked his tutor. 'I told her how much I liked her dress and what a lovely colour it was . . . how it exactly matched her gums', was the disarming reply.

Talking about emotions and dealing with abstract concepts

A major problem for almost everyone with autism is the ability to talk about or fully to understand abstract concepts, such as feelings or emotions or even pain. Even individuals of normal intellectual and verbal ability continue to show specific deficits in areas related to the deciphering and labelling of emotions (Hobson, 1993). Unless help can be provided to improve these skills, coping with physical, emotional or psychiatric problems in later life can present many difficulties. Again, the best solution seems to be to start young. Simon Baron-Cohen and colleagues (see Hadwin, *et al.*, 1996) have shown that after only a few sessions of teaching, children with autism aged between 4 and 9 years of age can be taught to understand and use mental-state terms related to other people's beliefs and emotions. Whilst this work was restricted to largely experimental settings, the fact that even brief training was effective suggests that more prolonged input might well result in substantial improvements in this area of communication and understanding.

Work with more severely disabled individuals also indicates that, even within this group, people can learn to express simple emotional concepts if given appropriate help. Pictures, photographs, audio or video tapes have all been used to help people decipher emotional states and to explain why certain situations arouse different feelings (Quirk-Hodgson, 1995). Teaching people to label emotions in structured, albeit somewhat artificial settings, may then help when they need to express their own feelings. Lorraine, a young woman with cerebral palsy as well as autism, was confined to a wheelchair throughout the day. Although generally relaxed, at times she would come to her day centre clearly feeling frustrated, angry or miserable. Beginning initially with photographs of happy, sad or angry faces, she has learned to identify these emotions, and to match them to situations that might provoke them. Subsequently, using a picture board portraying a wider variety of expressions, she has been taught to label emotions in different contexts, taken from photographs or stories in books. She is also encouraged to point each day to the face that best expresses her current mood and appears to do this with some reliability. It is now hoped to introduce a more complex set of 'emotional faces' in order to allow greater scope for expression. Figure 3.1 shows an example of the types of 'emotion boards' that have been used in other situations to enable people with learning disabilities to express their moods and feelings more effectively. Although this may be too complex for the majority of people with autism, it can be modified to suit a range of different abilities.

Unfortunately, help of this kind is often provided much too late in life for it to have a significant impact on people's ability to understand and express their emotions effectively. Greater attention to helping young children with autism develop their skills in these areas could well offer much greater chances of success. Many autistic children, for example, will spend hours watching videos of Disney cartoons or stories such as Thomas the Tank Engine, in which the characters tend to be highly stereotyped and actions and responses very repetitive and predictable. Because they relate in a very simplified way to specific events and situations, such materials can be of

Figure 3.1 Using picture charts to identify emotions
Source: Gaboney 1993

value, if used constructively by adults, to help children appreciate
that there are such things as emotions, to learn the names of these, and
to help them talk about feelings of happiness, anger, sadness, pain or
jealousy themselves.

Addressing other possible causes

Repetitive and obsessional speech patterns may, of course, stem from
a variety of other causes. Firstly, it should be remembered that in early
language learning, repetition or echolalia plays a crucial role in helping children to consolidate what they hear and, as well as enhancing

understanding, provides the opportunity to practise new words or expressions. For adults with limited language skills, repetition may continue to serve an important function and should not automatically be discouraged.

Secondly, repetition is, for all of us, an important factor in rehearsing potentially worrying situations, in dealing with feelings of anger, or in helping to allay anxiety. How many of us will repeatedly practise what we are going to say to someone the next day, if we know that a difficult situation is likely to occur or a personal problem needs to be resolved? If things do not go as planned, who has not gone over and over what they *should* have said, or rehearsed cutting and witty remarks that *could* have been used to devastate an opponent? In fearful situations, who has not continually reassured themselves that their fears are groundless; or tried to persuade themselves, for example, that the noises heard on the stairs in the dead of night are caused by the cat or a creaking floorboard, rather than admitting to their real fears? If stressed and anxious, sitting in a traffic jam while the deadline for arriving at the station or airport draws perilously close, are we not likely to ask the time repeatedly, even though we know the answer only too well? Autistic people also do all these things. Their problem is not that the behaviours are unusual, but that they are not carried out silently, in their heads, as is usually the case for the rest of us. Understanding *why* such behaviours may occur, recognising the normality, indeed the importance of them, may well help others to be more accepting. Greater understanding may also suggest alternative strategies that can be utilised. For example, desensitisation to feared situations or the teaching of relaxation techniques may be a more appropriate way of dealing with the problem of constant repetition than ignoring or 'time-out', which might well exacerbate the situation. Help with anger management may also be more productive, and techniques developed for use with individuals with other forms of learning disabilities may prove useful here (Clements, 1987). Alternatively, allowing the individual concerned to rehearse and practise the most effective ways of dealing with anxiety-provoking situations, but in a controlled way, facilitated by others, can also prove effective.

Finally, as noted above, providing permanent and concrete information via pictures, written instructions or other cues may also help to clarify situations when verbal instructions alone are inadequate, again reducing the need for stereotyped speech or repetitive questioning.

Developing communication skills in less able individuals

Although there are many texts available on the teaching of communication skills to people with autism (see Quill, 1995a) the majority of these have focused on young children, rather than adults. In adulthood the *acquisition* of novel, complex and spontaneous communication skills tends to be limited. This is hardly surprising, since anyone who has managed to cope with only minimal communicative ability for many years will hardly be greatly motivated to acquire new skills later in life. Although programmes designed to increase the communicative use of signs or pictures have had some degree of success, the spontaneous generalisation of such skills to untrained settings is often poor. And, even if alternative skills such as signing are acquired, they tend to be used in the same stereotyped, non-communicative and ritualistic way that typifies spoken language in autism (Attwood, Frith and Hermelin, 1988).

In recent years, the most promising results in improving communication skills have stemmed from studies examining the communicative functions (or 'functional equivalence') of so-called 'challenging behaviours' (see Durand, 1990 for a detailed account of this approach). It is apparent that many such behaviours, far from being *inappropriate*, may be the only way in which someone with very limited communication skills can rapidly, effectively and predictably gain control over his or her environment. Indeed, analysis of the function of these behaviours frequently indicates that so-called 'maladaptive behaviours' may be extremely *adaptive* and effective if an individual is unable to express his or her needs, feelings or emotions in any other way. Headbanging, throwing the TV across the room, pulling someone's hair, are all likely to result in rapid and usually predictable responses from others. An unwanted activity may be stopped, boredom may be relieved, and certainly attention will be received. Analysis of the possible reasons underlying these behaviours, and their subsequent replacement by alternative ways of communicating feelings of distress, frustration, neglect or anxiety can help greatly to decrease aggressive, self-injurious or stereotyped behaviours. In other words, if people can be taught alternative ways of communicating the same message, whether verbally, by gestures, tokens, signs, touch, or even by pressing a micro-switch, then appropriate communication is likely to increase, whilst challenging behaviours decline (Oliver, 1995). Carr and Durand and their co-workers have demonstrated, in a number of different studies, that teaching individuals to express their need for assistance by means of a simple word, phrase, sign or picture indicating 'help me', or enabling them to obtain attention or desired objects, or to escape unwanted situations by similar means has rapid and positive effects (Durand and Carr, 1991; Durand, 1990). Thus, as the communicative behaviours increase there is a concomitant decline in previously existing 'disruptive behaviours'.

Nevertheless, it is important to recognise that much of this work, although clearly very effective, has been conducted in highly intensive experimental settings. Detailed analyses of the possible functions of undesirable behaviours may require considerable time, expertise and technology and are often impracticable within mainstream settings (Owens and MacKinnon, 1993). In their attempts to overcome these practical difficulties, Durand and Crimmins have produced a 'Motivation Assessment Scale' (1988) which can be used by carers to classify the main functions of disruptive behaviours. They suggest that the majority of such behaviours can be categorised as attention-seeking, self-stimulatory, escape or avoidance, or as indicating the need for help or assistance. Once the primary function of a behaviour has been identified in this way, the individual can be provided with alternative forms of communication (signs, words, simple phrases, pictures, symbols or gestures) to obtain the same ends.

Despite its potential value, the reliability and validity of the Motivation Assessment Scale have received some criticism (Newton and Sturmey, 1991; Zarcone, *et al.*, 1991; Sigafoos, Kerr and Roberts, 1994). In particular, it has often proved difficult for different raters to reach agreement on the reasons for the behaviours assessed, and the four summary categories cannot encompass all the possible reasons for disruptive behaviours. Nevertheless, by helping carers to appreciate that such behaviours may be a function of poor *communication* skills, rather than being 'deliberate' acts of aggression or provocation, it may have a positive effect on both attitudes and approaches to intervention.

A similar, but less complex form of assessment, is the schedule devised by Schuler and colleagues (Schuler, *et al.*, 1989; see Table 3.1). Although designed primarily for *children* with autism there is no reason why a schedule of this kind should not be adapted for use with adults. By systematically questioning how an individual expresses his or her need to do something (sit by someone, obtain food or some other object, protest if something is taken away, etc.), this process can again help to indicate how behaviours that may be viewed as 'inappropriate' (screaming, self-injury, tantrums, aggression, etc.) can have important communicative functions. This information can then

Table 3.1 Assessing communicative behaviours (from Schuler *et al.*, 1989)

CUE QUESTIONS	Crying	Aggression	Tantrums/Self-Injury	Passive Gaze	Proximity	Pulling Other's Hands	Touching/Moving Other's Face	Grabs/Reaches	Enactment	Removes Self/Walks Away	Vocalization/Noise	Active Gaze	Gives Object	Gestures/Pointing	Facial Expression	Shakes 'no'/Nods 'yes'	Intonation	Inappropriate Echolalia	Appropriate Echolalia	One-Word Speech	One-Word Signs	Complex Speech	Complex Signs
1. Requests for affection/interaction: WHAT IF S WANTS																							
adult to sit near?																							
peer to sit near?																							
non-hand peer to sit near?																							
adult to look at him?																							
adult to tickle him?																							
to cuddle/embrace?																							
to sit on adult's lap?																							
other:																							
2. Requests for adult action: WHAT IF S WANTS																							
help with dressing?																							
to be read a book?																							
to play ball/a game?																							
to go outside to store?																							
other:																							
3. Requests for Object, Food, or Things: WHAT IF S WANTS																							
an object out of reach?																							
a door/container opened?																							
a favourite food?																							
music/radio/tv?																							
keys/toy/book?																							
other:																							
4. Protest: WHAT IF																							
common routine is dropped?																							
favorite toy/food taken away?																							
taken for ride w/out desire?																							
adult terminates interaction?																							
required to do something doesn't want to?																							
Other:																							
5. Declaration/Comment: WHAT IF S WANTS																							
to show you something?																							
you to look at something?																							
other:																							

be used to plan ways in which alternative and more acceptable responses might be established.

Increasing general communicative ability

The need to increase communicative skills is not, of course, restricted to individuals who exhibit challenging behaviours. Often, once they leave school and are relieved from the daily pressure on them to communicate, the language of less able people with autism ceases to show major improvements, and may even decrease in frequency or complexity. Because care staff working in adult units may be unaware of the previous capabilities of the individual concerned they may accept relatively impoverished language levels as being quite normal. Utterances may also become very abbreviated, so much so that their meaning can be quite obscure to people who do not know them well. Peter, for example, on moving to a new adolescent unit confused all the staff there by repeating constantly the phrase 'Morris Mummy, Morris Mummy', becoming very distressed when no-one responded. Enquiries to staff at his previous unit revealed that the phrase had originated many years earlier when the family lived in the country and an old Morris car was his mother's only source of transport. Many years (and cars) later, the same phrase was still used to indicate his wish to go out. Only when staff at the new unit began systematically to prompt and encourage more appropriate requests did his use of language begin to improve.

In other cases it is crucial that new staff or carers are made fully aware of an individual's potential ability and ensure that an appropriate level of skill is maintained. In the long term it will not be helpful if people with spoken language are allowed to take whatever they need without asking, or to communicate simply by means of signs or gesture. Similarly, if non-speaking individuals possess even very rudimentary gestures, staff should make sure that they are familiar with and respond to these; otherwise they are likely rapidly to disappear. If existing signs are not adequate within the new environment, then new and more appropriate ones may need to be taught. This may require staff themselves becoming trained in sign or symbol systems such as Makaton (Walker, 1980), but if this can be achieved the results can be very positive for all concerned.

For some individuals, even simple sign or symbol systems may be too complex. Layton and Watson (1995) provide a useful breakdown of the different skills required for using signs, pictures or written words with children who are non-verbal, and a similar strategy may be helpful in choosing alternative communication systems for adults. On the whole, a system using pictures or photographs makes least demands on cognitive, linguistic or memory skills although it is essential that the pictures used reflect the individual's particular interests or needs if they are to be used successfully. The PECS (Picture Exchange Communication System) of Bondy and Frost (in press) also stresses the need for the person with autism actively to handle the pictures (using Velcro or such to place them appropriately) if they are to make the association between the picture and the relevant item. Wall charts with photographs indicating the daily timetable, the staff who will be on duty, or the food on offer at meal times can ensure better understanding as well as enabling people to indicate their own choices more effectively. Individuals can be provided with their own personal set of photographs or pictures to enable them to indicate basic needs or wishes (for example, to leave the building, have a drink, go to the toilet, etc.). These must be easily accessible for both the staff and the individual, and might be attached to a key-ring on a belt, or on a clip-board, or even a long neck-chain (the sort that is often used for identity badges in large companies) – anything that is age-appropriate. A 'Triple Print' film processing system (which provides one large photo and two smaller copies for every negative) is also useful, providing identical pictures for staff and clients as well as for a central display. Picture cards should be updated or replaced as necessary, and be properly protected, preferably on laminated board. Even if there is little spontaneous use by the individual concerned, consistent prompting can be effective in gradually establishing the link between the picture and the resulting activity. Cards of this type also have the advantage, particularly in large or busy units, that they can be readily understood or used by new staff, whereas signs or more complex symbols may require prior knowledge or instruction.

If funds are available, the ever-increasing range of computerised communicative devices, developed primarily for use by individuals with severe physical impairments, can also be adapted for people with autism (Shane, 1994). Indeed some are now specially designed for this group. Interchangeable and increasingly complex keyboards make it possible for individuals to proceed gradually from single-symbol boards (with, for example, a large red square or circle that will emit a sound to attract attention) to multi-symbol displays, indicating a wide variety of stimuli, which can be personally tailored to the individual's own environment, needs or interests.[1]

The use of specialist equipment of this kind, which also incorporates prompting and shaping procedures to build up *independent* communication skills, should not be confused with the use of 'facilitated communication', discussed in Chapter 1, in which clients remain heavily dependent on the physical support of facilitators to type out messages. Despite extravagant claims, there is little evidence to suggest that the use of this technique does foster independent communication. Instead, 'messages' appear to be largely under the control of the facilitator, not the individual who is being facilitated.

Alternative, or augmentative, forms of communication may also be of help for individuals who are able to talk, but for some reason are reluctant to do so. Stuart, who had developed speech late in his childhood had never been a fluent speaker, but, during a period of severe depression, refused to utter anything other than an occasional 'Yes', 'No', 'Hello' or 'Goodbye'. When his depression finally responded to treatment he continued to resist speaking, becoming virtually non-communicating. In the past he had seemed to enjoy reading and writing and so, rather than insisting that he speak, which resulted in much anxiety and even aggression, his parents and day-care staff encouraged him to communicate in writing. This he was able to do quite effectively and, although he is still reluctant to talk spontaneously, he will read out what he has written and is able to express his needs and wishes very competently in this fashion. Recently he wrote a long letter to the BBC, pointing out a mistake in the rules of one of their quiz programmes (quiz games being his main obsession in life). He was delighted when they read this out to viewers and changed the rules accordingly!

Written communication, in a simpler form, may also be effective in helping other individuals to communicate their needs by single words. Computers, too, can be used to develop written ability in more able individuals, although care needs to be taken to ensure that their use also involves interactive skills; otherwise communication may be with the machine, and no-one else!

NOTES

1 See, for example, the range of Lightwriter equipment made by Churchill Ltd.

4 Social functioning in adulthood

Autism is associated with many different impairments in social functioning, and social deficits are at the core of all diagnostic systems, such as DSM-III-R and DSM-IV (American Psychiatric Association, 1980, 1994) or ICD–10 (WHO, 1993). Amongst the specific deficits noted are the failure to understand or respond appropriately to others' feelings or emotions, the lack of ability to share emotions or experiences, and poor integration of social, emotional and communicative behaviours within an interpersonal context.

Difficulties in all these areas tend to persist over time, even in the most able of individuals, and the pervasiveness and profundity of the social impairment continues to have a marked impact on almost every aspect of adult life. Nevertheless, as individuals approach adulthood many of the grosser social abnormalities evident in young children become less apparent. No longer are they likely to shrink away from all physical or social contact, or remain happiest left alone in a corner to indulge in ritualistic or obsessional behaviours. Problems lie instead in the understanding of social rules, in the ability to comprehend why others behave as they do, and in the interpretation of even the simplest of social situations.

The analogy of being like a stranger from outer space occurs in a number of personal accounts of autism. Therese Jolliffe, a postgraduate student with autism writes:

> Normal people, finding themselves on a planet with alien creatures on it would probably feel frightened, would not know how to fit in and would certainly have difficulties in understanding what the aliens were thinking, feeling and wanting, and how to respond correctly to these things. That's what autism is like . . . Life is bewildering, a confusing, interacting mass of people, events, places and things with no boundaries. Social life is hard because

it does not seem to follow a set pattern . . . I find it as difficult to understand the things I see as I do in trying to understand the things I hear. Looking at people's faces, particularly into their eyes, is one of the hardest things for me to do . . . People do not appreciate how unbearably difficult it is for me to look at a person . . . It disturbs my quietness and is terribly frightening.

(Jolliffe *et al.*, 1992)

In Oliver Sacks's (1993) interview with Temple Grandin in the *New Yorker* the notion of alien beings crops up again:

She said she could understand 'simple, strong, universal' emotions but was stumped by the more complex emotions and the games people play . . . She was bewildered, she said, by Romeo and Juliet ('I never knew what they were up to') . . . 'Much of the time . . . I feel like an anthropologist on Mars'.

Jim Sinclair (1992) a young man with autism comments in a similar vein:

I didn't need a cattle shute [referring to the support this offered Temple when she was younger]; I needed an orientation manual for extraterrestrials.

SOCIAL INTERACTIONS IN THOSE WHO ARE LESS ABLE

Social behaviours in those who are less able, of course, also continue to give rise to many difficulties. In this group there may continue to be avoidance of contact with others, and this, together with their lack of understanding of group situations, can make integration into community settings very difficult. In small group homes individuals may become very unhappy and distressed because of the social demands made on them. In Social Education Centres or other forms of day provision they may be equally out of place. Activities that other clients, students or residents particularly enjoy, such as holidays, special treats, birthdays or Christmas, may incorporate the very things that someone with autism finds most difficult: change, noise, unpredictability, novelty, crowds. Having to live or work in large groups, or in close proximity to people with whom they are unfamiliar can cause much distress, and may well produce aggressive and other disruptive behaviours. For those caring for them, their inability to take part in community or group activities, their failure to relate to other clients, and often their need for one-to-one staff input can produce intense strains on staffing.

Many of these problems are described by Hugh Morgan (1996) in his recent book on working with adults with autism in day and residential settings, and carers involved with this group should find much valuable information there to advise them. In the following chapter, therefore, the focus will be on individuals with autism who are more able. For them, making friends, talking to people and being engaged in social activities may become of supreme importance. In their case it is not *avoidance* of social interactions that poses problems, but the *quality* of these interactions. It is the desire for friendship, without the necessary social competence, which leads to many difficulties.

QUALITATIVE IMPAIRMENTS IN SOCIAL INTERACTIONS

Problems with peer relationships

The inability of young autistic children to engage in social play, to join in with the activities of their peer group, or to form close friendships is well documented (Schopler and Mesibov, 1983; Lord and Rutter, 1994). Indeed, many autistic children may avoid contact with others of their own age, preferring adult company, or, if they play at all, will tend to try to join in the games of much younger children. Aggression towards other children may also be a problem. Often, young children with autism have so few appropriate social skills that they may attempt to make contact with others simply by hitting them, or taking their belongings. As they grow older difficulties with peer relationships persist, but whereas in the case of young children there may be an active attempt to *avoid* contact with peers, later they may become much more anxious to be accepted, to join in with others, and to make friends. The problem is that often they are not sufficiently aware of their own social difficulties, and have little idea of the very complex sequences of interactions that are involved simply to enter into a social group (Dodge *et al.*, 1983).

Donna Williams (1992) remembers trying to make friends with a young girl in her neighbourhood:

'I did not know how to make friends, so I would stand there calling this girl every four-letter word I knew . . . Eventually [she] would take to her feet and chase me for several blocks . . . One day she caught me. She was about to 'smash my face in' when she decided at least to ask me why I had tormented her so persistently for so long. 'I wanted to be your friend', I blurted out furiously'.

Appreciation of the many complex and intertwined factors involved in the development of more intimate relationships is often entirely lacking. However, this is perhaps hardly surprising in that the skills necessary for forming and maintaining close friendships are so subtle and complicated that even most social scientists would admit to only partial and limited understanding of the 'rules' involved. Most human beings are born with a fundamental ability that enables them to understand why others feel or respond as they do and what their own responses, in turn, should be. Without this inborn understanding, and in the absence of any formal rules to guide social interactions, the simplest of personal contacts can, for someone with autism, become a frightening and confusing experience.

Even in more structured activities, such as games or sports, where rules are more explicit than in other social settings, people with autism can experience many problems, which again hamper integration. Christopher's mother reported that as a child he loved to play hide-and-seek but always accused other children of cheating when he was discovered. On one occasion he had a loud attack of coughing in the wardrobe where he was hiding but completely failed to understand how the other children could possibly have found him. As he grew older he was still only half able to grasp the rules of other games. In cricket he tended to run *away* from the ball if it came near him, and in football would always aim the ball for the nearer goal, regardless of team positions. Gradually he became vaguely aware that other children objected to having him in their teams, but he had no idea why this was the case. Similarly, although George was a very able cross-country runner, having a remarkable memory for routes and directions, he could never be relied on to win a race, because once he got near the finishing line he would wait to see who was coming next, often losing his place. Eventually, when he started work, his colleagues realised he would make a good member of their orienteering team, and this proved much more successful since there was then no need for him to come first.

Understanding friendship

Definitions of friendship vary but the qualities of closeness, sharing, helping, sympathy and empathy are fundamental to almost all descriptions. A real understanding of such abstract and elusive concepts, however, may be almost impossible for many people with autism. They may well realise that friendships exist, and indeed be aware that they *should* have friends, but without any true appreciation of the complexity of the relationships involved. Thus, whereas many adults with autism will describe themselves as having friends, detailed questioning generally reveals that although they have acquaintances to whom they can talk, there is rarely evidence of shared experiences or mutual understanding.

Considerable problems can arise because of this naive assumption of what constitutes a friend. If someone speaks in a friendly tone, or wishes them good morning on a daily basis, this may be mistaken as a token of much greater intimacy. Individuals who were simply being kind or polite may become the focus of the autistic person's wish to have a friend, and may be pursued unremittingly because of this.

Susie took the bus to her special college course every morning and another young woman who waited at the bus stop, recognising her disabilities, always made the effort to say 'Hello'. Susie asked where she lived and what time she got back from work and, eventually, somehow, also managed to get her telephone number. As time went on she began to wait for the young woman's return from work and would follow her home, or telephone her as soon as she knew she was in the house. The woman involved became more and more upset by this intrusion and eventually contacted the college authorities. Although the tutors tried to explain that this behaviour must stop, Susie insisted that the woman was her friend, and showed no perception of the distress she was causing.

Phillip, who lived in semi-sheltered accommodation, was allotted a support worker living in the same complex to help him in case of difficulties. He became more and more attached to this young woman, following her to work each morning and waiting for her to come home. If she were late he would become very distressed and he would stay up until two or three in the morning waiting for her. On one occasion he telephoned her grandparents in the early hours of the morning to tell them she had not yet come home.

Stanley, who had just begun a college course was allotted a 'buddy' – a volunteer student – who would keep a check on him and ensure that all was going well. On one occasion, feeling sorry for his isolation, the student suggested that Stan came along to the pub with him to meet some of his friends. Once he realised that the group met every Friday night, Stan would appear there without fail, despite their obvious annoyance at this intrusion.

Danny went to his local pub regularly once a week and would try to engage any young women there in conversation. On one occasion he was threatened with being beaten up after he had moved into their boy friends' seats during a darts match. After some weeks the barman asked him not to return because of complaints that he was 'harassing' women customers. Danny could not accept this, insisting that the women enjoyed his company and conversation (mostly concerning 1960's pop-music). Because they had not wished to be offensive they had not complained to him directly, and he remained oblivious to indications of irritation and annoyance. He refused to obey the barman's instructions and when he attempted to return to the pub as usual the following week, the police had to be called to eject him.

Even the tolerance of individuals with a specific goal of helping others can be stretched to the limit by the uncomprehending demands of someone with autism. Gerry, a young man in his early twenties, had become involved with a small religious organisation, after members had called at his house. Delighted by the attention and 'friendship' offered by people of his own age group, Gerry enthusiastically joined in the group's activities. He was constantly at the house of one member or another and when a vacancy arose in the flat shared by some of them Gerry immediately moved in. The group members seemed to have a sincere desire to help people in difficulties and they offered Gerry much support over several years. Eventually, however, even they found the constant demands for their time and attention too much, and reluctantly they had to ask Gerry's father to take him back home. Gerry himself could not understand this 'betrayal' and was left confused, saddened and embittered by his experience.

Understanding who is NOT a friend

Not only do people with autism have innate difficulties in understanding the nature of friendship, they may also have profound problems in interpreting whether someone is being unkind or even malicious. As is evident from the scenarios above, if someone simply speaks to them they may interpret this as a sign of great friendship. Similarly, if asked to do something for someone they will feel obliged to comply, because 'that's what friends are for'. Such naive interpretations clearly make the person with autism highly vulnerable to the demands of others. In mainstream schools it is not uncommon for children with autism to be deliberately led into trouble by other children who take a delight in exploiting this vulnerability. As the child with autism is frequently unable to appreciate the difference between children laughing *with* them and *at* them, they can be easily led into all sorts of outrageous behaviours. Attempts to 'buy friendships' with money, sweets or other goods are also common. Other people with autism may fall prey to the wiles of others simply because they do not know how else to behave. Mark was a young man in his mid-teens whose main activity was cycling. On his fixed cycling route he frequently passed a group of youngsters belonging to the local 'gang'. One day one of them stopped him and asked for a ride on his bike; another asked if he would lend them some money. Mark handed over his bike and wallet and only when he returned home without either several hours later did his parents realise what had happened. Having a good idea who had taken his belongings his parents managed to get the bike and his wallet (now empty) returned. However, despite warnings to avoid the gang in future, or at least to protect himself by hiding his money, Mark took no such precautions, and much to his parents' exasperation similar incidents continued at regular intervals. His only explanation was that since the boys talked to him they must be his 'friends' and therefore he should not refuse their requests.

This fear of displeasing people is a powerful factor in the lives of many able people with autism. Margaret Dewey's autistic son, Jack, is quoted by his mother (1991) as saying, 'It has always been one of the worst traumas for me to feel I have displeased somebody. I tend to remember it years afterwards. It hurts more than I can bear, practically. One thing I do is day dream about how I can be reconciled with people I have displeased, and change their opinion of me.'

This obvious vulnerability may lead to increasing anxieties for parents as their children grow older and demand greater independence. Owen had always had a fascination for Welsh rugby, and had been known to the men in his local club since he was a young child. Before a match he would wander into their dressing rooms and chat to them, and was much liked and accepted there. As he grew older, however, he began travelling alone to matches around the country, and it was only when his father accompanied him one day that he realised he was still wandering into changing rooms and talking to players. He showed no awareness that this behaviour might lead him into difficulties and his parents did not even attempt to explain the possible risks of engaging in friendly conversations with unknown young men.

Failure to understand or respond appropriately to others' feelings or emotions

Even within family settings, where there may be much greater understanding of the individual's difficulties, the lack of empathy and social understanding can continue to cause hurt and distress.

In the earliest months of life young infants will spontaneously show their delight at seeing familiar adults and they rapidly learn to respond in socially appropriate and effective ways. Subsequently they learn, too, to be more discriminating in their greeting behaviours: who to hug and kiss, who to tell more intimate secrets to, who to remain more restrained with. People with autism often lack this natural ability to respond to others appropriately, or to differentiate between interactions with familiar and unfamiliar adults. Often, they may fail to show any clear response to people, unless they are directly addressed. As children, few will rush to greet their parents returning from work or even a prolonged trip away, and this apparent 'coldness' or 'insensitivity' may continue into adulthood.

Jack, for example, has a father who is a deep-sea diver. He can be away for long and unpredictable periods of time, but Jack always insists on being given an exact time and date for his return. When his father comes home his only comments relate to whether his return is too early, too late or on time. His father recounts with some sadness that 'he has never once just said "Hello"'. Robbie's mother admits her mistake in once asking him whom he loved best, her or the Hotpoint washing machine (his particular obsession). His reply was unequivocal, but not the one she had hoped to hear! Jim's parents, on the other hand, were delighted when he came to meet them at the airport after they had been abroad for some weeks. He did not say 'Hello' or ask them if they had had a good trip, and as soon as they got in the car he began telling them of the new records he had bought. However, his presence in itself was enough to reassure his mother that he did indeed love them: 'He just doesn't know how to say it'.

Even if individuals with autism do recognise the need for greetings, or other expressions of emotion, this is often done in a highly formalised and hence inappropriate way. Ben, a young man now living independently, writes frequently to his mother and sister, of whom he is clearly very fond. After his sister's marriage he always writes to her as 'Dear Mrs Brown' and he always concludes his letters to both of them by: 'Yours Sincerely, Ben Smith (Mr)'. He cannot understand why his mother and his sister find this formality strange, and despite their suggestions has continued to insist that this is the 'correct' way to write a letter.

Even strong emotions such as grief may be very difficult to express appropriately. When Joe's father was dying everyone in the family was distraught. Joe himself could not talk directly about his sorrow or anxiety, but instead dealt with his feelings by constantly asking his mother for details of why his father was dying, what parts of his body were affected, exactly when he would die, and how much he would leave him in his will.

Joshua's father was a news cameraman on war assignment in Bosnia. When he went missing for several days Josh never once tried to comfort his mother or sister, but constantly asked them instead how many heavy weapons each side had and how many people they thought would be killed. When his father finally returned all he did was question him about how many dead bodies he had photographed. Some time later Josh was asked whether he had felt anxiety about his father at the time. He replied that of course he had, and that he had been aware that his mother and sister were upset. But he did not know what to say to them, or how to explain his own feelings, and he thought if he talked about dead bodies they would know he was upset. His mother and sister also report that although, deep down, they understand Joshua's difficulties and knew that he was not being deliberately callous, at the time they could not help but feel very hurt and angry at the way he behaved.

Sometimes, this apparent lack of feeling can prove the final straw for carers. Kenny's mother, who had looked after him with patience and understanding throughout his 15 years, resorted to calling Social Services late one night, saying that she could no longer cope with him at home. The duty social worker quickly managed to calm things down and it transpired that the crisis had arisen after mother's late return from work. She had had a particularly difficult week, but had nevertheless stopped to do the weekly shopping at the supermarket which stocked Kenny's favourite brands. On the way home her car had broken down and it was some hours later before she was eventually towed home. Kenny helped her unload the shopping as he usually did, although complaining about the lateness of the evening meal. However, when he realised that she had not got his favourite brand of orange juice he returned with her coat, telling her that if she hurried she could just get to a delicatessen some miles away before it closed. His mother, normally a quiet and gentle woman, had responded by throwing the rest of the shopping at him and then, in desperation, ringing Social Services. The next day she was very abashed by her response, knowing that he had not acted out of deliberate malice. However, Kenny was totally incapable of understanding why his mother should have reacted in this way to such a reasonable request, and he still refers to it, rather patronisingly, as the time when his mother 'went a little bit mad'.

Accurate recognition of others' emotions, unless these are very extreme, is often seriously impaired. Signs of irritation or annoyance in other people often go unheeded; then when they finally give full vent to their feelings, the person with autism is often genuinely surprised, having no prior inkling that anything was the matter. Moreover, even if problems are recognised, what to do about them presents major difficulties. David, a young man in his twenties, has finally learned to bring his mother a box of tissues if she is upset. He will still not attempt to comfort her, but stands poised with the tissue box until she takes one, then quickly goes away. Ruth, a woman of normal intelligence, now in her twenties is pleased that she has finally learned to recognise when her mother is upset or ill (although she still fails to recognise signs in other family members). Her mother, who is a frequent sufferer from migraine, confirms that this is the case, but admits somewhat ruefully that it might be better if she did not. The problem is that once Ruth realises there is a problem she will constantly question her mother about what it is, why it has occurred, or what she might do to help, when the last thing her mother wants to do is talk to anyone.

Knowledge that different emotions exist may also be limited. Justin, a man in his mid-twenties, who had suddenly begun reading fiction instead of his usual books on astronomy, admitted that he had not known before about people having feelings of love or hatred or jealousy, until he actually read about such things. Because of this failure to understand how others think or feel, even the most ordinary of social interactions presents enormous difficulties. Temple Grandin, in her interview with Oliver Sacks, is reported as believing, when a child, that other children must be telepathic because of their ability to communicate together in ways that she totally failed to follow or comprehend. Howlin and Rutter (1987) also quote the example of a man in his late thirties who had come for their advice on 'how to read people's minds'. He was working in an office, and was astute enough to recognise that he was having problems in interpreting what was said to him. Told sarcastically 'You just do that again . . .' after he had done something particularly foolish, he would obediently do so! Because other people in the office seemed to know when it was not appropriate to follow instructions, and because of his interest in science fiction, he had concluded that the others had learned to read minds; hence his request for help. Of course what they were reading was not minds, but the shrug of a shoulder, the raising of an eyebrow, the inflection of the voice – things about which he knew, or had read, nothing.

Another aspect of the failure to empathise with other people's feelings is reflected in the inability to assess the impact of one's own actions on other people. Robert, an 18-year-old, whose obsessional behaviour and constant questioning at home continually intrudes into family life, is unable to understand why these behaviours are unacceptable. He claims that his parents are just trying to 'treat him like a child' and that they should realise he is now an adult. To him, being an adult means doing exactly what *he* wants, and as he has no recognition of the needs or indeed rights of other family members, he views any attempts to modify his behaviour as unreasonably restrictive.

The failure to share emotions or experiences

A lack of 'shared attention', or the failure to participate in the activities or enjoyment of others, has been highlighted as a particular deficit of children with autism and is a problem that tends clearly to distinguish them from children with other developmental or communication disorders (Sigman *et al.*, 1986). Few children with autism try to share their own enjoyment with others; nor do they seem able to share in other people's feelings of pleasure or happiness. Rarely will they attempt spontaneously to point out things of interest to others. And, if they are ever invited to parties (an uncommon event for most) they are unable to participate in the group enjoyment in a normal way. Either they will remove themselves from the situation altogether or, alternatively, 'go over the top', becoming far too excited and overactive, often ruining everyone else's enjoyment. Danny, now in his late teens, remembers hiding under beds or tables whenever he went to a party, and says 'I never could understand what all the fuss was about'. Charles is described by his mother as always hating Christmas when he was a child. However, as he grew older he began to take a more active role in the yearly ritual, and now rather enjoys it. Unfortunately, 'ritual' is exactly what it has become. The family still have to eat, open presents, and play games exactly as they did when he was a child. He now spends a lot of money buying them presents, but in turn is very concerned about the cost of the gifts they give him. After wishing everyone 'Happy Christmas' he will quiz them on how much they spent on his presents, becoming very upset if he feels they have not spent enough.

Spontaneous pleasure in other people's happiness or excitement seems to be rare, and although some may try to share interests or activities with others this is often done in a rather stereotyped way. Danny, who is now in his twenties and still living at home, claims that he always tells his parents about things in which he thinks they will be interested. Although his mother and father admit that he does this, the problem is that he has no real understanding of what *does* interest them. If they are watching a favourite programme on the television he will interrupt to tell them about an exciting computer or computer program he has just heard about, or try to get them to read something in his computer magazine. When they appear less than enthusiastic he complains that they never take any notice of him.

Just as they are often unable to share pleasurable experiences, many people with autism are unable to share pain and distress in the normal way. Examples of inappropriate responses to other people's distress are described above but people with autism are just as likely to have problems talking about their own feelings or experiences. In discussions with young adults with autism, it is often apparent that they were badly teased and bullied at school, sometimes by teachers as well as other pupils. However, very often they were quite unable to explain to their families what was happening, or to seek help. For example, although Leonard attended normal school and seemed to have adequate language skills, the only way his parents knew if he was upset by events or people at school was when he bit the teachers. Even years later, when he was experiencing problems with a supervisor at work, he resorted to threats to bite her, and remained unable to resolve the situation by talking over his difficulties.

Poor integration of social behaviours

In many cases, it is not that *what* the person with autism does is wrong in itself, but that it is inappropriate within a particular social setting or context. Understanding where, when and how it is appropriate to act in a particular way requires much more subtle and complex social understanding than is often available to someone with autism.

Sharon, a woman in her thirties, had always had great difficulty in talking about personal issues but, over the years and with the help of a very supportive social worker, she has learned to express herself much more effectively. What she has never learned to do is discriminate *when* or *with whom* such personal revelations are appropriate.

Gerry, as a young child, was very aloof and remote and was deliberately encouraged by his parents to tolerate being hugged and kissed by visitors or friends. Now, a much more outgoing individual in his early twenties, he hugs almost everyone he meets, calling them 'Darling' or 'My lovely'. Whilst his mother's older female friends are rather gratified by such behaviour, younger women find it much less politically correct, and men are even more unsure how to respond.

The potential drawbacks of allowing behaviours that may be quite socially acceptable in a young child to continue into adulthood are often overlooked but they can have serious implications. Sarah, when younger, had a very poor appetite and in order to get her to eat her mother used to encourage her to take tempting items from other people's plates. Now a relatively socially competent student attending college, she is still likely to lean over and remove food from her neighbour's plate without warning.

Another example is Laurie who had always had a fascination with earrings. As a young child his mother had often been able to calm his tantrums or distress by encouraging him to play with her earrings and certain teachers at school had also allowed this. By the time he was 20, being allowed to touch earrings was still a very effective way of calming him down. However, when he began attending a local Social Education Centre, problems quickly arose when he started to fondle the earrings, or sometimes the ears of other students and staff, both male and female.

Other problems occur because of the poor ability of someone with autism to integrate different modes of communication in socially or contextually appropriate ways. The problems of inappropriate or poorly modulated intonation in speech have been described in the previous chapter but many other aspects of non-verbal communication may also be impaired. Gestures, if used at all, may be very stiff and stilted or, alternatively, far too dramatic and exaggerated. Eye-contact, facial expression or smiles may also be affected. Many autistic children go through a stage of actively avoiding eye-contact with others, or they may have a very limited range of facial expressions. As they grow older such skills do emerge, but often with impairments in timing or sequencing. Janet had, from the time she was little, been instructed to 'Look at people when you're talking to them'. This she now does, but lacking any innate awareness of the subtle and complex rules governing eye-contact, her direct and unremitting gaze is far more disconcerting and socially disruptive than if she were to look away.

Jonah, now in his thirties, had also been told at one stage to 'smile' when talking to people. This he now does, frequently with incongruent effects. When his favourite cat died he recounted the sad story with a large grin on his face and, more seriously, when he became depressed it proved very difficult for an unfamiliar psychiatrist to assess his mental state, as he smiled unwaveringly throughout the interview.

Problems in the appropriate use of facial or vocal expression have also been illustrated in a number of experimental studies. Work with children has indicated that they have difficulties in expressing even simple emotions such as happiness and sadness correctly and that their range of gesture or facial expressiveness is also limited (Langdell 1978; Attwood, Frith and Hermelin, 1988; Snow, Hertzig and Shapiro, 1987). Macdonald and colleagues (1989) found that adults with autism, all of whom were of normal intelligence, showed many more unusual aspects in their expression of emotion than did controls. The appropriateness of their facial expression, as related to different social situations, was also significantly more impaired.

Failure to interpret cues

These problems in emotional and social expression are parallelled by difficulties in recognising or responding appropriately to the emotional expressions of others. Hobson, in a series of studies, has explored the problems shown by children with autism in identifying and recognising emotions, or in matching emotional states to social contexts (Hobson, 1993). Macdonald and colleagues (1989) also examined the ability of adults with autism to interpret how people were feeling from their facial expression or tone of voice. Although there was considerable individual variation, the autistic group was found to be significantly more impaired on such tasks as compared with control subjects of similar intelligence and verbal ability.

Although many able people with autism are aware that smiles, gesture, touch, facial expression and eye-contact play a crucial role in social interactions it may still prove very difficult for them to interpret these correctly. Jeanette, for example, is a science student at university studying for a doctoral degree. She is fully aware of the importance of social cues such as eye-contact and smiles but admits that she lacks the ability to interpret such cues correctly, and is painfully aware of her own difficulties in expressing emotions in an appropriate way. She describes her situation as being similar to that of someone who is blind. 'It's like knowing that other people can see, but not understanding what it's like to be able to do so. It's like that for me when it comes to understanding what other people are thinking or feeling.'

Rules, 'morality' and deception

A further and paradoxical twist to this inability to understand or follow normal social rules, is that once a rule is acquired, it may be adhered to rigidly and inflexibly, regardless of other social factors. When someone with autism knows something is 'right' or 'wrong' they may often cling avidly to this view, whatever the circumstances. Lorna Wing cites the example of someone in the police force, who finding that the parking meter where he had left his car had expired whilst he was on a case, immediately wrote himself a parking ticket! As described in more detail in Chapter 6, children with autism in mainstream schools encounter many difficulties because of their insistence on sticking rigidly to rules, and trying to ensure that others do the same. Correcting other children for talking in class or inform- ing the head if any are seen smoking is not usually done out of any sense of malice, but because of the belief that if a rule is being broken, those in charge should be aware of this. In work situations, too, strict adherence to working practices can result in conflict with both staff and employers (see Chapter 8).

At home, as well, it can produce problems. Johnny's mother had told him *never* to open the door unless she or his father were in the house and, because of his vulnerability, she had deliberately practised this with him on several occasions, pretending to be a stranger asking for admittance. When one day she returned home without her key she refused to open the door and despite her protestations she had to wait outside until her husband returned. Oliver, who lived with foster parents, had been told that he must always come in quietly at night so that he did not wake the younger children. One evening he returned from his social club without his key. Although the lights were still on in the house he made no attempt to rouse anyone. When found next morning, sleeping in the large rabbit hutch in the garden, he explained that ringing the bell would have woken the other children and he had been told never to do this. His only complaint was that the rabbits 'had moved about a lot in the night' and had kept him awake.

David had a much younger brother with whom he enjoyed playing chess and computer games. However, he invariably won such games and when his mother suggested that he should let his little brother 'win' from time to time he became very upset, insisting this would be a form of cheating. There was no appreciation of the fact that no harm could come from acting in this way, and that it would help to encourage his young sibling. Indeed, understanding that there are rules, but that in some circumstances rules need to be broken, is for many people with autism a perplexing and confusing concept, which they may never adequately grasp.

Deception, too, is a skill that may never be acquired. Deception involves understanding not only one's own actions but the impact of what is done or said on other people's behaviour. This complex sequence of events is likely to be beyond the scope of most individuals with autism. While the notion of innocence may have its attractions, in a world that is far from innocent, the vulnerability and honesty of people with autism can be too easily exploited or abused. They are the ones left holding the brick outside the video centre whilst the other youths have made off with the goods; it is they who may be used to shop-lift, or even drive a stolen car whilst other people wait in the background. While such incidents are rare, they do occur, and again reflect the inability of people with autism to understand what is in other people's minds.

'Mindblindness'

The belief that other people must be able to 'mind-read' in order to interpret social situations, as expressed by one of the individuals described above, gives some indication of the profundity of the deficits in this area. Possible reasons for this failure to understand how other people think or feel, or why they respond in the way they do have been explored in much detail (Frith, 1989, 1991, Happé and Frith, 1995, Baron-Cohen, Tager-Flusberg and Cohen, 1993). It is clear that individuals with autism, whatever their intellectual ability, are seriously impaired in their ability to understand other people's beliefs, knowledge, emotions, desires, intentions or feelings. This ability to attribute mental states to oneself or other people is crucial for social understanding, and in normal child development is well established from the age of 3 to 4 years. In autism, however, the ability to 'understand minds' remains profoundly affected throughout life. 'Mindblindness' is the term used in Simon Baron-Cohen's inspired essay on theory of mind mechanisms and autism to convey the enormity of the deficit (Baron-Cohen, 1995). Of course, 'theory of mind' is not actually a theory as such, nor does it help to explain *why* individuals with autism suffer from this particular deficit. (For a discussion of possible mechanisms involved see Baron-Cohen, 1995; Baron-Cohen *et al*. 1993; C. Frith, 1995.) Nevertheless, it provides a crucial groundwork for understanding the extent of the social impairment in autism. Without the ability to comprehend the meaning behind what someone is saying, without the realisation that other people have different beliefs, or emotions, or feelings, or share different backgrounds or experiences, almost every social interaction is likely to result in difficulties and misunderstandings.

At the most fundamental level, even superficial social encounters will be marred by the inability to appreciate the need for basic contextual information. Thus, the individual with autism is likely to embark on detailed monologues referring to his or her special interests, without any attempt to ensure that the listener has any background knowledge or interest in the topics raised. When more complex social interactions are involved the pervasiveness of the deficit may be even more apparent. A characteristic example is the case of Arthur, who was a very competent computer analyst. His particular role at work was to identify the 'bugs' in other peoples' computer programs, a task at which he was remarkably skilled. Unfortunately, his inability to understand *that they could not understand what was wrong* made it almost impossible for him to explain the problems or help people to correct their errors. Many other examples, taken from clinical practice, of the impact of the failure to understand mental states on social interactions are described by Baron-Cohen and Howlin (1993).

WHAT CAN BE DONE TO IMPROVE SOCIAL FUNCTIONING?

Although the previous section has concentrated on the profundity and pervasiveness of the social deficits in autism, this should not be taken as an indication that there is little that can be done to improve the lives of people with autism or their families. It is true that intervention is unlikely to 'cure' the fundamental deficits in social understanding, but nevertheless much can be done to minimise difficulties, and, in particular, to prevent the occurrence of secondary problems arising from social impairments.

Begin at the beginning

Without doubt, the most crucial component of any social intervention programme is the need to provide clear, simple and concise guidelines of what is and what is not acceptable from as early an age as possible. The natural social awareness of normal children means that they readily learn to modify their behaviour according to social context almost from infancy. Behaviours indulged in at home, such as baby-talk, object attachments, immature patterns of interaction, are all rapidly dispensed with when the child enters the world of other children and adults. Few, if indeed any, explicit rules exist on *how* or *when* behaviours should change, nor are there guidelines on how to assess the complex (and often conflicting) requirements of differing social interactions. Nevertheless, most children have no need of such guidelines: they are born with an innate sense that enables them to recognise unwritten social rules, to appreciate subtle changes in social interactions, and to adapt their behaviours appropriately. In autism not only is recognition of these implicit rules impaired, so too is the ability to change behaviours accordingly. Thus, patterns of behaviour that are accepted, perhaps even encouraged as a child, will remain part of the social repertoire as they grow older, no matter how socially unacceptable these may become. A young child who enjoys running his hands up and down women's legs, because he likes the feel of their tights, or one who enjoys putting his hands down the front of women's jumpers, because they feel soft and warm is likely to be viewed with amused tolerance; a 12-year-old who does the same is unlikely to be treated so indulgently and a 20-year-old will find himself in serious trouble. However, the individual with autism will have little ability to recognise *when* or *why* a previously accepted behaviour suddenly becomes unacceptable. The onus is thus firmly on carers to ensure that behaviours that are likely to give rise to pro-blems in the longer term are discouraged from an early age. Unfortu-nately, this is a counsel of perfection that is not easy to follow. It is not difficult to understand why the parents of a previously withdrawn child should praise and encourage him when, eventually, he begins to talk to, greet, or even hug and kiss everyone he meets. However, it is subsequently extremely difficult for an autistic teenager to understand why such behaviours are suddenly *discouraged,* and he or she may understandably resent such apparent inconsistency. The ability of parents to see into the future, and to predict the possibility of later problems, can be a crucial factor in preventing or at least minimising social difficulties but this may be at the cost of placing restrictions on the few social behaviours shown by the child earlier on.

At about the age of 7, Harry began to copy his older sister's habit of hugging and kissing all her friends, much to the amusement of the family and the entertainment of visitors. However, his mother, aware of his tendency to become fixed in routines, worried that this behaviour could lead to problems in other settings as he grew older. Much against the wishes of her daughter and her friends she insisted that Harry should not be allowed to respond in this way. Instead he was taught to shake hands and say 'Hello, how are you?', a much less spontaneous and natural response, but one which his mother recognised would stand him in better stead in years to come.

A similar dilemma was faced by Kieren's mother. Because of his behaviour problems she had great difficulty in finding baby-sitters for him. The only reason she was able to retain one or two was that, no matter how much trouble he caused during their stay, as they left he would always tell them how much he loved them and give them a great hug and kiss. By the time he was 12, she realised that it was time to discourage these behaviours, and rather reluctantly placed an embargo on physical interactions of this kind. Other behaviours, such as removing clothing, revealing intimate personal or family details, approaching strangers, wandering into other people's houses or gardens, whilst acceptable, if not always desirable, in a 3 or 4 year-old, may become a source of embarrassment, rejection, or even personal danger in later years. Thus, basic rules of behaviour must be established from as early an age as possible.

Learning the rules of social behaviour

Unfortunately, the fundamental problem in attempting to formulate rules to guide social interactions is that, in the majority of cases, such behaviours are not governed by formal or explicit rules. There is an inborn sense of what is or is not acceptable in different situations, and an innate ability to recognise when social demands change, even though the setting and the people involved are apparently the same. Even if rules do exist, these are so complex, and so dependent on innate social sensitivities, that there is rarely any point in trying to operationalise them. However, without this innate understanding, rules will be all that the person with autism has to guide his or her behaviour, and, imperfect as they are, they will be crucial for acceptable social development.

Individuals may also need to be given specific guidance on when, how often or how to carry out tasks that are necessary for social acceptance. Maurice, as a teenager, had many problems because of his ritualistic washing habits. He would only shave every three days, bath once a week, and wash his hair once a fortnight. This routine was strictly adhered to, whatever activities he had been involved in.

Over the years his parents had slowly managed to increase the frequency of his washing but they were worried that he might develop equally unhelpful routines when he moved into semi-sheltered accommodation. In collaboration with Maurice and his care-workers a daily timetable was drawn up, specifying what activities should be done on each day of the week. In order to avoid the routine becoming too rigid, a slightly different timetable was organised for each week. Eventually, provided with a list of tasks that had to be completed on a daily or regular weekly basis, Maurice was able to design his own monthly timetables, without help from others.

Often, even for very intelligent individuals, there is little point in offering detailed explanations of *why* certain behaviours are unacceptable. This may have no impact on the behaviour, and may lead to prolonged and futile arguments. Gerald's parents, for example, tried to stop him walking around the streets at night whenever he could not sleep. The problem was made worse because they lived on the edge of a very rough area of south London and although Gerald did not actually go out in his pyjamas he would don any item close to hand, including his mother's pink tracksuit and on one occasion a black plastic bin-liner. When they tried to explain to him the potential danger of this behaviour he immediately produced detailed and lengthy statistics on the relatively low risks of a 16-year-old, such as himself, being 'mugged' in that particular area.

Unsuspected difficulties may arise, of course, when it becomes necessary to *bend or break* established rules. It may be essential to take off one's clothes, or to talk about intimate personal details, for example, when visiting the doctor, or if in hospital; it may be necessary to approach strangers if one is lost or needs help; similarly it may be acceptable to take off most of one's clothes on a beach, or, as relationships develop, to begin to reveal more about personal feelings. In such circumstances rules may well prove counter-productive.

Daniel's parents experienced difficulties when he was a little child because of his tendency to take off all his clothes whenever he could. From his early teens, therefore, they made a rule that he could strip down to his underpants or shorts *only* in the house (and then only if there were no visitors there), *or* in the swimming pool, *or* in the gym at school, *or* if he was examined by a nurse or doctor. As they lived in the north of England they felt they could cope with occasional visits to the beach, where his insistence on remaining fully dressed was a sensible precaution. Problems arose, however, when the family moved to Australia. In order to encourage him to wear fewer clothes when the weather was hot, they provided him with a wrist watch with an integral thermometer and when the temperature reached a certain level he was told he could strip down to his under-shorts. By ensuring that these were the same style as other young men's shorts, his appearance in underpants was socially quite acceptable and Daniel's parents rightly congratulated themselves on their imaginative approach to the problem. Unfortunately, sometime later they returned to England around Christmas time. In the middle of a shopping expedition to Harrod's, Daniel realised that the temperature had reached the required level, and it was only with extreme difficulty that his parents managed to remove him before he had stripped completely.

Bob was taught by his parents, after some worrying episodes were reported in the local paper, that if a stranger ever spoke to him in the street he was to run straight back to the house. This rule worked relatively well throughout his childhood, but began to backfire when he reached adulthood. If someone innocently stopped to ask him the way he would immediately take to his heels, even if several miles from home.

Nevertheless, despite such drawbacks, rules of some sort are a great deal better than no rules at all. And, as time goes on, it may be possible to add riders or modifications to the original guidelines to make these more flexible. In Bob's case, as he was a hefty young man over six feet tall, his parents felt there was little risk of his being taken advantage of; moreover, his flight and panic when asked the simplest question by a stranger made him appear very abnormal. They eventually persuaded him that he should first stop and listen to what he was asked, and if he could answer (he was very knowledgable about local routes) he should do so and then *walk* on.

In another case, Sarah had caused a lot of problems when she was a young teenager because of her fascination with babies. She would approach babies in their prams and pick them up whenever the opportunity arose. This behaviour was not appreciated by their parents and as she grew into a young woman there was a danger that she could get into serious trouble because of it. Her family and the staff at her day centre made an absolute rule that she was not to approach *any* prams or *ever* touch a baby, and with much vigilance they were able to enforce this. Sometime later, Sarah's sisters began to have children of their own, and as it seemed very *inappropriate* to adhere strictly to the rules in their case, she was told she could pick up the babies *if* she asked first and as long as someone from the family was there 'in case she needed help'; the rules were further adapted when two staff members from the day centre, of whom Sarah was very fond, also had babies of their own.

On the whole, it seems more successful to begin with a very strict but simple rule, which must be rigidly followed initially, and then gradually to relax this as appropriate, rather than to begin with more flexible or complicated guidelines which then have to be made more stringent.

Other 'rules', relating to dress, appearance, how to greet people, contact with strangers and so forth, are also best laid down at an early age. Help may also be required in learning to distinguish between different types of 'stranger'. Thus, while it may be acceptable to talk to or even take sweets from the owner of the local newsagent while out shopping, it is not allowable to talk to a stranger who approaches you on the street. Specific help may also be needed to cope with apparently straightforward activities, such as using a public lavatory. For example, although Matthew's mother had suspected that he was being badly teased at school, it was only when another pupil told her that this was because he always pulled his trousers right down before urinating that she realised why.

Although the value of early guidance or preventative strategies cannot be overstated, the rule 'better late than never' also applies. People with autism, even those of normal intellectual ability, often remain much more dependent on their families than other young adults, and may accept parental advice long after others would reject it. If this is not the case, and some individuals decide early in their teens that parents should no longer 'interfere' in this way, they may be more receptive to instructions from others, particularly figures in authority.

Personal hygiene

One area in which many adults who are living independently or in semi-sheltered accommodation may need help, is in organising their weekly activities to ensure they manage to cope adequately with tasks such as washing or cleaning. Advice on constructing a daily, weekly or monthly timetable can prove helpful in ensuring that time is effectively and efficiently structured, and experience indicates that few people resent what might otherwise be construed as an intrusion into their lives. Even with such apparently clear-cut tasks, however, it is important to ensure that the individual *fully* understands what is required. Gerald had a fixed routine (largely organised by his mother) for shopping, going to the launderette, bathing, cleaning his flat, etc.

She had taken great pains to ensure that everything was fitted in, and was therefore most upset to hear that he was having problems at work because of poor personal hygiene. He assured her he did go to the launderette once a fortnight and that he changed his shirts and under-clothes on a daily basis, as agreed. A visit to his flat, however, revealed that although he *changed* his clothes every day he did not necessarily wash them. If the linen basket were full he would place soiled clothes neatly back in his drawers, and these could well be worn several times before eventually being taken to the launderette. Supplying him with a larger laundry basket, and instructing him to *wash* clothes before re-wearing them effectively overcame this problem.

Although, as noted earlier, the failure to appreciate potentially embarrassing situations can lead to problems, it can also be an asset at other times. Explicit explanations that a behaviour is not acceptable, that clothes are dirty or inappropriate, or even that personal hygiene is inadequate, would be deeply resented by the majority of individuals. But because Gerald, like many other people with autism, showed no embarrassment following the complaints from his manager, and was not at all bothered by the involvement of his mother, he was able to return to work without the slightest qualms. Moreover, *only if* the person with autism is given direct guidance will he or she appreciate the need to change.

Responding to cues from others

As far as social communication is concerned it may well prove impossible to provide someone with autism with a complete under-standing of when it is, or is not, appropriate to talk to someone, or whether a particular topic should be discussed or not. Nevertheless, it is usually possible, at the very least, to teach ways of responding to guidance from others. Simply learning not to speak so loudly, so that comments are not broadcast far and wide, can be a great advantage. Similarly, responding to a cue from parents, siblings, teachers or others, that discussion of a particular topic should cease forthwith, may help to avoid giving offence to others. As a general rule, attempts made *at the time the problem occurs* to explain *why* a topic is not appropriate for discussion simply tend to exacerbate matters, as the individual with autism will then demand reasons for the interrup-tion, or vociferously defend his or her right to continue. A clear and unambiguous signal that it is time to stop may help to deal more effectively, and immediately, with problems of this nature, whilst explanations can be given after the crisis has been resolved.

Appropriate responses to guidelines from others generally need to be established in settings that do not, in themselves, give rise to problems. With time the behaviours learned in this way can then be generalised to situations in which difficulties actually occur. However, sometimes individuals may be very resistant to 'intrusion' of this kind unless they are fully aware of the possible consequences. John, who was a very able teenager, had an unerring knack of saying just the wrong thing to everyone he met. His mother had tried to teach him to introduce himself appropriately and to make compliments to people he met or to try to talk about topics in the news, but these frequently misfired. When told that a friend of his mother had lost a stone in weight he immediately said it would be a very good thing if she lost another two. To a colleague who called to take his mother to work he suggested it would be a good idea if she became a 'Page Three Girl' because she had such a nice figure, and at social gatherings organised by his left-wing parents he would regale visitors with his Thatcherite political opinions. Matters finally came to a head when, on a visit to his brother at university in Dublin, he was asked to play the piano in the local pub. He had exceptional musical ability, but unfortunately the first tune he tried to play was 'God Save the Queen'. He could not understand the offence that this obviously caused, and resisted attempts to silence him. Without his brother's intervention he would almost certainly have been badly beaten.

On-the-spot explanations of why such behaviours were unacceptable simply led to further arguments and remonstrations, but, away from the situation he was able to accept that he did 'sometimes say the wrong thing'. Because he became quite fearful after the incident in the pub his family managed to persuade him that if he said or did something inappropriate they would say loudly 'Well, I think it's time to go now' and he would then follow them out of the room or building. He would still try to argue with them when he was removed from the situation, but at least this tactic reduced the embarrassment that his behaviour so frequently caused.

Helping more complex social understanding

Formulating rules that are likely to be successful across a range of different situations is difficult enough, even when relatively straightforward social behaviours are involved. Improving more fundamental understanding presents even greater problems. Temple Grandin is reported as trying to deal with the problem by building up a vast library of experiences over the years . . . They were like a library of video tapes, which she could play in her mind . . . of how people behaved in different circumstances. She would play these over and over again, and learn, by degrees, to correlate what she saw, so that she could then predict how people in similar circumstances might act. 'It is strictly a logical process' she explained.

(Sacks, 1993)

However, much social understanding takes us beyond the realms of logic. For example, although recognition of whether or not someone is a friend comes naturally to most people, few of us could actually define how this understanding comes about. In autism, where such awareness is impaired, perceptions of friendship are often based on superficial and often misleading cues. The fact that someone speaks to them in a kindly fashion, greets them on a regular basis, or even sits next to them at work or in class, can quite erroneously be taken as evidence of close friendship. If no such signs exist, the individual with autism may take to approaching people directly, and asking them 'Will you be my friend?', a tactic that is almost guaranteed to ensure they will not be.

Some help in dealing with social problems may be obtained from the series of books, written for people with learning disabilities, by Sheila Hollins and colleagues. These illustrate clearly and explicitly problems of social rejection and can be used to discuss the emotional and practical issues surrounding this. However, teaching someone how to recognise whether or not someone is truly a friend is probably an impossible task. Indeed, most of us will have had experiences of our instincts being wrong, and of being let down in the trust we have placed in someone. For most of us, however, persisting errors of this kind are rare, in that we are able to learn and profit from earlier mistakes. Often, this is not the case for people with autism. Specialised social skills training, as described in a later section, may help to some extent, but is available only for very few. For others, helping them to recognise explicit signs of rejection or acceptance may be all that is possible, and even this may well require considerable assistance. Giles, for example, was always approaching young female members of staff at his day centre and asking politely if he might sit next to them, a request which they could hardly refuse. It was obvious in his talk with his mother that he believed them to be his 'real friends', unlike the clients at the centre, to whom he considered himself greatly superior. He would become very distressed if a 'friend' subsequently left, or had to deal with him firmly. At the request of his mother, the staff discussed the problem and decided, against the better judgement of some of them, that they would have to be more honest in their dealings with him. It was made clear that although they liked him very much, because they were staff they could not be 'real friends'. Attempts to encourage activities with some of the more able clients at the centre were not at all successful, but developing his role as assistant to those who were more disabled helped to improve his self-esteem and reduced his tendency continually to pursue staff members.

Danny had been in trouble on several occasions for approaching women in his local pub, and asking if he could sit next to them, whether or not they were accompanied. His siblings, who were much concerned about the situation, did their best to offer practical guidance. Their first rule was that he should *never* approach a woman who was already sitting next to, or in a group with, other men. The next rule was not to ask if he could sit next to someone – most of the women he asked tended not to give an outright refusal – but to ask instead 'Is someone else going to be sitting here?' (which seemed to give people the excuse to say 'Yes' even if no-one actually appeared). ONLY if they said 'No' *and* they moved up to make space for him, could he take this as an invitation to sit down. Otherwise, he was to go and find somewhere to sit by himself. On the few occasions when someone actually did move up, he was instructed to ask them *one* question only (usually something as banal but inoffensive as 'Have you been here before?' or 'Do you come here often?', if he had seen them on previous occasions). If they did not ask him any further questions he was then told just to sit and read his book or newspaper. His sister and brother kept intermittent checks on his behaviour when they could and their rules did seem to help to keep him out of further trouble.

Learning to say 'No'

Other social difficulties arise from the fact that, in their desire to make or keep friends, people with autism may try to comply with any request that is made of them. Many find it extremely difficult to refuse requests for help, as they believe this will make them appear rude or ungrateful. This desire to please can obviously lead to difficulties, and not necessarily only with strangers. Damien, who had always been very careful with his money and had acquired considerable savings, was approached by his cousin who had recently come to live in the same town. He explained that he needed some cash, and as the banks were closed he asked if Damien would give him money in exchange for a cheque. Damien parted with £100, but despite the fact that neither this nor subsequent cheques were ever honoured, his cousin still managed to persuade him to part with similar sums on many occasions. Damien admitted that he knew the money was unlikely to be paid but was too anxious about upsetting a member of the family to refuse.

Helping people to say 'No' politely but effectively, when they are aware that a request can lead them into trouble, is an essential requirement. Experience of more able people with autism suggests that they are usually aware, or at least they eventually become so, that what they are asked to do is unwise or can lead them into trouble. Giving them the opportunity to discuss the problem, helping them to work out what they should or should not do, and providing them with strategies for avoiding or getting out of the situation, can all be beneficial. Because many people seem to find it difficult to say 'No' directly, an alternative way of excusing themselves from the situation may be useful. Jack, who on a number of occasions had been used as a scapegoat for other children's misdemeanours, was encouraged to say 'I'll just check with my mum first' if ever members of the local teenage gang asked him out. If they were up to mischief this response tended to make them depart with speed.

It may also be necessary to enlist the help of other people. Although Damien was encouraged to respond negatively but politely to his cousin's requests for money, he was not able to tell him that he had no cash available unless this was actually true. He was finally persuaded to tell his parents about what was happening and, as well as approaching the cousin directly, they tried to ensure that Damien did not have enough money available in his current account to make such payments. For a while the problem subsided, but eventually the cousin returned, this time asking for cheques instead of cash, and telling Damien how 'hurt' he had been by his 'betrayal' to his father. Unfortunately, this emotional blackmail resulted in large additional amounts of money being wasted until his parents eventually found out what was happening.

Sometimes, too, it may be necessary to take steps to avoid the problem situation occurring altogether. Robert's mother began to realise that his dinner money was not arriving at school, and suspected that this was being used to 'buy' friendship from other people. She arranged with his teacher for the money to be taken in the first lesson each morning, rather than at lunch time, and again, for a while, this seemed to work. However, he then began to be waylaid on his way to school and in the end the only solution was for the school to collect the money in advance directly from his parents.

Working with older people with autism, it is clear that almost all experience great difficulties in attempting to be appropriately assertive. Much earlier intervention, when they are children, could perhaps help to reduce later difficulties. Basic strategies such as providing clear guidance on what is right and wrong, when to say 'No' to other children, help to understand that money or goods will not bring them friends, or that saying 'No' will not necessarily make them enemies can all help to reduce the risks of more serious problems in adult life.

Respecting individual difficulties

One way in which more able individuals with autism are able to help themselves is to be explicit with other people about the nature of their social difficulties. Many individuals, for example, are uncomfortable at having to meet direct eye-gaze, dislike physical contact or proximity, or find it difficult to cope with loud noises. If they can be encouraged to explain these problems to those with whom they come into contact, unnecessary conflict can be averted. Judith, a young woman currently studying for a post-graduate degree, finds direct eye-contact with others very disturbing, but is able now to explain this, and to warn people in advance that she would prefer not to look at them. As long as this request is met her interactions with other people are greatly enhanced. Veronica, another extremely gifted woman who writes both music and poetry, cannot bear physical contact or being in crowded situations of any sort. However, as long as she is able to make clear beforehand that she cannot tolerate people shaking her hand or touching her in other ways, and as long as she has some pre-determined 'escape route' in social gatherings, she is able to tolerate and sometimes even to enjoy these.

This approach clearly contrasts with the methods sometimes used to encourage social interactions, particularly in children with autism. In the past, for example, direct eye-contact was often specifically encouraged. However, although behavioural techniques can be used to increase eye-contact, such methods can never teach the subtleties of eye-gaze – when it is appropriate to look, when to shift gaze, when to look away. Instead, what tends to be achieved is a fixed and unblinking stare, which is socially much more disconcerting than someone who explains simply that they do not like to make eye-contact. Children with other handicaps are usually taught ways of circumventing their difficulties. If a child has physical or sensory impairments they are provided with aids to ameliorate these, they are not forced to see or hear without help. In contrast, enormous pressures may sometimes be placed on people with autism to confront their problems directly – pressures that can lead to anxiety, aggression, withdrawal or greater social disruption. Sensitivity to individual needs, and offering ways of avoiding or minimising social pressures, may prove as important for social integration as the teaching of specific skills.

Modifying the demands of the social environment

Whatever strategies are employed to improve social functioning, it is important to recognise that the fundamental deficits are likely to remain throughout life. A focus on changing the expectations or behaviours of others may play as important a role in intervention as concentration on the deficits of the person with autism, but this requires considerable flexibility on the part of carers. Avoiding those social situations which, although highly enjoyable for others, may cause distress for people with autism, can be very effective in reducing unnecessary conflict and disruption. However, this may mean a reduction in the variety of activities or outings undertaken, and as such can pose ethical problems for staff members. Similarly, activities involving a high level of participation with others, exposure to crowds or even novel experiences can all place untold stress on someone with autism. Asking carers to allow someone with autism to spend more time alone, to let them follow a less intensive programme than other clients, or even to avoid birthday or Christmas celebrations again raises many difficulties, and may well produce feelings of failure and frustration. The balance between pressure and passivity becomes all important – not making demands that will result in conflict or distress, whilst at the same time attempting to improve the general quality of life. It is essential to offer the person with autism the opportunity to choose between various options. But, in order for that person to be able to make choices he or she must be able to experience the options available. If fear, obsessionality, social impairments or communication difficulties interfere with the ability to choose, these problems will need to be addressed directly. Some pressure, too, may also be required in order to persuade the individual with autism to depart from their normal routine long enough to experience, albeit briefly, other possibilities. Some sort of 'escape hatch' seems to be essential here, for if the individual has sufficient control over what is happening, if he or she has access to a place of privacy, can escape from social demands if these become overwhelming, or can terminate a novel experience if it all becomes too much, then it is much more likely that they will be persuaded 'to give it a go'. Over time, exposure to activities that seem to offer some potential for social enjoyment can be gradually increased, whereas activities that invariably precipitate anxiety and distress should be avoided and replaced by more acceptable alternatives.

Learning from mistakes

Because of the pervasiveness of the social problems in autism it is inevitable, whatever help is provided, that difficulties will occur from time to time. However, instead of being discouraged by failure it is important to recognise that errors can in fact be used very productively. Individuals with autism almost always have problems in coping with abstract or hypothetical concepts and hence attempts to teach rules in isolation are likely to have limited impact. If a problem has arisen this can be used much more effectively as a teaching opportunity: to discuss what may have gone wrong, how cues may have been misinterpreted, or how the situation might be improved in future.

Barry, for example, had attended a number of 'social skills' sessions to help him greet other clients in his day centre more appropriately. When he first began attending the centre he had irritated many people by addressing them, quite deliberately, by the wrong name or title (Mrs Kat, the head of the centre was always addressed as 'Mr Dog', and clients' names would frequently be distorted in a variety of ways). Attempts to teach him more appropriate forms of address failed entirely, until he was hit by a large and usually docile client, whom he had teased for some time. This direct experience of the possible repercussions of his behaviour subsequently made him more responsive to the teaching of alternative responses. Similarly, John, whose unfortunate experience of playing the British national anthem in a republican bar is described above, became much more responsive to his family's suggestions once he was made aware of the potential dangers of his social naivety.

Social skills training

Another approach to improving the social awareness of people with autism is the use of social skills groups. Probably because the social impairments in autism are often so different from the social difficulties associated with other disorders, there is little evidence that social skills training in mixed groups is particularly effective. Instead, the groups that seem to have had most effect are those that have focused specifically on the deficits related to autism (Williams, 1989; Frankel, Leary and Kilman, 1987). However, these can clearly cater only for a tiny minority of individuals. An additional problem is that the skills taught have often been far removed from real-life situations (Foxx *et al.*, 1989; Lalli *et al.*, 1991). Brown and Odom (1991) have discussed a number of problems related to social skills training programmes; these include the circumscribed nature of the skills often taught, limited evaluation, the problems of generalisation to and maintenance in real-life settings, and problems in encouraging the use and development of such programmes by care staff, teachers and others. Wider-ranging social skills programmes for adults and adolescents with autism are few and far between, although work by Quill (1995b) and Quirk-Hodgson (1995) on solving social problems and developing relationships in children may be usefully adapted to working with adults. For the more able, written scripts or instructions may also be of help in improving relatively complex social skills, such as interactive behaviours with peers (Krantz and McClannahan, 1993).

Mesibov (1992) describes in some detail, group and individual programmes designed to develop social competence in high-functioning individuals enrolled in the TEACCH scheme. Their teaching focuses not only on direct social interactions, but also on ways of analysing and organising their thinking, understanding the relationships between events and behaviours, learning about perspectives, and developing trust and rapport. Other programmes have made use of a wide range of different techniques, but there is a general focus on role-play procedures. Unlike many students, individuals with autism do not seem to be daunted at having to take part in role-play exercises, or by appearing on video. Such adjuncts to therapy are valuable in demonstrating and rehearsing the skills required in social settings such as restaurants, pubs, work, shops or parties; in encouraging problem-solving and the development of more appropriate strategies to cope with difficult situations (including assertiveness training); in developing listening, conversational and turn-taking skills; in improving perception of non-verbal cues, such as eye-contact, body language, facial expression and tone of voice. Ways of dealing with situations that are stressful or anxiety-provoking also play an important part in intervention. Although the evaluation of these programmes remains limited, they do indicate that improvements in various areas can be achieved over time. Figure 4.1 illustrates the

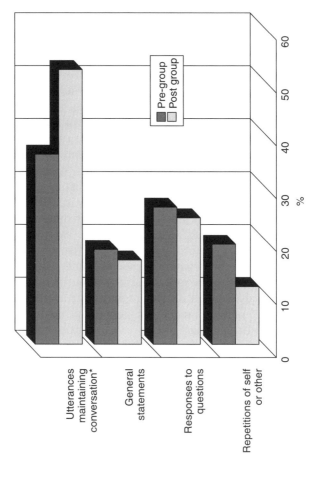

Figure 4.1 Changes in social conversation following attendance at a social skills group
Note: * significant change between assessments (*p*<0.05)

changes made in the use of more appropriate conversational skills by a group of adults attending a social skills group over a period of about a year. Generally speech became less repetitive, and contained significantly more attempts to maintain conversations, such as by offering information, asking questions, initiating new topics or developing existing themes. Of the 9 individuals who attended this group consistently over the year (more were involved altogether but their attendance was less regular), changes were also reported in their social competence in other areas. Four left home to live in supported or semi-supported accommodation; 2 spent some time living abroad and one managed to cope at home by himself when his father moved away. Four managed to find at least part-time employment or embarked on further training schemes (one for a post-graduate qualification). When asked for their own comments on what they had gained from the group individuals reported improvements in their communication skills, their ability to interpret other people's emotions, their problem-solving and decision-making abilities, and improvement in their ability to relate to people at home and outside. Families also reported improvements in their sons' conversational and social skills, in their self-confidence and general independence, and in their decision-making and problem-solving strategies (Howlin and Yates, 1995).

Despite these positive indicators, however, there continued to be difficulties in generalising the skills acquired in the group to settings outside. The individuals attending this group all had good language skills and their intellectual ability was well within the normal range. It was clear that in group discussions and role-play sessions they were able to demonstrate good understanding of social rules and that they also had some perception of other people's feelings and emotions. Nevertheless, once the supports of being in a group were removed, and they were left to cope alone with the demands of social interactions, their ability to apply these skills remained limited. For example, in discussion it was clear that group members were fully aware that unsolicited approaches to unknown young women were unlikely to be successful, and could well lead to frightening or offending the person approached. However, reports or observations of some individuals in other settings indicated that such behaviours still tended to persist.

Attempts to improve assertiveness skills also seemed to have limited effects. All the group members said they found such interactions very difficult, and they disliked having to try to stand up for themselves, usually for fear of giving offence. For example, Damien, whose cousin had for some time been taking more and more of his money, was helped to recognise that this was both dishonest and manipulative, and that he would never get back the money he was handing out. Strategies were practised that would enable him to say 'No' more effectively, as well as teaching him ways in which he might try to avoid the problem (such as ensuring that he did not have access to large quantities of cash). However, although Damien said that he tried to use these tactics he found it almost impossible to remain firm under pressure and the loss of money continued until his parents actively intervened.

There is also a risk that social skills groups of this kind may run into problems by providing training in certain areas of social inter-action whilst failing to address more fundamental issues. Jerome, who had previously attended another social skills group for people with a mixture of social problems, largely unrelated to autism, had been given help and coaching on ways to initiate and maintain conversations with young women. The problem was that Jerome rarely met women as he lived alone with his family and had few outside activities. His solution for finding the best place to meet as many single women as possible was a simple one – inside the local ladies' lavatory! When arrested by the police he clearly had no perception of why this behaviour had got him into trouble, espe-cially as he had been rather proud of himself for solving the problem in this way.

Finally, too, it is crucial that such groups do not appear to promise more than they can actually offer. Teaching young men how to improve their conversational and social skills is no guarantee that they will then be able to find a girl friend or establish a permanent relationship. From the outset, therefore, it is imperative to make absolutely clear what the group can *and cannot* offer. People with autism suffer constant setbacks and disappointments throughout their lives, and it is all too easy inadvertently to raise false hopes. Clar-ification, from the outset, of the group aims and limitations is essential if tutors are to avoid the risk of undermining, yet again, their confidence and self-esteem.

Improving the ability to 'Understand Minds'

Although there have been many investigations of the problems related to 'theory of mind' in both children and adults with autism (Baron-Cohen *et al.*, 1993) there have been relatively few attempts to explore whether such deficits can be improved in any way by training.

Those studies that have taken place have concentrated almost exclusively on children and have usually focused on very specific areas, such as understanding false beliefs or distinguishing between appearance and reality (Bowler, Stromm and Urquhart, 1993; Starr, 1993; Swettenham, 1995; Swettenham *et al.*; 1996) Teaching in these studies has utilised a number of different approaches, including computers, actors, behavioural and emotional cues, direct instruction, task repetition and feedback. Almost all the children involved were able to learn to pass the tasks and, in some cases, to maintain the skills over a period of several months. There was little evidence, however, that children could generalise what they had learnt to novel tasks or situations.

A more recent study by Hadwin and colleagues (1996), involving children between the ages of 4 and 9, suggests that a developmental approach to teaching may be more effective. Teaching was based on the stages of development normally involved in the acquisition of imaginative, emotional and belief understanding (Table 4.1), and by using a range of different teaching strategies the authors were able to

Table 4.1 Levels of training on theory-of-mind tasks

	Emotion	*Belief*	*Pretence*
1	Face recognition	Simple perspective taking	Sensorimotor play
2	Schematic facial recognition	Complex perspective taking	Functional play (< 2 examples)
3	Situation-based	Seeing leads to knowing	Functional play (> 2 examples)
4	Desire-based	True belief/action prediction	Pretend play (< 2 examples)
5	Belief-based	False belief	Pretend play (> 2 examples)

Table 4.2 Increases in theory-of-mind level with training

Teaching group	*Emotion*	*Belief*	*Pretence*
Pre-test	2.5	0.9	2.4
Post-test	3.7[a]	2.1[a]	3.3
Follow-up	3.3[a]	1.6[a]	3.0

Notes: No differences between the groups in initial levels. No significant transfer across training groups. [a] = significance of change from initial level ($p < 0.05$)

demonstrate improvements in the understanding of beliefs and emotions (Table 4.2). However, although there was some generalisation to non-taught tasks within the same domain, there was little generalisation to other, non-taught aspects of theory of mind. Furthermore, few improvements were found in the development of imaginative play activities. Nevertheless, the fact that even a very brief intervention study of this kind could make a significant impact on certain aspects of children's learning is promising.

The value of these techniques in improving social and emotional understanding in adults has yet to be demonstrated, and work from other sources (Peterson and Siegal, 1995) suggests that initial impairments in theory of mind may be further exacerbated in adulthood by poor expressive and receptive language abilities, which, in turn, progressively impede individuals' exposure to, and understanding of, mental states as they grow older. Whether or not, therefore, training in adults is likely to have even the limited beneficial results found in studies of children is questionable, but they clearly offer the potential for more effective intervention.

Dealing with loneliness

As all the example cited above must indicate, life for the majority of people with autism is devoid of many of the most basic human comforts, which for the rest of us are so essential for happiness and fulfilment. Social impairments affect relationships within the family, success at work or college, and acceptance within residential settings or in the day centre. Even the most casual of interactions are likely to be affected, and the chances of ever enjoying the pleasures that come from close intimate or sexual relationships are severely curtailed. The accounts of more able people with autism make very clear how much some of them, at least, miss the opportunity to be like other people, to have friends, or develop relationships, particularly with the opposite sex. Therese Jolliffe (Jolliffe *et al.*, 1992) writes: 'contrary to what people may think, it is possible for an autistic person to feel lonely and to love somebody'.

However, many also recognise the conflicts that a close relationship might entail. Maria, a young woman in her twenties, described how much she sometimes longed for someone to talk with but she is perceptive enough to admit to the difficulties that intimacy involves: 'Half of me would like to have a close friend but the other half knows that it would be too much hassle'. Previous relationships had always ended in acrimony; at school because she would try to dominate the interaction and exclude all others, and later, when she tried sharing a flat, because of her obsessional and ritualistic activities.

Anne, a young woman described by Margaret Dewey (1991), notes:

> I don't feel as if I have enough friends but I've been feeling a lot better recently because of all the things I've been doing. I work part time organising the library for the Autistic Society. And I do some part-time work with the Developmental Disability group. There are some benefits in being alone, too, I can think through and be more ready to go out again. I often feel lonely for a man. I would really like to have somebody but I'm glad I haven't gotten attached yet so I make further progress and be more acceptable.

Other people express the view that they may be better off alone. Margaret Dewey's son Jack is quoted in the same paper as saying:

> Actually, I don't suffer from loneliness. If I have to relate to people too much I become nervous and uncomfortable . . . It is important for me to please people [but] it is not important that I see them often.

Still others confess that if it were not for outside social pressures they might be much more contented with their way of life. Irene, a woman in her mid-twenties, who has had a number of disastrous relationships in the past noted that:

> I don't usually feel lonely, and in some ways I'm better by myself; I couldn't cope with the demands of a close relationship . . . I'd be awful . . . Sometimes I think that if I didn't know about friends, or knew other people had them, being alone wouldn't bother me at all.

At least such individuals are able to talk about their loneliness and feelings of exclusion or rejection. The majority of people with autism, even those who may possess relatively good spoken language, have little ability to express their feelings in this way. Indeed very often, in settings catering for people with disabilities, clients with autism are often described as being 'happiest if left alone', or as having no desire for contact with others. The anecdotal accounts or writings of more able people, however, suggest that such views (which of course can help to reduce the burden on professional carers and sometimes even families) may not entirely reflect the needs of the individuals concerned.

Making use of existing skills

Given the complexity of intimate human relationships, and the pitfalls they present even to the most socially accomplished of individuals, it is unrealistic to expect, and certainly dishonest ever to promise, that any form of therapy or training can help to furnish the individual with autism with the skills of empathy, understanding, sensitivity and the countless others that are needed to establish successful relationships. Help can, however, be provided to ensure that as many opportunities as possible exist to increase the opportunities for social contacts, and to ensure that the person with autism is as well equipped as possible, both socially and in terms of other skills.

Even when working in specialist day or residential settings it is crucial to overcome, as far as possible, any behaviours that will make individuals socially unacceptable within their peer group. It is also important to ensure that the person with autism is encouraged and if necessary taught the skills required to interact with other clients. Often, people with autism spend much of their time alone, or in one-to-one interactions with members of staff. For some this may be entirely appropriate, but others may never have had the opportunity to work *with,* rather than simply alongside, others in their daily activities. Very many activities, however, do offer much more scope for sharing, turn-taking and co-operation than is often recognised. Music, cooking, gardening, yoga, art and crafts, as well as more obvious activities such as dancing or games, offer many opportunities for skilled staff to promote joint working between clients. Many individuals with autism in institutional or day-care settings are often much more capable in many ways than other clients, and helping them develop a supportive or care-taking role can also foster integration. Jenny, for example, developed considerable skill in using massage and simple aromatherapy techniques with physically handicapped clients at her day centre, and became a very useful source of additional help to the therapist. Denny is a young man who will spend hours pushing wheelchair users around, as long as he is allowed to follow his own repetitive routes.

Encouraging a wide range of activities, in which social interactions may be further developed, is crucial for individuals of any level of ability. Making use of specific skills or interests in areas such as music, chess, computing, transport, wildlife or environmental issues, can also be invaluable in offering individuals the opportunities to mix with other people. Jonas had always had a fascination with railways since a young child and as he grew older accompanied his parents to local groups campaigning for better transport systems. He is now an active lobbyist in the campaign against new motorways, and spends much of his time travelling around the country attending meetings on these issues. Peter, who initially had an obsessional interest in deer and sheep, is now a devoted supporter of the Worldwide Fund for Nature, and is a tireless fund-raiser on their behalf. Leslie, a gifted musician, spends several evenings a week playing for local orchestras or choirs, or in residential homes for the elderly and handicapped. Dominic spends almost all his time in activities related to the local church, and weekends and holidays are spent helping individuals with physical disabilities. In the week, he attends French lessons so that on the annual trip to Lourdes with the church he will be able to offer better help. All these individuals describe themselves as having many friends, and although the quality of these friendships may be questioned, it is clear nevertheless that their time is fully occupied, that they are accepted and appreciated by the groups involved, and most importantly, that they view themselves, with some justification, as popular and valued members of society.

5 Obsessional and ritualistic behaviours

PATTERNS OF OBSESSIONAL AND RITUALISTIC BEHAVIOURS IN ADULTHOOD

A characteristic, but oversimplistic, view of ritualistic behaviours in autism is that of a solitary child lining up rows of bricks or coins, spinning the wheels of toy cars, posting objects down the backs of radiators or chairs, or collecting coins, leaves, pieces of string or plumbing equipment. However, with age, particularly in the case of individuals of higher intellectual ability, the obsessions tend to become much more involved. The causes of ritualistic behaviours, too, are often highly complex. For some individuals they play a crucial role in keeping fear and anxiety under control. As Therese Jolliffe notes:

> Reality to an autistic person is a confusing, interacting mass of events, people, places, sounds and sights. There seems to be no clear boundaries, order or meaning to anything. A large part of my life is spent trying to work out the pattern behind everything. Set routines, times, particular routes and rituals all help to get order into an unbearably chaotic life. Trying to keep everything the same reduces some of the terrible fear.
>
> (Jolliffe *et al.* 1992)

Environmental and developmental factors also play an important role. The degree to which individuals are able to develop their social, communication and cognitive skills, for example, can have considerable impact on the extent of obsessional behaviours in later life. The more limited an individual's skills in these areas the greater will be their dependence on ritualistic and obsessional behaviour patterns. Similarly, the emptier their lives, the more such behaviours will predominate.

Collecting facts

Instead of large collections of *objects*, many older people with autism collect *information*: knowledge about all the different seating systems on British Rail Western Region trains since 1960; the hit songs of particular pop-groups or the records published by specific recording companies; rugby scores; the trophies won by Torvill and Dean; Les Dawson; albinoism; sporting events or personalities; astronomy; poisons; quiz shows; pedigrees of Arab stud horses, are but a few examples of topics about which individuals may possess a wealth of knowledge. Memory for or fascination with birthdates, or with travel routes and timetables are also characteristic. Many of the more intellectually able people with autism will avidly buy books or magazines related to their special interests, or spend hours in the library reading about them. In contrast to the obsessional behaviours of childhood, when the obsession itself is a problem (so that families may have the house filled with unlikely objects such as left-foot red wellingtons, or blue rubber sink-plungers) difficulties in adulthood tend to arise because of the time spent thinking, talking or worrying about these interests, sometimes to the exclusion of other activities.

Damien, for example, was a young man with an obsession with airlines and aeroplanes. Given the registration of a particular plane he could recall with complete accuracy not only where and when it flew, but its flight history, the company that owned or leased it and its repair and accident record. The extent of his knowledge was so impressive that as part of a job experience scheme he was given a placement at his nearest airport. His careers adviser had, understandably, thought that his fascination and knowledge of planes would prove a major advantage there; instead the opposite proved to be the case. Instead of completing the jobs assigned to him, Damien spent the whole day watching or talking about planes and eventually managed to hack into the airport's computer system to gain even more information. Stuart, who had an obsession with the seating systems on British Rail trains, carried around with him albums full of photographs of these. Whenever the opportunity arose he would go through these in detail, and at great length, with anyone who was close at hand.

Generally, the effect of such obsessions is to induce boredom, or at worst irritation in the listener; however, there may be even less desirable effects. Sandy, who had always been interested in warfare, developed a particular interest in the regime of Pol Pot in

Cambodia in the 1970's. He would regale anyone he met with the atrocities committed during this period, providing graphic, horrific and unwanted details about the methods of slaughter and the numbers of victims murdered. His glee in recounting this information, and his obvious fascination with violence could make listeners feel most uncomfortable, and there were concerns that he might begin to enact some of his violent fantasies. Obsessional interests can also lead to financial difficulties. Oliver, a young man with a fascination for computers, spent all his time and money buying computer magazines, and agonising over which computer he should buy next, even though he had no money with which to do so.

Involving others

Whilst most obsessional interests will have at least an indirect impact on other people, some may involve others more directly. Owen was a young Welshman whose obsession with rugby had persisted since a child. He knew everything there was to know about teams, players, scores or league tables, and was a devoted attender at his local club. His 'conversations' were dominated by rugby and he would try to involve anyone he met in talk about this. However, he was also very pedantic about the precise terminology used. Players had to be called 'boys' not 'men', jerseys described as 'jumpers', boots as 'footwear', scarves as 'colours' and so forth. If his mother, in her attempts to talk with him, used the 'wrong' word, this could lead to hours of correction and recrimination, often disrupting family activities for the rest of the day.

Sally was a 25-year-old woman with a fascination for TV quiz games. Since she was very young her parents had watched these with her, as this was one of the few situations when she would enjoy talking to them. Although she became much more sociable as she grew older she continued to insist that they all watch quiz games together. Twenty years ago, when the obsession first began, there were relatively few quiz games to watch and the habit was not particularly disruptive. As the frequency of these games on TV increased, however, and as her insistence on the family's involvement became more pronounced, the intrusiveness of this obsession became considerable. Even if they went out she would insist on the programmes being recorded on video and these would then have to be viewed, often until late into the night.

Dislike of change

Although, as they grow older, many people with autism come to accept and even enjoy greater variation in their lives, they may continue to resist changes in particular settings, or in certain aspects of their environment; unpredictable changes, too, frequently provoke considerable distress.

David was a 40-year-old man, who, after many years of living with his mother, was helped to buy his own apartment. Before leaving he had taken numerous photographs of his previous house and these were displayed throughout his new flat. He also ensured that the layout of his bedroom was as similar as possible to that of his old room. Through the help of his photographs, and with his mother's support, David coped remarkably well with the move. However, unforeseen problems occurred when his mother herself later moved house. David insisted that all the rooms were arranged exactly as they had been previously and he became so upset that he had not taken enough photographs of the old house that he wrote to the new owners asking permission to take some more. He was then horrified to discover that they had already begun major alterations to the kitchen, bathroom and garden. He was so distressed at not having enough photographs of the original layout that he spent all his free time searching old photo albums for pictures and cutting them out (ruining his mother's photo collection in doing so).

Martin had learned to cope with many changes in his life and after leaving college had succeeded in finding work in a local office. However, at holiday times he still insisted that the family go to exactly the same place, and carry out the same activities as they had done when he was a child. This was a small, isolated caravan site, not far from their home in the south of England, which, in his more disturbed days had been the only place they had been able to risk taking him. The only activity, apart from sitting on the beach, that he would take part in was 'Crazy Golf' which they were forced to play for hours on end. Although the holiday was the highlight of Martin's year, for the rest of the family the mere thought of a whole fortnight there became a nightmare.

Simon, by the time he was in his mid-twenties was living alone, with relatively little support. He had learned to clean and shop for himself and had begun attending day courses at his local college. However, the one area which he never changed was his diet. At home he would cook only a certain brand of frozen food and when out ate only chips and cheeseburgers from a particular fast-food chain.

Unfortunately, as this was not one of the major chains, it severely restricted opportunities to eat out, and in turn imposed major limitations on trips or holidays away.

Bonnie was a young woman who, despite having a marked resistance to any changes in the home when younger, had learned to cope with alterations over time. However, in her own room everything was kept in strict order, and although she spent much of her time in a residential unit, her family were not allowed to move any item, no matter how small, in her absence.

Matthew was an 18-year-old who since a young child had been used to being washed at the kitchen sink. His self-care skills had developed considerably since he had begun attending a Social Education Unit and he was quite able to bath and wash himself. On bath nights (Tuesdays, Thursdays and Saturdays without exception) there were no problems in his using the bathroom. On the other nights, however, he insisted on stripping off completely and washing at the kitchen sink as he had always done. This gave rise to untold embarrassment if his teenage sister had friends around at the time.

Collecting

The tendency to collect objects of various kinds can persist well into adulthood. Sometimes the focus of interest may remain much the same as in childhood; for others collections may vary over time, or become more sophisticated. Sally, a middle-aged woman with autism and moderate learning difficulties, has continued to collect 'diaries' throughout her life. These contain lists of the names and birthdays of everyone with whom she comes into contact, and if the current book is lost or removed (other residents in her group home have learned that this is a very easy way of upsetting her) she becomes very distressed. Sarah, another young woman with learning disabilities, collects small stones wherever she goes, which she keeps in jars all over her room. Stevie, a young man with a degree in electronics, is an avid collector of pop-records, of which he now has many thousands. Each of these is catalogued according to its date, publishing company and singer, and identified by a complex numbering system. If new editions of any of these records are produced Stevie is unable to rest until he has acquired these, sometimes at considerable expense.

Many families report that the obsession with collecting seems to decline somewhat as individuals grow older, but sometimes the opposite may be the case. Emma, for example, loved collecting notebooks and shiny pieces of paper as a child. In her teens she developed a passion for ball-room dancing and collected any leaflets relevant to this activity. Then, because she worried lest any leaflets became damaged, she began to collect several copies of each. Eventually, she became unable to dispose of pieces of paper at all and as she worked in a printing company would bring home large parcels of waste paper each week. The house and garage became full of boxes of paper, but although she recognised the problems that her collections caused for herself and her family (paradoxically she loved everything around her to be neat and tidy and this had become increasingly impossible) she could not bear to throw anything away.

Rodney was a middle-aged man who had lived alone since the death of his father. As a young child he had had a fascination with collecting tools and electrical equipment and when older had found work as a porter in the supplies department of a large electrical company. When equipment became obsolete he was often allowed to take this home. The problem was not too bad while his father was alive because he refused to allow new items into the house unless an old item was disposed of first. However, after his death Rodney continued to collect everything he could, until it became almost impossible to enter the house because of the huge piles of equipment stacked everywhere.

Routines

Routine is essential for almost everyone if they are to organise their lives in an effective way: leaving the house at a certain time, eating at regular intervals, developing regular patterns for washing, dressing, going to work or even pursuing leisure activities can be crucial if life is to run smoothly. It is only when such habits become so fixed that they disrupt other activities, or when a behaviour that was once acceptable can no longer be tolerated because of changing circumstances or expectations, that problems occur.

Jim had had a fascination with watching the sun set for many years. At school this had not been a problem, because for most of the year lessons finished well before sunset. When he moved to an adult residential unit, however, and was expected to be engaged in work or other activities, or to catch the coach home later in the day, his insistence on waiting to see the sun set became much more of a problem. Similarly, Bob had been fascinated with the weather since he was tiny and he spent much of his childhood listening to weather forecasts and informing everyone what the next day's weather would be like. As the family lived in Western Australia at the time the predictability of weather conditions was fairly good. Their move to England, however, resulted in enormous disruption when Bob quickly realised that the correlation between the forecast and actual weather conditions was far from perfect. Marion was a very able young woman whose autism was hardly apparent except to those who knew her well. By her mid-twenties her main rituals were confined to night-time activities which had little impact on other members of her family. Eventually, through her church group, she met a young man who, much to her delight, asked her to marry him. Her parents then realised that these remaining 'habits' could be a source of considerable difficulty. The main problem was that before going to bed she would draw and re-draw the curtains until they were in *exactly* the 'right' position and she also had to pick up every piece of fluff on the floor. Her parents had imposed a time limit on these behaviours in the rest of the house, but in her bedroom at night she would spend hours engaged in these activities. However, it was apparent that her fiancé would find such behaviours very difficult to understand or cope with.

Susan was another young woman who had left her family to live in a large residential unit. As a child she had always been given pocket money by her parents and although she had little interest in the money itself, she took great delight in depositing it in her post office account and watching her savings grow. The money was never removed as she was always provided with everything she needed. In her new Home she continued, like the other residents, to deposit any money remaining from her benefit payments into the local post office. However, persuading her to *withdraw* this money produced enormous problems. Even taking out enough money to contribute to a birthday card for another resident would require days of wrangling and she would refuse to go on trips or outings rather than withdraw any of her money.

Other stereotyped behaviour patterns may present problems in adulthood because behaviours that are acceptable in a child later become entirely inappropriate. Joey, for example, loved to watch the washing spinning around in his mother's machine, and this could keep him still and quiet for hours. The family lived in a small country village and if his mother's machine was not in action the neighbours were happy to let him watch theirs. In his teens he would wander off to the launderette in the nearby town and happily remain there for an hour or two. When this closed down Joey was resourceful enough to seek other ways of indulging his passion. He would wander around the neighbourhood looking through kitchen windows and if he saw a washing machine working would do his best to gain entry. His family only became aware of the problem when he was brought home by the police, having terrified an elderly pensioner who came home to find him sitting in the middle of her kitchen floor.

Stereotyped movements

Stereotyped movements, such as rocking, flicking or flapping are often less in evidence as individuals grow older and if they do occur may be an important indicator of distress or anxiety. Bella was a young woman with moderate learning difficulties who had always flicked and flapped her hands as a young child, but by the time she reached her late teens and was well settled in a local day centre she rarely did so. After a holiday away, however, these behaviours suddenly returned, together with other signs of stress. Having little speech, Bella was unable to explain what had happened but it was later revealed that a number of clients on the trip had been abused by a worker there. It was never established whether Bella herself had actually been abused, but it was apparent that the distress surrounding these incidents was responsible for the upsurge in stereotyped behaviours.

Precipitating factors are not necessarily as serious as this, of course. A change in routine or an unexpected event which would be of little significance to most people, may easily trigger a return to stereotyped motor behaviours in someone with autism. Jeremy was a middle-aged man working in a large office as an accounts clerk. With his formal suit, rolled umbrella and smart attaché case he appeared much the same as all the other commuters at his local railway station. However, unlike them, he could never behave with the same equanimity over cancelled or delayed trains, and it was at these times that he would revert to the rocking and flapping that had been so characteristic in childhood.

Boredom or inadequate stimulation may also be a problem. Individuals who showed little sign of motor mannerisms in a structured school setting may begin to display these behaviours if they are subsequently placed in situations with inadequate stimulation. Raymond, for example, had rarely rocked since a child, but this behaviour became very pronounced after a few months in a residential unit. On visiting him, his social worker found that he was unable to join in most of the day activities at the unit because of the noise and general overcrowding there, and this was when the behaviours were most in evidence.

Although problems related to stereotyped behaviours may lessen in adulthood, or be important indicators of other, hidden anxieties, the main difficulty is that they appear much more out of place as individuals grow older. Whilst flapping and rocking may go almost unnoticed in a very young child, they will rapidly draw attention to an adult with autism, often exacerbating their social difficulties and reducing their chances of integration and acceptance.

Anxiety, fears and phobias

Another major problem related to obsessions in older people is the high anxiety levels that these behaviours may produce, often for a variety of different reasons. Obsessions and fears often become inextricably linked, so that children who have an obsession with a particular object at one stage can develop a great fear of it later. Mark's first word was reported to be 'Hoover' and for years his mother would let him play with the vacuum cleaner to calm him down. She even turned it on in order to get him to sleep! However, when she switched from an upright to a cylinder model he became quite distraught, and thereafter the noise of the cleaner would induce such panic that his mother could only clean when he was out of the house.

Martin had developed an obsession with video game machines as a young boy and was well known as an expert player at the local games centre. His presence there would attract large numbers of on-lookers, keen to see what his scores would be. However, he became increasingly anxious about maintaining his high level of scores and although he loved playing, his fear of 'failing' to meet his on-lookers' expectations became so intense that every visit became more and more stressful.

Adam, a young man in his early twenties and of well above average intelligence, had had an obsession with things electrical since he was tiny. By the age of 6 he would create havoc when his family visited other people's houses by attempting to re-wire lamps or other equipment. At the age of 7 he wired up the Christmas tree lights to the video recorder to see whether inserting a video tape would make the lights come on! Although, as he grew older, he began to take more heed of his parents' warnings about the potential danger of such behaviours, he then became obsessional about *never* touching electrical equipment unless it was entirely safe. He would not use any equipment in the kitchen or bathroom because of the proximity to water and was therefore unable to make himself even a cup of tea or piece of toast, bathing was difficult because he refused to have the light on in the bathroom, and he would only use an electric shaver in his bedroom. Eventually he refused to go into the kitchen at all, becoming far more dependent on his mother for cooking and washing than he had ever been when younger.

Robin as a child had developed a very strict sense of 'honesty'. This was so strong that he kept rigidly to every rule he was ever given at school, much to the annoyance of his peer group (continually informing the headmaster of the other children's favourite place for illicit smoking did not enhance his popularity!). When he reached his teens, if he was ever given the wrong change in buses or shops he would always seek to remedy this, whether it meant his trying, often at considerable inconvenience or expense, to return or get back just a few pence. Over time he became more and more anxious that he might inadvertently walk out of a shop without paying for something and be arrested for this, and he would insist on being given receipts for the smallest transactions. He then became worried that if the receipt were lost he could still be charged with theft and began to hoard every proof of purchase he could, becoming extremely agitated if any of these became mislaid.

Anita had always been described by her parents as a 'perfectionist' and could not bear anything that was damaged in any way. As a child she would refuse to wear clothes with any marks or faults at all, but as she grew older and began to grow fond of certain garments, she became very anxious about what would happen if these wore out. Her solution was to insist on buying at least two or three copies of every garment, so that her wardrobe became full of unworn shoes, trousers, jumpers and T-shirts. The problem then extended to buying food, as she could not bear the thought that she might have bought inferior produce. She would spend hours choosing a chop or pack of bacon, and would often return home with pounds of these items, to ensure she had bought the best in the shop.

Finally, the utter uselessness of certain obsessions can be very difficult for families to tolerate. Living in a house filled with collections of stones, shells, pieces of cardboard or sink plungers is hard enough, but it may be even more frustrating when a potentially useful interest develops into a meaningless activity. James's mother was a keen and skilled gardener and she had encouraged him as a child to share her interest in gardening. In his late teens he developed an obsession with daffodils and narcissi, and knew everything there was to know about the many different varieties and their flowering habits and so on. He was provided with space in the garden to grow his own and he spent considerable sums of money acquiring rare or new varieties. However, as soon as the bulbs sprouted he would dig them up and replace them with others, rarely allowing anything the opportunity to flower. His mother could not bear the wanton destruction of plants in this way but could do little to prevent him or teach him to appreciate the aesthetic value of the flowers.

COPING WITH OBSESSIONAL AND RITUALISTIC BEHAVIOURS

Work with children suggests that direct attempts to prevent or prohibit obsessional or ritualistic behaviour frequently prove counterproductive (Howlin and Rutter, 1987). Deprived of the opportunity to take part in the few activities that may provide them with enjoyment or relief from stress, individuals may become even more disturbed, agitated and anxious. Even if attempts to stop one form of obsessional behaviour are apparently successful, children may then proceed to develop new rituals or obsessions, which can be even more disruptive than the original ones. Similar effects are found with adults. Moreover, as individuals become bigger, stronger, and better able to control their environment, attempts to prevent these activities will become ever more difficult. Locking cupboards or doors or trying to place things out of reach are unlikely to hinder a large and determined adult.

A more productive approach is to attempt gradually to modify the behaviour, so that it no longer interferes to the same extent with the lives of individuals or their families. A variety of different approaches can be adopted in order to achieve lower levels of disruption, and often a combination of strategies will be required. Determining the best approach will require careful assessment of the problem behaviour and detailed knowledge of the individual involved.

Addressing underlying causes

Obsessional and ritualistic behaviour in adulthood may persist simply because the individual concerned has always done things in a certain way or has always had an interest in a particular topic. However, as noted above, an upsurge in obsessional activity may well be an indication that someone is particularly anxious or under stress. In such cases, little progress will be made unless the underlying source of stress is identified and if possible eliminated.

Sometimes quite simple modifications to the environment can result in a rapid diminution of obsessional behaviours. Sally, who had moved to a residential home, became increasingly ritualistic at meal times. She would insist on sitting in a certain place, eating only from particular dishes, and had a variety of motor mannerisms that became more pronounced as the meal progressed. If attempts were made to calm her down she would immediately throw her meal across the room. Staff realised that the behaviours did not occur to the same extent at weekends, when many of the other residents were away. Sally's parents also reported that she generally disliked eating when she was surrounded by too many people or too much noise. Allowing her to sit at a table by herself, well away from the others, and in a position that allowed her to leave the room easily if noise levels got too high, quickly helped to reduce the problem.

In other cases it may be necessary to modify the expectations or attitudes of other people in order to bring about change. Jonathon was a young man who had recently moved to a residential unit where staff were particularly concerned about his inability to cope with money. Because this restricted his ability to go out alone, they decided that teaching him to use money appropriately should have a high priority. What they did not know was that at school Jonathon had had an obsession against maths and had become expert at making himself sick in almost every maths lesson. Shortly after the money coaching was introduced, Jonathon began complaining that 'maths made him sick' and he would repeat this over and over again to anyone he met. It was decided simply to ignore these comments, with the result that Jonathon soon put his words into action, vomiting every time money training was introduced, and rapidly losing weight. When staff sought help to deal with the problem the advice given was to reduce the emphasis on using money, at least in the Home, and simply to ensure that Jonathon always had sufficient funds when he went to the shop to buy his favourite magazines and sweets. The vomiting quickly stopped and although he quite often returned without any change he was unperturbed by this. The staff remained torn between the desire to help Jonathon develop his independence and the need to keep him healthy, and they in turn needed support to accept that few normal adults reach their full potential in all possible fields of competence, and that being able to choose which skills we develop, and which we do not, is a fundamental human right.

At times, of course, it may not be possible to modify the environment sufficiently to ensure that obsessional behaviours do not occur and it may be necessary to address underlying anxieties more directly.

Desensitisation techniques

There are many effective cognitive and behavioural strategies that can be used to decrease fears and anxieties. However, many desensitisation programmes rely on the ability of clients to *imagine* themselves in fearful situations and this clearly poses problems for people with autism. Instead, 'real-life' exposure is usually required.

In the case of Adam, whose obsession with the dangers of electrical equipment resulted in his becoming less and less able to take care of himself, a desensitisation programme was devised to help him overcome his fears. A simple 'hierarchy' of fears was established by getting Adam to indicate, using stick-on faces, how he felt about certain activities involving electrical equipment (see Table 5.1). A chart was pinned on the kitchen wall, indicating the task to be worked on each week. In order to reduce his anxiety as far as possible, a selection of his favourite tapes was kept in the kitchen to be played whenever he was there. As the tapes were not available elsewhere this increased his motivation to enter the kitchen. After 3 months he was able to make toast, put food in the microwave, and make toasted sandwiches as long as his mother was close by, but he refused to use a kettle until a circuit-breaker was installed. Once he was assured that this would instantly cut off the flow of electricity if problems arose, he began to make himself hot drinks and to stack the dish-washer. The process up to this stage took 6 months and Adam remained dependent on his mother's presence. When he began to approach the stage of attempting these tasks without his mother, however, he became increasingly agitated, constantly talking about what would happen if anything went wrong, or if the circuit-breaker failed, and he once more began to resist entering the kitchen. It was decided that this level of stress was unacceptable, and that it would be better to maintain his current progress rather than pushing him too far and perhaps causing his behaviour to regress. Although the ultimate goal of the programme was far from being attained, at least some level of independence had been reached, giving Adam a greater sense of self-esteem and allowing his mother some extra freedom.

A 'graded change' approach

Just as obsessions and rituals tend to grow gradually, often almost imperceptibly over time, programmes to reduce them are best if carried out in gradual and carefully planned stages. Graded change

Table 5.1 Hierarchy of fears relating to electrical equipment

Fear hierarchy	*How feeling*
	1 Happy and relaxed
	2 Not VERY happy, but not upset either
	3 Bit tense; tight feeling in stomach
	4 Very tense and nervous
	5 Very upset and panicky/Want to run away and scream

Fear rating
1 = *no anxiety*
5 = *panic*

	(*Mother present in kitchen*)
1	Making dry toast
1	Making a toasted sandwich
2	Making a toasted sandwich with tomatoes in
2	Putting dry food (e.g. cooked rice) in the microwave to heat
3	Cooking a prepared meal in the microwave
4	Heating a cup of coffee in the microwave
4	Putting a cup in the dishwasher
4	Turning on the dishwasher
5	Making a cup of tea/coffee
	(*Mother absent*)
4	Making dry toast
4	Making a toasted sandwich
4	Making a toasted sandwich with tomatoes in
4	Putting dry food (e.g. cooked rice) in the microwave to heat
4	Cooking a prepared meal in the microwave
5	Heating a cup of coffee in the microwave
5	Putting a cup in the dishwasher
5	Turning on the dishwasher
5	Making a cup of tea/coffee

is particularly useful in helping individuals to cope with environmental changes or alterations in daily routine.

David, who became very upset when his mother moved house, began to insist that she placed all her furniture in the same position as in their old home. To begin with, his mother tried to comply with his wishes, despite the inconvenience this caused. However, as time went on David became increasingly resistant to her changing anything. Remembering how difficult it had been to stop his obsessions as a child she decided she must draw a halt. Indeed, drawing, or taking photographs, was exactly what she did. Beginning first in the downstairs kitchen and dining room, where David's 'plans' were particularly inconvenient, she took photographs or made drawings of the layout, explaining to David exactly what she was doing and the changes she planned. As long as David had a pictorial representation of how things had been he agreed to accept some minor alterations. His mother made it clear that she would make no changes without telling him first, and that she would ensure that he had enough photographs or drawings of the original layout. David accepted this and gradually over a period of several months she was able to organise most of the new house as she wanted. The exception was the spare room which David used when he visited and which he was allowed to preserve exactly as it had always been.

Introducing alternative and more acceptable behaviours

Obsessional behaviours are frequently at their worst when individuals have no access to other, more productive activities with which to fill their time. Attempts to modify rituals or obsessions without replacing them with alternative behaviours are unlikely to prove successful, and without careful planning there is a real risk of even more disruptive behaviours taking their place.

Tessa was a 30-year-old woman whose fascination with hair-cutting had persisted since childhood. She frequently cut her own hair and, whenever the opportunity at her day centre arose, she would take aside uncomplaining students and cut their hair too. If scissors were not available, knives or razor blades removed from the craft room served equally well. It was apparent that this behaviour occurred mainly at lunch times, when staff supervision was minimal and when no other activities were timetabled. Once the 'danger periods' had been identified additional help was enlisted to ensure that Tessa was appropriately supervised during the lunch break. A detailed timetable was drawn up, to ensure that the time was filled more constructively and staff managed to obtain some old wigs and wig stands, together with a supply of styling equipment (heated rollers, driers, etc.) that could be used by Tessa to indulge her interest without endangering others. At the same time, the whereabouts of potentially vulnerable clients was closely monitored and security in the unit was improved in order to restrict her access to scissors, knives or razor blades. Since staff were aware that Tessa was capable of breaking into drawers or cupboards, or searching through staff's possessions to look for scissors, they took the additional precaution of routinely asking her, each meal time, whether she had a knife or scissors in her bag or pockets. Tessa would always show them if she had, and this combination of strategies brought the behaviour successfully under control.

Sally was a 35-year-old woman, with a severe learning disability, who had lived with her parents since leaving school. Because of the inadequacy of local day-care facilities she spent almost all her time at home with her parents, with only occasional input from local services. Whenever she was bored through lack of occupation, or stressed by being pushed into activities that she did not enjoy, Sally would pull or pick her hair until she had become almost bald. The only time she did not hair-pull, apart from when she was asleep, was when she went swimming. Her parents and relief workers attempted to try to develop a more appropriate daily programme that was neither over- nor under-stimulating, and which involved as many visits as possible to the hydro-therapy pool of a local hospital. It was not possible for Sally to use a public pool as the noise or presence of too many people, and especially children, was very distressing for her. As Sally never tried to pull her hair whilst wearing her bathing hat she was encouraged to wear this for much longer periods each day, a nylon hat replacing the less comfortable rubber one. Over time, the combination of the hat with a more constructive daily programme, resulted in a marked diminution of the hair pulling, apart from her fringe which remained an easy target. Some activities outside the house were then re-introduced, but Sally's appearance was not enhanced by her red and black striped swimming cap. Because attempts to remove this resulted in much distress, it was covered with a more age-appropriate baseball cap. Eventually, as the seams of the bathing hat began to fall apart, Sally was persuaded to wear just the baseball cap when out, although she still preferred the bathing cap in other circumstances.

Keeping obsessions out of sight

In some cases, the main problem with obsessional behaviour is not so much that it is particularly disruptive, as that it may bring unwanted attention to the person with autism. Whilst this may not concern the individual concerned, it can cause problems for other family members.

David was a young man who had made good social progress in many ways, and who worked in a voluntary capacity at a day centre for people with more severe learning difficulties. He got on well with his two brothers and shared their enjoyment in going to the cinema or the local pub. However, he had a number of facial mannerisms and grimaces that tended to occur if he were not otherwise occupied, and on buses or in queues these were a source of considerable embarrassment to his brothers. Although when younger David had learned to bring his hand mannerisms under control (by developing greater awareness of them and ensuring he always wore trousers with pockets into which he could put his hands) his awareness of his odd facial movements was much more limited. Eventually his brothers insisted that, wherever they went, he carry with him a daily newspaper and if the grimacing began they would make him disappear behind this. If the paper contained something of interest for him this tended to reduce the amount of grimacing, but even if it did not, at least no-one else could see him, which was all that mattered to his brothers!

Alan was an adolescent attending mainstream school where, although rather isolated, he was respected by other pupils because of his academic ability. He had always had an obsession with 'Sooty and Sweep' puppets, but had learned that taking these to school led to teasing or worse and he was content as long as he always had them at home at night. Problems arose when his class went on a geography field trip. His mother was concerned that if other boys found his puppets he would be teased unmercifully; on the other hand she knew he could not possibly sleep without them. Eventually she sewed them up into a pillow-case, with a gap into which Alan could place his hands, and she hoped that the other boys would not notice. When she discussed the situation with the teacher in charge sometime after their return, she was upset to learn that Alan had soon revealed his secret to other children. However, it then transpired that several others had teddy bears, old blankets or other 'comforters' tucked away and Alan's revelation had made it possible for them to talk about their special objects too.

Shaping: contracts and compromises

For anyone, attempting to get rid of a long-standing habit, no matter how undesirable, inconvenient or even health-threatening it may be, is no easy task. For someone with autism, in whom patterns of behaviour are particularly entrenched, the difficulties are even greater.

Often by the time families or individuals seek help, patterns of obsessional behaviour may be so intractable that almost every area of functioning is affected. Attempts to solve many different problems at once usually lead to frustration and failure, and the first important step is to accept that progress will be slow (although it can also be steady) and is generally only made possible by working on one aspect of one problem area at a time. Over-ambitious attempts to stop behaviours that have had a strong hold for many years will almost certainly prove unsuccessful. Instead, behaviours need to be carefully broken down into their component parts and these then tackled step by step, with the ultimate goal perhaps taking many months or even longer to achieve.

Matthew was an 18-year-old man whose insistence on washing in the kitchen sink caused such embarrassment to his teenage sister that she threatened to leave home. Although he bathed regularly on three nights a week, he persisted in stripping and washing at the kitchen sink every other evening. In this case the stages of intervention were as follows. Firstly, the red plastic bowl with which he washed himself in the sink was replaced with a different bowl which he accepted without too much resistance. The original bowl was then transferred to the basin which had been installed some years ago in his bedroom, but which he had consistently refused to use. Initially he also refused to use the bowl here, until his mother (knowing that he loved to be able to lock the bathroom door when he went for a bath), offered to let him fit a lock on the bedroom door too. She also supplied him with some favourite towels and soap from the bathroom. When the lock (which could easily be opened from the outside) was fitted, he began to wash himself in his bedroom, but only with persistent pressure from his mother, and he continued to try to get to the kitchen sink. However, following an electrical fault, all the lights in the kitchen ceased working, and as he hated the dark he became more willing to wash in his room. Rather than having the fault mended, his mother left the lights unfixed for several months (at considerable inconvenience to herself), until his new washing patterns were well established.

Because Matthew had very limited speech, his involvement in the

planning of this intervention was fairly minimal, although his agreement was sought at every stage. However, with more able individuals
it is often helpful to draw up more formal 'contracts' in which the
roles of all those concerned are agreed and specified from the outset.

Emma's paper collection had, as noted earlier, grown to such an
extent that the garage was full of boxes of theatre, sport and dance
programmes, printing leaflets from work (she estimated she had
around 18,000 of these) and old school textbooks. Her parents were
insistent that something had to go and Emma herself accepted the
need for this. Firstly, a hierarchy of items was drawn up, specifying
the materials that would be most difficult for her to relinquish and
those that would cause less distress. The most disposable were her old
school textbooks, the least dispensable her dance programmes.
Although she could not bear to throw anything away herself, she
agreed to allow her mother to remove the boxes containing school
books over a three-month period. The next stage was to work on the
theatre and dance programmes. She had many duplicate copies of all
of these and after a lengthy discussion agreed that she would throw
away any copies in excess of two, thereby reducing the number of
boxes by about a third. The next stage involved the removal of all but
ten boxes of printed labels from work. If Emma wished to bring more
paper home this was accepted only if she allowed her mother to
remove an equivalent amount. Again she could not bear the thought
of the paper being thrown away but agreed to give them to her mother
so that she could use them for notes 'or other purposes'. She stipu-
lated that her mother was not to throw any paper away but that she
could take it to the recycling depot, as long as she did not tell Emma
if and when she had done so. In turn, Emma had to agree not to ask
what had happened to the paper (her mother knew this would lead to
anxiety and persistent questioning). Future theatre programmes could
be collected, but no more than two copies of anything were to be
brought home. Each stage of the programme, including planned dates
for action, was specified in writing, with both Emma and her mother
signing their agreement to the proposed plans. Emma had little
problem coping with the removal of her school books, but the loss
of her precious theatre programmes proved too traumatic and she
asked to re-negotiate the plan so that she was allowed to keep three of
each. Rather than increase her anxiety to a level when she would
refuse to co-operate altogether, this was agreed. Eventually the
programme resulted in a large quantity of paper being removed
from the garage and the level was kept fairly stable thereafter.

Marion, whose impending marriage was causing her mother such anxiety because of the time she spent before bed, drawing the curtains and picking up fluff, finally agreed that this might irritate her partner. With her parents' help she rather reluctantly attempted to reduce these behaviours. For a few weeks she kept a record of how long it took her to get to bed each night, the average length of time being about two and a half hours. With advice from her psychologist, Marion drew up a bed-time schedule, on which the time for getting to bed was reduced by five minutes each night. By using this, and with guidance from her parents, she was able to reduce the nightly ritual to about thirty minutes, a time period that it was hoped would be more acceptable to her new spouse. Finally, they invested in a very powerful vacuum cleaner as a wedding present in the hope that this would speed up her carpet cleaning, thereby reducing the time even further.

Anita, whose anxiety about having to wear damaged garments resulted in drawers and wardrobes overflowing with clothes, agreed to attach a 'wear by date' label on each item purchased. The negotiated expiry period was two years after the original purchase date; thereafter Anita agreed that her mother could take any unworn garments to a local charity shop. On the whole this agreement worked quite well, although occasionally she would buy back certain garments from the charity shop and re-date them, pointing out that this had not been restricted in the terms of the original agreement.

Making rules

Although discussion and compromise are the most desirable ways of effecting change, there may be times when the level of resistance shown is so strong that a firmer approach is required if families or carers are to gain any degree of control. As already noted, attempts to restrict an obsession entirely are rarely successful, but it may be necessary to establish rules about when, where, with whom or how often certain activities can take place. Stuart's obsession with photographs of British Rail seating systems, for example, was beginning to discourage people from visiting the house, as he would bombard them with his pictures as soon as they arrived. Finally, in exasperation, his sister demanded, in no uncertain terms, that he must not show *any* train photographs to *any* of her friends ever again. He was so upset by this that she relented somewhat, promising that he could talk to them about any other topic for *five minutes only* before they went out. She also promised to look at his pictures with him every Sunday afternoon. She primed her friends to say 'I don't like photos of trains' if he broke the rule, but also encouraged them to talk to him about other topics. This approach proved so successful that the family began gradually to impose further restrictions until the obsession became far less intrusive.

Discouraging obsessional behaviours by imposing limits on where and when they can be carried out often proves very effective, and if restrictions are introduced in a planned and gradual way they should not result in too much distress or resistance.

With effective planning, obsessional behaviours can also be used to reward periods of more productive activity. Caroline, who attended a local day centre, would spend all her time, if left alone, ripping up pieces of paper. Over time, staff dealt successfully with the problem by insisting first that she did not tear paper in the kitchen whilst making or drinking coffee (an activity that was also very important to her). Opportunities for tearing were also reduced by removing paper towels, kitchen rolls or newspapers from the room. Once she had left the kitchen, Caroline was allowed to return to her paper-tearing. Next, tearing was restricted in the dining room and later during musical and craftwork activities, which she also enjoyed. At the same time her involvement in other tasks, such as completing chores, was rewarded by providing her with a small pile of paper to rip up. As the time spent in other activities increased, and as the paper supply grew steadily smaller, her obsession with the activity gradually reduced, until it no longer caused any disruption. However, it could still be used to fill up time if she were not otherwise occupied, or to calm her if she became agitated or distressed.

As noted in the chapter on communication problems, however, there is one class of obsessional behaviour that proves particularly resistant to modification, and that is verbal obsessions and routines. Whilst it may be relatively easy to restrict the time spent lining up bricks, or to insist that the collection of jam jars be kept in a specified place, placing limitations on verbal behaviours is much more difficult, and the problems of developing *consistent* management strategies should not be underestimated. No matter how hard one tries to resist it is extremely easy to be drawn into obsessional conversations, before even realising it. Particularly if the subject matter is interesting, or novel, the individual with autism usually has little problem in finding an audience. Dan, who was fascinated by the subject of albinoism, could readily attract the attention of people who did not know him with his extraordinary knowledge of this subject. Aaron, who spent all his time watching films on or reading about 'Batman', showed remarkable skill in turning any conversation around to this topic. Obsessive questioning also tends to 'feed' the obsessional behaviours themselves. Thus, Adam's obsession with electricity and the potential dangers of this was heightened rather than diminished if he was given the opportunity to talk about the subject at any length. Establishing rules early in childhood, or when an obsession first begins to emerge, about *when* a topic can be discussed (e.g. only after a discussion of other topics, or only at bed times), *where* discussions take place (only in the house and never outside), or *with whom* (e.g. with the class teacher, but only at the end of the day's work), is crucial if later difficulties are to be minimised. Attempts to prevent the individual from ever talking about his or her special interests, or asking the ritualised questions, are likely to result in overwhelming anxiety and agitation. But, as long as the established rules make it clear that the obsession is allowed at specified times, and as long as carers keep to their side of the agreement too, then a reasonable degree of control is usually possible. However, if complete freedom is allowed in the early years, or if obsessional discussion or questions reach a level when they totally dominate all conversations, intervention in later life becomes far more difficult.

Enlisting the help of others

As is evident from the examples above, reducing obsessional behaviours to an acceptable level can be a very complex process, involving detailed assessments and a variety of different strategies, including environmental restructuring. In order for programmes to succeed, information, help and support are needed from everyone concerned. Family and carers may also be required to change their behaviours or expectations at least as much as the person with autism. Changing the habits of many years is not easy for anyone, and careful discussion with and agreement from all the relevant parties will be required. Adam's mother had great difficulty in *not helping* him in the kitchen, as she could not bear to witness his distress and anxiety. Over the years she had protected him more and more from the need to use electrical equipment but in doing so had greatly curtailed his self-help skills. Her agreement *not* to offer him support was as difficult to achieve as his agreement to try to use the equipment, and although with time some measure of success was achieved, he continued to remain dependent on her presence in order to be able to carry out the necessary tasks.

For older parents, too, the practicalities of offering support can present problems. Although Emma's parents were very willing to help reduce her paper collection, they lived some distance away, and it was not easy for them to visit their daughter on a regular basis to ensure that the terms of the agreement were consistently complied with.

Compromise may well be needed on both sides and it is not always possible to predict, at the start of a planned programme, the degree of stress that may be experienced. However, if anxiety, or distress (on either side) become excessive, intervention will almost certainly fail; hence the need for back-up and professional support, frequent reviews and a rapid re-negotiation of plans if problems arise.

SELF-CONTROL TECHNIQUES

Because of the strains that an intensive programme can impose on other people and the problems that can occur if external support is unavailable for some reason, it is also crucial to provide the person with autism with as many ways as possible of controlling his or her own behaviour.

Sometimes these strategies can be purely practical. Emma, recognising the pain that parting with her paper collection produced, realised that it would be easier for her to *stop* taking papers home, rather than then having to throw them away. If offered leaflets or papers on the street she began either to refuse these, or to discard them immediately she had read them, instead of taking them home. Whilst this strategy did not reduce the amount of paper still left in the garage it helped to avoid the situation worsening any further.

Predicting and dealing with change

Although it is often stated that people with autism have extreme difficulties in coping with change, in many cases it is the inability to cope with *unpredictable* change that gives rise to most problems.

Jeremy, whose agitation when the train failed to arrive on time made him appear so odd to other commuters, was helped to deal with his problem in a number of ways. Firstly, he began to get up 15 minutes earlier each morning to listen to the travel news on his local radio station; if problems were predicted he would ring up his workplace to let them know that he 'might' be late. He also listened to the weather forecast before going to bed each night, as rain or bad weather was also likely to cause delays. Secondly, instead of sticking invariably to a single route to work, he planned out some possible alternatives that could be used in the case of major disruptions or cancellations. Next, he made sure that he always had a spare phone card in order to be able to contact work if problems arose. Finally, in order to reduce his own agitation, he began to listen to his 'Walkman' on the way to work, as this helped him to relax. Being able to predict problems, at least to some extent, together with the provision of some simple, practical hints on how to deal with these, greatly improved the journeys to work. Although difficulties were not entirely solved – totally unforeseen delays, for example, continued to cause major disruption – they were significantly reduced.

Bob's distress at the inadequacy of weather forecasts in England was dealt with by his family in the following way. Firstly they agreed that his complaints were not without foundation, and they did not attempt to argue with his frequent suggestions (accompanied by letters to the BBC and the Met Office) that all forecasters should be instantly dismissed. Instead of trying to reassure him that the forecast would probably be correct, they reinforced the idea that it might well be *wrong*. They encouraged him to keep daily records of the weather conditions that had been predicted and what they had actually been like. As the obsession shifted from distress at inaccurate predictions to a statistical analysis of the inaccuracy of the forecasts much of the disruption that this problem had previously imposed on family life was removed.

Relaxation

Perhaps the major problem associated with obsessional and ritualistic behaviours is the high level of stress that they can engender. In particular, intense anxiety can occur if the individual is prevented, or has fears of being prevented, from carrying out the activity; because of worries about change, or because of fears of what will happen if the activity is not performed in a certain way. Relaxation techniques, which have proved so effective in dealing with the fears and anxieties of non-autistic people, can readily be adapted to meet the needs of someone with autism. The principle underlying relaxation techniques is that of 'reciprocal inhibition': that is, alternative responses can be elicited in order to reduce, inhibit, or otherwise interfere with the physiological and psychological symptoms of anxiety (Sheldon, 1995). Many tapes and books are commercially available to help individuals develop more effective means of relaxation. These involve physical relaxation methods to reduce muscle tension or to improve breathing techniques, as well as psychological methods. The latter may involve developing powerful visual imagery (e.g.

of pleasant and tranquil scenes), which can then be used to disrupt anxiety-provoking thoughts or images; auditory stimulation, involving calming music or other sounds, can be used in a similar way.

For individuals with autism, however, some of the physical muscle-relaxation exercises may be too lengthy or complex, or demands on visual imagery and imagination too abstract, for these techniques to be of much practical use (Clements, 1987). Some, even amongst the most able of individuals, complain that the tapes are just boring or meaningless, and seem to be unable to persevere with these. However, the basic techniques can be modified to suit people with autism. For example, simple breathing techniques – showing individuals how to take four or five deep breaths in a way that decreases rather than increases chest tension (many pull in their stomach muscles when they inhale, which simply increases tension), can be a rapid and effective way of inducing feelings of calmness or relief, and avoids the need for more prolonged relaxation exercises. Instead of trying to promote visual *images*, which often proves too abstract a task for people with autism, looking at a photograph, post card or picture of a pleasant or familiar scene may be much more helpful. The picture needs to be small enough to be carried about easily, and may need covering or reinforcing in some way if it is not to fall apart. Alternatively, a series of easily replaceable pictures may be used instead, and postcards can be particularly helpful here. Some people find the 'Magic Eye' postcards (where the apparently abstract foreground of the card needs to be stared at intensely before a 3-D image can be seen) useful sources of distraction. Similarly, although it may be difficult to arouse auditory images, individually made tapes of music or other relaxing sounds can be used instead.

Whatever exercises or images are found to be helpful, the crucial aspect of relaxation training is that it *must* be carried out at frequent and regular intervals if it is to be of any practical use when anxieties actually arise. Ideally, a daily session should be established, when the individual goes through his or her 'exercises', and as people often find it difficult to set aside special times for these, bath or bed times are often the best periods to utilise. Supervision and guidance will usually be needed at first, but once appropriate techniques are developed, individuals should be able to put these into practice themselves, at least with some reminding, as time goes on.

The main problem then is to encourage them to make use of these strategies when anxiety-provoking situations occur. For individuals who have some supervision throughout the day, direct prompts can be given by carers when the first signs of anxiety are recognised. Experience indicates that it is much more effective to intervene immediately the first signs of agitation are apparent, rather than to wait until anxiety has reached a higher level. However, for individuals who are living independently or who do not have access to input of this kind, other options will need to be explored. One alternative is to make use of role-play situations that deliberately provoke anxiety or stress, and then to encourage the use of relaxation strategies. Perhaps surprisingly, many people with autism respond well to simulation exercises of this kind and seem to have little difficulty in summoning up the appropriate emotional responses. David, for example, had an obsession with 'always being right', and if anyone seemed to be critical of him in any way he would become extremely agitated. Sessions with his psychologist were used to help him cope in situations when someone spoke to him in an angry or annoyed voice or when they had criticised something he had done. As soon as he started to become visibly agitated he would be prompted to put his deep-breathing and distraction exercises into action. The psychologist also helped him to recognise his own internal and external symptoms of stress (in his case facial grimacing and a feeling of tightness in his stomach) and to respond more rapidly to these. The programme also involved practical advice about ways of responding to criticism.

Another possible solution for adults living relatively independently is to enlist the help of relevant individuals at work or home. Timothy had a job as a computer programmer, but became very agitated if certain problems over data input arose (usually when he considered that someone else had made a stupid or avoidable error). At such times he would grimace, shout and even throw things, behaviours that were particularly unacceptable if there were visitors in the office. After discussions with his line manager, one of the older secretaries volunteered to take Timothy aside whenever she saw him becoming agitated and would suggest he went outside to the corridor to calm down. Because of her seniority Timothy was quite willing to accept this guidance and the impact of the problem was greatly reduced.

At the other end of the spectrum, for people of lower intellectual and linguistic ability, self-directed relaxation techniques may be difficult, if not impossible, to implement successfully. Instead, direct help with ways to relax will need to be provided by other people. Massage, aromatherapy, physical exercise, music and dance, and various arts and crafts are all activities that have been reported to be valuable in reducing agitation and distress.

Distracting techniques

A further way of attempting to reduce ritualistic behaviours is to use distracting techniques. Again, these can be of a variety of different kinds and should be adapted to the needs of the individual involved. As with relaxation, the chosen strategies should be employed as soon as the first signs of the obsessional behaviour or the anxieties related to it are noted. Monica was a young woman with severe learning difficulties as well as autism, whose main obsession was 'posting' things (mainly paper items) down the backs of chairs, radiators or cracks in the walls or floors. Many important documents and the occasional five pound note were thought to have disappeared in this way. If she were fully occupied the problem tended to diminish, and it arose mainly at times when the unit was poorly staffed. Although the main aim of her care programme was to keep her fully occupied this was simply not possible throughout the entire day. A large wooden container was constructed, full of holes of different shapes and sizes, and if other activities were not readily available, Monica was encouraged to post items into this. Whilst the behaviour was not stopped by this technique, it did at least ensure that the items posted could be easily regained.

John, a young man attending a day centre, had an obsession with coins and would 'collect' these whenever the opportunity arose. Understandably, this caused considerable resentment amongst some of the other clients at the centre. His key worker noted that the 'collecting' tended to occur after John had begun to talk about money and what he would do with this. He found that if he then occupied John in making shopping lists for purchases for the centre, and arranged for a time when he could be taken to the shops, the problems greatly diminished.

Thought stopping

Another technique, developed from cognitive behavioural work with adults with depressive or obsessive problems, is that of 'thought stopping'. This, as its name suggests, involves interrupting the train of distressing or intrusive thoughts by introducing conflicting thoughts or self-instruction (Sheldon, 1995). Again, however, reliance on internalised verbal techniques of this kind can be difficult for people with autism. Martin, whose anxiety about achieving the highest possible number of points on video games was described earlier, was advised to try to use thought-stopping techniques to reduce his anxiety. However, telling himself 'I'm the best' if a lower-than-expected score was achieved did not prove helpful, and he even began to argue with his parents about the 'untruthfulness' of such statements. Instead, it was decided to encourage him to keep a notebook in which to record every score, so that he could then work out his *weekly* average (which was almost certain to be extremely high). Delaying the opportunity for worry, by writing scores down, proved much more effective. Other thought-stopping strategies can also be employed. Jason, who had an obsession that any aeroplane flying overhead might crash, had found aromatherapy helpful in teaching him to relax. His insistence on rushing outside every time he heard a plane proved very disruptive, especially during group activities, and instead he was encouraged to carry a small pad soaked in a perfume which he could smell whenever he heard an aeroplane. Staff's reminders to 'have a good sniff' would often distract him long enough for the plane and the anxiety to disappear!

For other people, the use of picture postcards as a distracter, or cards containing a simple written instruction (e.g. 'Relax', 'Don't panic', 'Take a deep breath' or 'Count backwards from ten') may be helpful. Other cues can also be used. Sally, who tended to get very agitated if she were not allowed to line up objects whenever she went somewhere new, was instructed by the staff at her home to 'count to ten' in order to calm her down. As she could only count to ten by looking at her digital watch, and as she insisted on waiting until the seconds were back to zero before doing this, her outbursts could often be delayed long enough for some other distracting techniques to be employed.

Further descriptions of other self-control techniques, which can be adapted for use with individuals of different ability levels can be found in the books of John Clements (1987) and Brian Sheldon (1995). Tryan (1979) also provides a useful review of simple thought-stopping techniques, including non-verbal strategies such as wearing on the wrist a thick elastic band, which can be pulled and released if obsessional thoughts begin to intrude.

IMPROVING THE GENERAL QUALITY OF LIFE

Possibly the most crucial element in any intervention programme for obsessional or ritualistic behaviours is the need to develop and encourage other activities as far as possible. The importance of appropriate stimulation is illustrated in many of the examples above and there is considerable experimental evidence to indicate that obsessional and ritualistic behaviours increase when individuals are inadequately occupied (Chock and Glahn, 1983).

However, once obsessions and routines become established they can prove remarkably resistant to change and hence attempts to expand alternative activities may be strongly resisted. Again, a 'graded change' approach can often prove effective.

Adam, whose obsession with the dangers of electrical equipment was described earlier, spent almost all his time talking about the problems of electricity and its potential perils. In addition to the practical desensitisation programme, attempts were made to increase activities that might distract his thoughts from electrical matters. His other main interest was tennis, but because of his fear of losing he would only play members of his own family (whom he could fairly easily beat). Fortunately, a neighbour discovered that a local residence for people with learning disabilities needed volunteers to coach them in sports such as tennis, and suggested that Adam might give this a try. Since he was almost certain to win every game, he was only too happy to spend his spare time at the unit, where his quietness and gentleness were much appreciated by the residents. As he became more involved in his tennis coaching, his electrical obsession became less intrusive and his previously overwhelming anxiety about this also seemed to subside.

For individuals of lower ability, attempts to develop alternative activities may also be helpful. Clyde had many problems in settling into a home for people with learning disabilities, and his obsessional behaviours became very difficult to deal with. Before leaving each morning he insisted on lining up all the chairs on the ground floor in straight lines, their backs a few centimetres from the wall. Because of his anxiety that other residents might disrupt the furniture, he refused to leave the house until everyone else had gone, often missing the coach to his day centre because of this, and if anyone remained at home because of illness he would not leave at all. Recognising his need for order, and for greater solitude, staff gave him the responsibility of organising the equipment in the greenhouses and garden sheds. As each item already had a set place, identified by silhouettes or pictures, Clyde did not have the opportunity to impose his own idiosyncratic placement systems and seemed content to replace everything in its allotted position. Few other residents went into the sheds so that Clyde was generally left alone and he knew that equipment was unlikely to be moved. The combination of an ordered environment and greater isolation from other residents helped to reduce his other obsessional behaviours to a more manageable level.

EARLY PREVENTION

The effective modification of obsessional and ritualistic behaviours in adults with autism will almost always require strategies that are complex and specifically designed to meet individual needs. The more pervasive and entrenched the problems, the more imaginative and resourceful management programmes will need to be. However, there are a few basic rules, which, if followed, could prevent many subsequent problems.

The first is to ensure that, from the child's earliest years, obsessional behaviours are under the control of those caring for the child, rather than carers themselves being controlled by the obsessions. Although this may sound far-fetched there are many examples of families whose lives, over the years, can become dominated in this way. Raymond, now in his fifties, had always shown a marked resistance to change. Even when he was still in his push-chair his sister remembers walks being dominated by his insistence on never taking left-hand turns, and his protests if his mother tried to retrace her steps rather than returning by a different route. He was not diagnosed as having autism until he reached his late forties, and although his family had always recognised the fact that he had problems, no explanation and, more importantly, no help for these was ever provided. By the time he was 50 he lived alone with his widowed mother and had absolute power over her, dictating who came to the house, what food they ate, where they shopped, where they went on holiday, and refusing ever to let her throw away anything so that the house was full of old clothes, newspapers and useless equipment. In the end, as his mother's health deteriorated, she was removed by Social Services for her own protection. Eventually, too, because of his inability to function adequately alone, he required hostel accommodation. Perhaps if the family's need for help had been recognised at an early age and if appropriate advice and support had been offered, the obsessional behaviours would never have been allowed to develop to the level where they virtually destroyed the lives of an elderly woman and her only son.

The second rule, which admittedly requires some ability to see into the future, is never to allow or encourage behaviours in young children that will be unacceptable in later life. All too often, obsessional or ritualistic behaviours present difficulties as people grow older, not because the intensity or frequency of the behaviours has increased, but because other people's attitudes have changed. Behaviours that are acceptable in a little child (such as an obsession with the feel of women's tights, or publicly removing all clothing) will be viewed very differently when the same individuals reach late adolescence or adulthood.

Joey's obsession with washing machines, for example, had provided his mother with much needed respite when he was a child. However, by the time he was a large, active teenager he was well able to break into other houses to indulge his obsession, so that a previously innocuous behaviour became a threat to both himself and others. Adam, whose skill in 'mending' electrical equipment was considered a real party trick at the age of 7, by the age of 12 required constant attention and supervision both at and away from home because of the potential danger of this behaviour.

Without help, parents are unlikely to be able to identify the potential problems related to obsessions and routines and in order to avoid distressing a young child will very naturally tend to give into these, perhaps with disastrous results in the future. It is up to professionals who are knowledgeable about autism, and the pattern that behaviours are likely to take in later life, to advise, to warn, and to develop appropriate strategies for families, schools and others to follow. Coping with an obsession of a few weeks' duration may be hard, but it is nothing like so difficult as attempting to eliminate a behaviour that has been well entrenched for many years!

The third point is to remain vigilant and sensitive to the emergence of new or potential problems. Most people with autism will develop new interests, obsessions or rituals over the years. Some of these may be short-lived, others may become very pervasive and disruptive. Knowing when or whether to intervene depends principally on knowledge and understanding of the individual concerned. In some cases it is wisest to pay little attention to new behaviours, in that if ignored they will tend to disappear again fairly rapidly. In contrast, obsessional behaviours in other individuals quickly become entrenched, and rather than allowing this to happen intervention in the very earliest stages (specifying rules about when, where and with whom) will be crucial if the problems are not to escalate.

A final guideline is to make the best use of any externally imposed changes on the individual's environment or life style. The move from home to a residential setting or from school to college provides many valuable opportunities for change and even individuals with very fixed routines in one setting may show surprisingly little resistance to modifying these in a totally different environment. However, for such changes to occur it is crucial that steps are taken to ensure that there are no opportunities for the old behaviour patterns to re-establish themselves. If allowed in the new environment the behaviours will be strengthened even further. On the other hand, if different and more appropriate routines are established *from the outset*, major behavioural changes can often be implemented with relatively little difficulty. Sandra, a woman in her twenties, had developed very rigid patterns of behaviour at home with her elderly mother. She would watch television, with the volume on high, until the early hours of the morning; she had lengthy and complex routines for washing and going to bed; and she insisted on her mother cooking meals at exactly the same times each day. Recognising the importance of such routines for Sandra, staff at the Home to which she was to move constructed detailed timetables, in collaboration with Sarah, specifying the times for each of these activities on a daily basis. The times were changed somewhat from day to day, to avoid encouraging over-rigidity, but ensured that TV watching was limited to times that did not disturb others (a mark was also placed on the volume control to indicate acceptable levels of loudness) and that the time involved in dressing and washing was not excessive. Because she was aware, well in advance, of what the routines would be, Sandra accepted the changes with little difficulty.

USING OBSESSIONS

Although obsessional behaviours may, if not adequately controlled, become the source of considerable disruption, they can play an important role in providing the person with autism with comfort, self-occupation or entertainment, which, because of their lack of other creative, social or imaginative skills would be almost impossible to obtain by other means. Longer-term outcome, too, can be positively affected by the way in which obsessional interests develop. Leo Kanner, in his 1973 follow-up of young adults with autism, found that many of those who had made most progress had done so via their obsessional interests. Special interests in music, memory or mathematics had, in a significant number of cases, led to the development of valuable work-related skills; others with a fascination for topics such as chess, history, politics or transport, succeeded in building a range of social interactions around these.

Asperger, too, reports on cases where early obsessions led to later success in life. For example, one individual with a childhood fascination with mathematics subsequently became an assistant professor in a university Department of Astronomy, despite severely impaired social skills, after having proved a mathematical error in Newton's work.

Similarly, in a London-based follow-up of young adults (Goode, Rutter and Howlin, in preparation) several individuals who had done particularly well had made use of their earlier obsessions. Danny had, ever since he was a small child, been fascinated by angles and directions and from about the age of 3 his drawings consisted almost entirely of room plans or the angles made by doors or furniture. By his mid-twenties he was successfully employed in a cartographer's office and despite some problems was a popular member of staff. His popularity was also enhanced by his input to the company's sporting team, because of his remarkable skills in orienteering. Maurice, who had been fascinated with collecting scientific facts from an early age, had managed to obtain a Master's degree in chemistry and was currently working as a scientific officer for a major chemical company.

From a personal point of view, Temple Grandin (1995) also stresses the value of using obsessional interests.

> Fixations are powerful motivators. It is a mistake to try to stamp out fixations . . . When I was in high school many of my teachers and psychologists wanted me to get rid of my fixation on cattle shutes . . . I have made a successful career based on my fixation with cattle squeeze shutes. I have designed livestock handling systems for major ranches and meat companies all over the world.

Even if special interests do not lead to occupational success they can play an important role in developing hobbies or other activities to fill otherwise empty hours. Clara Park, writing of her daughter Jessy, tells of how her unusual artistic skill was put to little use until she discovered that it brought her money, one of the few items she did have a particular interest in. Although art for art's sake held little meaning for her, art for money's sake did, and by the age of 20 painting and drawing had become an important and fulfilling part of her life. Many other people find their obsessional activities a source of comfort if they are anxious, or tired, or have to cope with novel or stressful experiences. Others use their obsessions in order to relax. Jonah, who works as an accounts clerk in a busy company, spends an hour or so at the end of each day at his local railway station, collecting train numbers. Caroline, who was always fearful of the dark when younger, now reports that it is much easier for her to sleep if she has managed to watch the moon in the sky for half an hour or so on clear nights.

Obsessions can also offer support at times of severe stress or loss. Dennis, who worked for his father in their small family firm, was the victim of a vicious attack, in which both he and his parents were shot and wounded. Although unable and unwilling to talk about his suffering or fears after this incident, his obsession with collecting and drawing a particular make of old-fashioned radio clearly gave him some relief. Over time his desire to talk about his obsession over-rode his avoidance of social contacts and eventually it became possible for him to make some use of professional counselling.

Sometimes, too, obsessions may serve to reduce anxiety as well as proving productive in other ways. Temple Grandin first constructed a 'squeeze machine' to reduce her own anxiety and obsessional fears but this later became the basis for her later, and highly successful, cattle restraining devices, which have won acclaim in the field of animal psychology.

Finally, particularly for less able individuals with autism, whose range of interests and abilities may be very restricted, the opportunity to indulge in obsessional activities can be an important means of increasing other skills. David Premack, in 1959, was one of the first psychologists to show that the use of ritualistic, obsessional, or other apparently meaningless activities, as a reward for more appropriate behaviours, may be a very effective strategy in increasing behavioural repertoires. Since then many other studies have shown how stereotypic, obsessional or attachment behaviours can be used to increase more constructive activities in people with autism. (Wolery, Kirk and Gast, 1985; Sugai and White, 1986).

Whilst such strategies do not aim to eliminate obsessional or ritualistic behaviour, they can be highly effective in reinforcing and encouraging short periods of alternative behaviours, with the result that the obsessions themselves gradually diminish in frequency or intensity.

As the examples above illustrate, dealing with obsessions and routines is by no means an easy task and successful interventions will require time, patience and often the implementation of several different strategies in tandem. The principal guidelines for success, however, are early intervention; a graded approach to the introduction of change; the provision of a more appropriate or stimulating environment in order to encourage other activities; the establishment of basic rules about where, when, with whom or for how long ritualistic or obsessional behaviours may take place. The aim should generally be not to remove the obsession entirely but to ensure that the behaviour no longer intrudes in a distressing or unacceptable way into the life of the person with autism or that of his or her carers. Once an acceptable level of control is reached, obsessional behaviours or interests may actually have many beneficial effects.

6 Education for adolescents with autism

The debate over whether children with disabilities should be integrated into mainstream schooling or receive specialist education has been a focus of controversy for many decades. However, although the proponents for and against full integration are equally vociferous, evidence in support of the arguments on either side remains limited. Both mainstream and segregated education have their benefits and drawbacks and these will vary according to the needs of individual children and the severity of their disorder (Howlin, 1994a).

The appropriateness of special education facilities will also vary during the course of the child's school life. Thus, whilst specialist provision, especially for those with severely disabling problems, may be valuable in the early school years, it may be less productive at secondary school age, where access to the normal school curriculum becomes crucial for entry to further educational and occupational opportunities.

In much of Europe, the United States and Australasia, legislation has swung steadily towards integrated education for all children, resulting in the closure or even abolition of specialist schools. The obligation to place children in 'the least restrictive environment, regardless of the severity of their disability', has had a dramatic impact on educational provision in the USA over the last two decades. Similar trends have occurred in many other countries. In England and Wales, the Education Act of 1981 implemented many of the recommendations of the Warnock committee (1978) which had concluded that the majority of children with special needs should be catered for, as far as possible, within mainstream settings. The more recent Education Act of 1993 places all local education authorities under a 'qualified' duty to secure integration of children with special educational needs in the mainstream, provided this is right for the child. The Act requires improved parental choice in placements, the establishment of an independent appeals tribunal and a new code of practice on the identification and assessment of Special Educational Needs. All schools must also develop and publish their own Special Educational Needs policy.

Nevertheless, despite greater recognition of the requirements of children with special educational needs, in practice there remains much room for improvement. In 1988 Elizabeth Newson and colleagues (Gilby, Jones and Newson, 1988) reported on a survey of educational provision for children with autism in England and Wales. Out of a total of 105 education authorities, only 12 claimed to be educating children with a diagnosis of autism in mainstream school. Only <u>17</u> children (out of an estimated population of 7,800 children with autism; Jones and Newson, 1992) were identified as receiving mainstream provision. Moreover, it was evident that in the majority of these cases, teachers had no prior knowledge of autism nor of the potential problems entailed. The amount of extra help provided varied from none to full-time, with 11 of the 17 children receiving additional (but rarely specially trained) help for half the time or less.

The failure of integrated services to provide children with autism with the additional and often highly skilled help that is required has resulted in many parents using the Act to obtain specialist rather than mainstream provision. Even those in support of integration find that, because of the failure to provide teaching staff with adequate training or support, it may be preferable for education in the early years to be provided in specialist units. If major difficulties can be brought under control in this way, gradual integration may then be feasible at a later age.

The crucial issue, of course, is not whether integrated or segregated education is best, but what can be done to ensure that the educational system available to children with autism is able to meet their social, emotional *and educational* needs. Research into effective school environments has consistently indicated that children do best in settings that are well structured, offer appropriately individualised programmes, emphasise 'on-task' activities, and have goals that are clear to both teachers and children and that can be modified according to children's needs and abilities (Rutter, 1983). Very similar factors appear to be important in educational programmes for children with autism. Over twenty years ago, Rutter and Bartak (1973) stressed the value of a structured programme that focused directly on educational goals in improving both academic *and* social competence. The highly structured teaching approaches that form the basis of the TEACCH programmes of Schopler and his colleagues (Mesibov, Schopler and Sloan, 1983; Short, 1984) have also proved extremely effective. Directive teacher intervention is also required (Meyer *et al.*, 1987), as is the use of behavioural strategies to decrease undesirable behaviours and to improve skill levels. Egel, Koegel and Schreibman (1980) concluded that behavioural models resulted in much more effective teaching than strategies derived from psychoanalytic or sensory-deficit models. Communication and social skills training, too, are important and progress may also be enhanced if the programme extends to the training of normal peers (Brady *et al.*, 1987; Wolfberg and Schuler, 1993; Lord, 1984; Howlin and Rutter, 1987; Williams, 1989). However, the development of effective programmes also requires detailed individual assessments, highly specialised teaching techniques and often considerable environmental restructuring (see Quill, 1995a for a number of excellent chapters on these topics).

Whilst a structured and behaviourally based approach to teaching is clearly important, caution is required in interpreting some of the claims put forward for special education programmes. Daily Life Therapy, as practised in the Japanese-run Higashi schools (Kitahara, 1983) is said to result in unprecedented progress in the education and integration of children with autism. The Boston Higashi school reports impressive outcomes in children who have been through their highly structured, intensely physical programmes (see Gould, Rigg, and Bignell, 1991 for details). The Option method of Kaufman (1981) also claims impressive, even miraculous, results. Unfortunately such claims are rarely supported by adequate experimental evidence (Quill, Gurry and Larkin, 1989).

Recently, Lovaas and his colleagues in California (Lovaas, 1987; McEachin, Smith and Lovaas, 1993) have reported dramatic improvements in a group of autistic children exposed to very intensive behavioural training and education (40 hours of one-to-one intervention a week for two years) from an early age. It is claimed that many showed significant increases in IQ and were subsequently 'indistinguishable' from their normal peers. Indeed, it is suggested that over 40 per cent of students 'recovered' from their autism. However, problems in group selection, the different measures used over time, and definitions of 'normality' make the interpretation of results very difficult. Not surprisingly, the study has given rise to considerable, and as yet unresolved, controversy (Schopler, Short and Mesibov, 1989; Mesibov, 1993). From a practical point of view, too, the project raises many important issues. Although some families are able to cope with programmes of this degree of intensity (see, for example, Maurice, 1993), for many others the demands made are such that even if the outcome is as positive as suggested, success can only be achieved at enormous expense. Thus, although the huge investment of time, energy and emotional involvement required may enhance the progress of the child with autism, at least initially (long-term comparative studies are not available), any benefits must be weighed against the inevitable disruption to normal family life and relationships.

Whatever the ultimate conclusions about the effectiveness of these methods, few families will have access to such intensive intervention programmes. For most parents the choice will be restricted to whatever their local education authority has to offer.

THE RANGE OF EDUCATIONAL PROVISION FOR CHILDREN WITH AUTISM

In a recent follow-up study of young adults with autism, Goode and her colleagues explored the types of school most commonly attended. Although, as children, they had attended a wide range of different schools, the majority had spent most of their school life in specialist autistic schools or units (see Figure 6.1).

Specialist schools for children with autism

In England, the National Autistic Society is directly responsible for 5 schools for children with autism and throughout England and Wales there are 7 additional schools run by local autistic societies, offering approximately 400 places in all (Jones and Newson, 1992). There are also a number of units or classes run by local education authorities, offering a further 600 specialist placements. Thus, in an estimated population of 7,800 children with autism in these countries (Autisme Europe, 1988), approximately 1,000 (12.5 per cent) are in specialist provision. Jones and Newson found that of a total of 105 local education authorities in England and Wales in 1992, only 37 per cent had any specialist provision for children with autism, 52 per cent would fund placements outside the authority, and 10 per cent funded no specialist provision, placing all pupils with autism in schools for children with learning disabilities, or in a few cases in mainstream provision.

In other countries where there is little or no specialist education

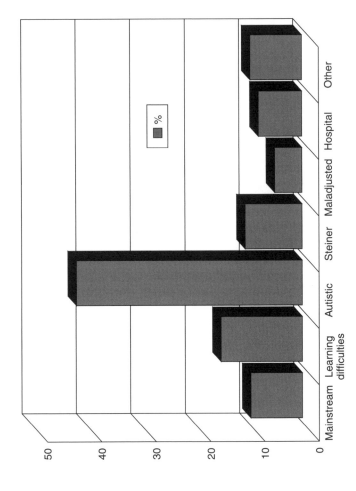

Figure 6.1 Principal school placements of individuals followed-up by Goode and colleagues
Note: 'Other' includes: private, 'delicate', home tutor, unknown

(for either economic or political reasons), small classes or units are often set up by charitable or parental organisations. The success of the TEACCH classes, which originated in North Carolina (Mesibov, 1992) and which have since been adopted by a number of countries in Europe, also demonstrates how research-based programmes can be adapted for use in schools.

As in any educational setting, the curriculum and quality of teaching offered within specialist schools or units is very variable. Although there have been attempts to evaluate the most appropriate types of teaching programme and school environment for children with autism (Newson and Jones, 1994), the small sample size of such studies, together with problems in experimental design, means that the conclusions are often contradictory or uncertain. There remains no firm evidence in support of the argument that the majority of children with autism are best educated in special autistic schools. Indeed, because of the heterogeneity of children with autism, it would be surprising if any one approach or system were to be universally effective. As Rutter pointed out many years ago (Rutter and Bartak, 1973), what is needed is task-oriented, highly structured teaching adapted to meet *individual* needs.

The unique advantage of autistic schools, however, lies in the specialist knowledge and expertise of the teachers who work there. Their training, and the experience that comes from being in daily contact with children with autism, places them in a singular position when it comes to dealing with behaviour difficulties, minimising ritualistic and obsessional behaviours, developing social and communication skills, and generally creating an optimal environment to reduce problems and maximise abilities. Support and guidance from colleagues working with the same problems helps to maintain a high standard of teaching and the emphasis on home-school links, which tends to be a particular focus of these schools, also ensures greater consistency in treatment and management. Small class-sizes and a very high teacher-to-pupil ratio are other advantages, rarely available in non-specialist provision. Many such schools also have strong links with other experienced professionals, such as social workers, GPs, paediatricians, psychiatrists and psychologists who are able to offer additional help to deal with other aspects of the child's or family's needs.

Many children with autism, even those with severe behavioural disturbances, show rapid improvement when placed in specialist autistic provision. Despite the advantages, however, there are also clear drawbacks to segregated units of this kind. Firstly, the peer group itself, by its very nature, is unlikely to offer opportunities for the development of social relationships. That is not to suggest, of course, that simply placing a child with autism alongside normal peers will automatically lead to improvements. As discussed later in this chapter, the development of social interactions requires highly skilled input from teachers. Nevertheless, if all the other children in the school also have profound social impairments, even the most expert of teachers will have problems encouraging social interactions. Many parents are also concerned about the effects of placing their child with others who may be even more severely handicapped. Autistic children, like any others, have a propensity for copying undesirable behaviours from their peers, and parents may be understandably anxious about the risk of new problems being acquired in this way.

Perhaps the most important drawback of special units, especially for more able children, however, is the limited educational facilities that they are able to offer. Small schools may have a great advantage when it comes to developing a consistent and individualised approach to teaching but these very factors make it difficult, if not impossible, to offer a wide teaching curriculum. Despite the fact that special schools are expected to incorporate the 'normal curriculum' into their teaching as far as possible, the extent to which this can be done is obviously limited. Few autistic schools are able to offer a child with autism the opportunity to take external examinations in maths, physics, computing or similar topics, since they are unlikely to have staff adequately qualified in these areas. The London-based study by Sue Goode and colleagues has shown that very few people with autism, even those of normal intellectual ability, leave school with any formal qualifications (see Figure 6.2).

But, since success in later life is highly dependent on the qualifications obtained in school or college, the inability of autistic schools to provide such opportunities has serious implications for at least a minority of their pupils.

Education in schools for children with severe learning disabilities

The majority of children with autism will, of course, never reach a high level of attainment. Around half of all children with autism have severe to moderate learning problems and because of this many education authorities argue against placement in highly specialised (and expensive) autistic provision, when places are readily available in schools for children with more general learning disabilities.

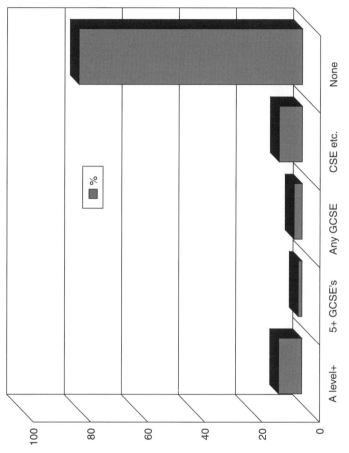

Figure 6.2 School qualifications of individuals followed-up by Goode and colleagues (highest level reached)

In principle, there might seem to be a number of factors in favour of this argument. Firstly, because there are more schools available for children with learning disabilities, it should be easier to find one relatively close to home, thereby avoiding the need for extensive travelling, or even boarding facilities. Secondly, proximity to the child's home means that it should be easier to develop the crucial links between parents and teachers. If other pupils live locally, this should also facilitate the development of peer relationships outside school. Finally, because such schools are larger, the physical amenities are often far better.

Nevertheless, in practice, the very specific pattern of disabilities shown by children with autism poses many problems in mixed settings of this kind. Most children with learning disabilities, especially those in the mild to moderately handicapped range, will show a fairly 'flat' profile of abilities. Thus, although delayed in all areas, their social, communication and emotional development will, in general, be on a par with their development in other areas. Teaching can therefore be relatively easily adapted to the child's overall cognitive level. In the case of autistic children, whose developmental profiles are characteristically uneven, this can prove much more difficult. Thus, certain aspects of motor development may be relatively unimpaired; there may be moderate delays in other areas of non-verbal development, whilst deficits in verbal, social and emotional development may be very profound. If matched with other learning-disabled children on the basis of their non-verbal skills, pupils with autism will almost certainly be far more handicapped than their peer group in terms of social and communication development. If matched for social or communication skills then they are likely to be far more capable in terms of their motor development. This can give rise to considerable problems for staff having to cope with very delicate or physically disabled children. In addition, if placement is in a special needs unit, then much of the staff's time is likely to be taken up with activities such as cleaning, feeding or toileting, so that the needs of the physically more able child with autism can easily be neglected.

Additional problems may occur in adolescence, when many children with learning disabilities will have developed good social networks and will be able to work co-operatively, thereby allowing more group teaching to take place. This is rarely the case in autism, where individually based teaching remains an essential requirement. The child with autism is almost certain to be lacking, too, in the imaginative and imitative skills of other pupils, making play and other joint activities very difficult. This progressive 'isolation' can lead to an upsurge of behaviour problems and staff are unlikely to have the specialist skills needed to deal with these. Specific training related to autism may not be available, and the mutual support and advice about effective strategies that teachers in a school for children with autism can offer each other will also be missing.

Schools for children with mild learning disabilities or emotional and behavioural difficulties

Again, in principle, such provision should be appropriate to meet the needs of more able children with autism whose general intellectual ability falls within the low-average to mildly handicapped range. Again, however, the very uneven developmental profiles of children with autism can make teaching, and learning, in such settings very difficult. Thus, while the communication and interpersonal skills of children with autism may be much less well developed than those of their peers, their cognitive development, at least in certain areas, may be significantly more advanced, leading to problems for class or group teaching.

Obviously, many pupils in schools of this kind will have behavioural problems but these are often very different in kind, or have very different causes, from the problems shown by autistic children, and hence may demand very different approaches to intervention. Similarly, the general goals of the school may be inappropriate. Thus, an emphasis on the development of independence and self-motivation may prove counter-productive for adolescents with autism who are simply not able to cope without a high level of continuing teacher support and guidance. Their lack of social understanding leaves them highly vulnerable to teasing and verbal or physical abuse, or of being 'set up' in some way by more socially aware peers. Moreover, because of their communication problems, pupils with autism are often unable to explain that they are being bullied or teased; they may even misinterpret such behaviours as 'friendliness' on the part of their peers. Indeed, it may not be until years later, when they are better able to describe feelings and experiences, that parents become aware of the traumas they have undergone.

Geoffrey had attended a boarding school for children with mild learning difficulties and had never made any complaints to his parents or teachers during his time there. While attending a social group for people with autism, in his mid-thirties, however, he gave graphic accounts of his cruel treatment by other children, and even by some members of staff. On one occasion he had even been caned by his teacher, after openly admitting that he had let his mother complete his geography project. Another young man, Tony, was excluded from his school for biting one of the teachers but it was not until many years later that he was able to explain that he had done so because of the anxiety and distress caused by continuous bullying from other boys.

Bullying and teasing, of course, are not insurmountable problems, especially if schools are small and well staffed. With due attention to these risks, accompanied by educational programmes that are specifically adapted to meet the cognitive, social and emotional needs of the autistic adolescent, successful placements can be achieved. However, this depends largely on the skills, care and flexibility of the staff involved, rather than the particular type of school. Certainly, in some cases, schools for children with mild learning disabilities, or for those with emotional and behavioural disturbance, can, and do, offer an effective educational environment; in other instances, such provision may go disastrously wrong.

Schools and units for children with language disorders

Because of their widespread communication difficulties it might be expected that placements in a 'language unit' might prove very suitable for at least some children with autism. However, specialist language provision for adolescents is extremely limited and the few schools or units that do exist are often unwilling to accept pupils with a diagnosis of autism, because of their additional difficulties, and in particular their lack of motivation to communicate. Whereas most children with specific language disorders show normal social reciprocity, imagination and make-believe play, and have only mild impairments in their use of gesture and other non-verbal skills (Bishop, 1994), children with autism frequently show severe delays and abnormalities in all these areas, even if their expressive language skills appear relatively intact. Thus, again, the skills required for teaching in a language unit may be very different from those needed for teaching children with autism. In addition, few school-leavers in language units obtain formal qualifications (Haynes and Naidoo, 1991), so that the intellectually able student with autism is unlikely to gain any academic advantages in such provision. Indeed, there is some evidence that pupils with autism may achieve more highly in an autistic school than in a placement for children with language impairments (Mawhood, 1995a).

Special autistic units attached to mainstream or other schools

An alternative to segregated schooling is the development of small units, specifically designed to meet the needs of children with autism, but on the same site as a larger school. This may be a mainstream school or a school for children with other forms of learning disability. The advantage of such units is that children can take advantage of the facilities offered by the parent school whilst continuing to have access to the individual support and specialist knowledge of the staff in the autistic unit. However, there is no hard evidence for the effectiveness or otherwise of units of this type. Clearly they do work well for some children but integration within the parent school is often less extensive in practice than in principle. There is also a tendency for teachers in the small unit to feel isolated from, and indeed sometimes even rejected, from the main body of the school.

Children with autism in mainstream schools

For the majority of high-functioning children with autism, their chances of living a full and independent life will be dependent on whether they are able to obtain academic qualifications at school, which will, in turn, allow them to progress to further education and eventually a job. With few exceptions, the only way in which this can be achieved will be by attending 'mainstream' school.

The push towards integration, particularly for children with fairly mild problems, has had a significant impact on education at the infant and junior levels and many primary schools have children with a variety of different disabilities on roll. Research evidence suggests that children with milder or less obvious disabilities tend to be more readily accepted by their peers (Howlin, 1994a) so that children whose autism is relatively mild are likely to be more easily assimilated. There have also been a number of studies indicating that input from normal peers can have very beneficial impact on the play and social interactions of young children with autism (Lord, 1984; Wolfberg and Schuler, 1993; Quill, 1995a). However, such interactions need to be carefully structured and reinforced by teaching staff; the type of play equipment used and the general structure of the classroom are also important, otherwise the enthusiasm of the normal children tends to be short-lived.

There are far fewer studies of integration involving older, secondary school children but such evidence as is available suggests that the risk of rejection rises with age. Discrimination by peers and teachers alike tends to increase for a number of reasons. Firstly, because of increasing pressures to perform well in academic 'league tables' or similar forms of assessment, schools have become more reluctant to accept pupils who are unlikely to do well. If a pupil has disruptive behaviours these, too, of course, can have a negative impact on the work of other children.

Secondly, in adolescence, the need to conform to group norms and to be accepted by peers becomes of paramount importance. Those who do not fit in are increasingly likely to be excluded. Recalling her adolescence Donna Williams writes: 'At school the other children had begun to pick on me. I'd become fairly insensitive to being called mad but I was now being called stupid and . . . this still hurt . . . My history at this last school was the same as at the others. I was a failure' (Williams, 1992).

Thirdly, the structure of secondary school is very different from that in primary school, and poses far more problems for pupils with autism. In primary school, children often remain with the same peer group for six years or more. Lessons are conducted in the same classroom, with the same teacher for almost every subject, and many children remain with the same teacher for two years or longer. Schools tend to be relatively small in size, so that teachers become familiar with all the children and their parents. Staff will usually learn to tolerate 'unusual' behaviours (such as making loud comments in assembly or correcting the teacher in the classroom) once they understand that this is not done out of malice or rudeness but because of a lack of social understanding. Classmates, too, often become used to, and accept the child's 'odd ways'. Indeed, these may prove a welcome distraction from the normal boredom of lessons. In such environments it is also usually possible (although by no means always easy) to keep a watch on bullying or teasing and for staff to agree on consistent approaches to education and management.

In contrast, secondary schools are large, sometimes on split sites; although there may be some familiar children from primary school most will be unknown; lessons, classrooms and teachers change at hourly intervals; most teachers will never get to know the children well, or understand the problems associated with an unusual and specific disability, such as autism. Thus collaboration between teachers in establishing an appropriate educational programme for a pupil with special needs can prove very difficult. Because of the numbers and ages of the other pupils it is impossible for teachers to exert the same amount of control over bullying or teasing. Furthermore, the very uneven profile of skills and difficulties shown by the child with autism can prove very disconcerting for teachers, possibly even undermining their own self-esteem. If the child with autism has the reputation of being an excellent French scholar, or one of the best mathematicians in the school, why is it that he cannot ever bring the correct books into lessons, or even learn to tie his shoe laces after gym? If he or she has an excellent spoken vocabulary, it can be very difficult to accept that *comprehension* of language may be much less well developed, or that problems in co-operation are due to the child's failure to understand, rather than deliberate disobedience. Instead of these problems being accepted as fundamental deficits over which the child has little control, teachers may understandably interpret the student's difficulties as being due to deliberate non-compliance. As the examples below illustrate, such difficulties may also be perceived as a threat to their own competence as teachers.

Thomas had progressed well at primary school where his teachers had shown considerable inventiveness in using his obsession with Dr Who as an incentive for working on every subject from art to maths to geography. At secondary school, however, such flexibility proved much harder to achieve. His teachers had been informed that allowing him to draw a picture of Dr Who at the end of each piece of work would almost certainly ensure his co-operation, but he was frequently banned from, or even punished for doing this. Deprived of his primary motivation, he became increasingly anxious and non-compliant, refusing to complete work assignments and eventually refusing to go to school at all.

Stevie was a child with autism and mild learning disabilities who had just been accepted by his local secondary school, with support from staff in the special needs unit there. One of his main problems was his inability to find his way in unfamiliar places and if he got lost or confused he would throw quite alarming tantrums. His mother asked that he be given some additional guidance, before the school opened in September, so that he could familiarise himself with the layout; she also asked for extra help in the first term to ensure that he was able to find his way from one lesson to another without difficulty. Although the head of the special needs unit was sympathetic to her requests, the head of the school was adamant that no child could enter the school during the holidays and additional funding for a school 'guide' was refused on the grounds that the special needs unit was already well staffed. In the first week of school Stevie became so distressed and violent that he was soon threatened with exclusion.

Giles was a 13-year-old of high intelligence, whose autism was relatively mild. However, his social difficulties had already led to his

exclusion from one secondary school on the grounds of 'gross rudeness to teachers' and he had been removed from another after his
parents found out that he was kept in the school building every break
and lunch time because teachers were afraid of physical bullying by
the other boys. Not wanting to have their son 'labelled' they rapidly
transferred him to another school without informing staff of his
problems. In the first week he marched up to the head master in the
middle of assembly and commented loudly, and publicly, on the
redness and spottiness of his face!

Peter was well known at his junior school for avoiding work of any
sort unless he was firmly pressured into doing it. His class teacher
monitored each page of work carefully and there were strict limits on
the amount of time he was allowed to complete each page. His
parents co-operated in this programme and each evening they
received a note from his teacher informing them of the amount of
homework to be completed. When he transferred to secondary school,
his Statement of Special Educational Needs made clear his problems
and the recommended strategies for dealing with these. Unfortunately, few of the teachers at his new school had the time or inclina-
tion to monitor his work or enlist the help of his parents in the same
way, with the result that his output declined rapidly and dramatically.

Stuart had a tendency to throw all his books and even strip off his
clothes when upset, and although pupils and teachers at his primary
school had learned to ignore such outbursts, it was clear that they
could not be tolerated in secondary school. One of the main reasons
identified for his becoming disturbed was a lack of structure and
predictability. If he knew where he was going, where he could sit
and what books he would need, such problems were much less likely
to occur. In the early months at the school a special needs teacher was
allotted to try to help him get to the appropriate classroom on time,
and she also attempted to ensure that he had the right books and
equipment. However, to avoid his being singled out as having problems she tried to avoid going into the classroom as Stuart was quite
capable of dealing with the academic requirements of lessons. Unfortunately he could not cope with the mad rush towards tables as the
children entered the classrooms for each lesson, and he was frequently left, distressed and bewildered, and still looking for somewhere to sit long after the other pupils had settled down. His mother
suggested that this problem could be readily overcome if Stuart were
allowed to have a fixed place to sit in every lesson. The best situation
was at the back of the class where he would be less of a distraction to
other children. She even offered to buy some tables and chairs for his

personal use if necessary. Some teachers were happy to implement her suggestions, and Stuart's behaviour in these classes improved rapidly. Others announced that they were not willing to change their teaching practices for anyone, with the result that his behaviour in these settings was generally appalling, and highly disruptive for the other children.

Fred also ran into problems over his tendency to correct other people's mistakes and his insistence on keeping firmly to rules. His memory and general knowledge skills were excellent, and he would continually correct teachers over minor errors of fact, or dates. This clearly did not enhance his popularity, and although his peer group were kept entertained by his arguments with teachers, they, in turn, were alienated by his constantly admonishing them if they broke any rules, and the fact that he would also inform teachers of any 'irregularities'. On one occasion he was badly attacked in the playground after he had openly informed the head teacher about certain pupils' smoking habits. He had no awareness of why his honesty had caused such problems, insisting that he was 'only doing his best to help the school'.

Damien was another child whose generally high intellectual ability tended to disguise marked deficits in specific areas. In particular, his understanding of language was extremely literal and in junior school he had frequently been in trouble because of this. When told to paint a flower vase in the art lesson he had done just that – and broken it in the process! When told to take off his clothes for gym lessons he would remove every item, unless specifically told what to leave on. He was even accused of ruining the school photograph because, having been told by the photographer to 'look up', he stared so intensely towards the sky that all the other children followed suit. In secondary school he ran into major problems with his maths teacher in the first week. The children had been told to go out into the playground and measure the area of tarmac – a task that Damien totally refused to do. The head master was asked to intervene, but Damien remained so adamant that his parents were requested to take him home for a few days or 'until he changed his mind'. Eventually his mother managed to elicit the reason for his rather uncharacteristic stubbornness. He explained that he could not possibly calculate the *area* of tarmac, since tarmac, being three-dimensional, could only be measured by its *volume.*

These examples are by no means isolated ones and many individuals with autism are able to give graphic accounts of the problems they have faced from both teachers and pupils in mainstream settings.

Many have been through multiple changes of school, with little understanding or proper planning to meet their educational, social or behavioural needs. Some have been lucky in finding a sympathetic teacher or school that has been able to offer them the support needed, and this has then enabled them to make the best use of their academic abilities. However, this has more often been due to chance rather than appropriate educational planning. Most others have struggled along miserably throughout their teenage years; unsupported, misunderstood and often mistreated.

Therese Jolliffe (Jolliffe *et al.*, 1992) writes:

> I hated school . . . the children cannot tell anybody they are suffering and if you do end up with A levels it does not really make people want you, so it seems you cannot use qualifications to obtain, let alone keep a job. Although ordinary schooling enabled me to leave school with . . . a few A levels and then to obtain a degree, it was not worth all the misery I suffered . . . The teachers pretended to be understanding but they were not. I was frightened of the girls and boys and everything there . . . I was kicked, hit, pushed over and made fun of by the other children. When I attended a place for autistic people life was a little more bearable and there was certainly less despair . . . Parents of autistic children should never think of sending their children to ordinary schools because the suffering will far outweigh any of the benefits achieved.

This places many parents in a terrible dilemma. All too often they are aware that the school will not be able to cater for their child's social and emotional needs, and they are terrified of the stress that this will almost certainly cause. On the other hand, if children of average academic ability are denied access to the normal curriculum, their chances of making progress in later life will be severely limited.

Clearly much needs to be done to improve existing support systems and indeed there are many practical approaches that, with some flexibility and imagination, can be used, at least to minimise the types of problems described above.

EDUCATING TEACHERS ABOUT AUTISM

Apart from those working in specialist autistic provision, or in schools with a high proportion of children with autistic features, understanding of autism and the problems associated with it tends to be limited. Few teachers in schools for children with mild to moderate learning disabilities, and even fewer in mainstream schools, will have had any special training on autism. Even educational psychologists, unless they are working primarily with children with special needs, are unlikely to have detailed knowledge about the condition. Since the incidence of autism within the wider spectrum (including children of normal intelligence) is now estimated to be about 3 per 1,000 (Wing, 1993; Gillberg, 1984) it is highly likely that most teachers will, in fact, come across several such children in the course of their careers. Much wider dissemination of information about the condition, and strategies for intervention, is clearly crucial. Although, since the introduction of the 1981 Education Act, many training courses for teachers have introduced modules related to children with special needs, time constraints mean that the time that can be allotted to any specific condition, such as autism, is very limited. Thus, continuing professional development courses clearly have a crucial role to play. The National Autistic Society and the TEACCH organisation run frequent teaching courses for teachers. Newly introduced programmes, including distance-learning courses, can also offer additional academic qualifications. In England, for example, Birmingham University offers a number of qualifications specifically in autism (Advanced Certificate, B.Phil. and M.Ed. in Education) for professionals working with older autistic children and adults.

Specialist training can be vital in helping teachers to identify and understand pupils with autism. Identification in secondary mainstream schools can be particularly difficult, because most pupils who have managed to stay in 'normal' provision up to this stage will show milder or more subtle handicaps than those who are diagnosed earlier. Although such pupils will almost certainly have been singled out as having behavioural or emotional difficulties in the past, unless the nature of their problems has been recognised they tend to be labelled as showing 'disruptive behaviours' or as being 'emotionally disturbed'. *If* any therapy is offered this tends to concentrate on the outward manifestations of problem behaviours, or on presumed difficulties within the family, rather than addressing the underlying basis of these. However, if the underlying disorder is correctly diagnosed and accepted, this can have a marked impact on teachers' willingness and ability to cope.

One particular problem for staff in mainstream school, for example, is the apparent rudeness of a child with autism. Constantly being corrected in class, having one's physical imperfections highlighted, or being faced with direct refusals to co-operate is not easy for any teacher to deal with. However, the knowledge that a child is acting in this way, not out of deliberate *malice*, but out of a *failure* to understand the impact of his or her behaviours on others can help to make the situation a little more tolerable.

Other difficulties may arise from children's social impairments or from their obsessional tendencies. Although these are fundamental to autism, there are many ways in which the impact of these problems can be reduced and approaches to intervention were discussed in the three previous chapters.

The failure to recognise autism can also present problems for staff and pupils in non-mainstream settings. Oliver was an 11-year-old boy with Down's syndrome, who had always been extremely difficult to cope with because of his 'stubbornness', his 'lack of co-operation' and his 'failure to join in with other children'. For many years his parents had felt that his progress was very different from that of other children with Down's syndrome and in desperation they finally sought a further diagnostic assessment. This revealed that he was clearly autistic, in addition to having Down's syndrome – a diagnosis that led to a much better understanding of his difficulties both at home and at school.

APPROACHES TO TEACHING

The mere understanding that a child has autism does not, of course, lead to the disappearance of problem behaviours. Changes in approaches to management will also be required and there are now a large number of books and pamphlets available that may be of help. The Current Issues in Autism series of books edited by Schopler and Mesibov (1992, 1983, 1986) contain many valuable accounts of teaching techniques, and two recently published books by Quill (1995a) and Jordan and Powell (1995) provide a wealth of information on both well-established and more innovative teaching strategies. All these provide many practical ideas to help children with autism and their teachers in a variety of educational settings. There are, however, a few fundamental principles that should be kept in mind at all times.

The need for structure

Since the work of Rutter and Bartak many years ago, numerous studies have stressed the importance of structure in teaching children with autism (Howlin and Rutter, 1987; Short, 1984; Jordan and

Powell, 1995). The TEACCH programme of Schopler, Mesibov and colleagues illustrates how highly structured teaching programmes can have a very positive impact on both the behaviour and the learning abilities of pupils with autism. The whole teaching system, including the physical design of the classroom, is designed to provide the students with visual cues to aid understanding. Work areas are clearly differentiated from play or leisure areas; individual teaching areas may be distinguished from group areas; there may be a clearly delineated 'time-out' area in which to be quiet or establish self-control. Partitions are used to indicate the types of work activities to be carried out in particular places and even the positions of chairs and tables may be indicated by the use of sticky tape on the floor. Work materials indicate the tasks to be carried out; their position indicates in what order tasks should be completed; and different coloured containers indicate where finished work should be placed. Although offering much useful guidance for teachers in specialist schools, 'packages' of this kind may be less appropriate for children in mainstream provision. Nevertheless many elements of this approach are of relevance in almost any setting.

The organisation of time

Experimental studies such as those of Durand and his colleagues (Durand and Crimmins, 1991) indicate that obsessional, ritualistic or other problem behaviours are most likely to occur at times when individuals are not fully or appropriately occupied. In a school setting, too, problems are usually most in evidence if the daily timetable is poorly organised. If difficulties are to be minimised the programme for the entire school day should be clearly specified, so that the tasks required for any time period are made absolutely explicit. Thus, in addition to the regular school timetable, the student with autism may need to be provided with an extra, personalised timetable, indicating the amount of work to be produced by a particular stage of each lesson. As indicated in the earlier chapter on communication skills, instructions of this kind can be much enhanced by using picture cues indicating the tasks to be completed, particularly if these require direct action from the child. For example, 'tear-off' clock faces, indicating the passage of each quarter of an hour, can help students keep a much better track of time than if they are simply asked to watch the clock.

Because of their dependence on structure, major problems can arise for children with autism outside lesson times. Although breaks from lessons are designed to provide normal children with the opportunities they need to relax and to interact with their peers, for a child with autism such periods can be extremely stressful. Children who are able to behave quite acceptably when involved in guided and structured activities, frequently appear much more 'odd' or unusual at times of free play. Obsessional and ritualistic behaviours may become more apparent and exposure to teasing or bullying is much more of a risk, especially because staff supervision at such times is greatly reduced.

It was because of such problems that Giles, mentioned earlier in this chapter, was deliberately kept in by his teachers because of fears for his physical safety. If, as is often the case, it is simply not possible to offer greater structure or supervision in the playground, avoiding the problem by allowing children *not to go out to play* may be the best solution. Play times, after all, are intended to offer children relief from the pressures of the classroom; they are not designed to increase stress, although this is just what they may do for children with autism. Carol was a 14-year-old girl in a school for pupils with mild learning difficulties. Although able to cope in lessons, at play times her inability to join in with the other girls, and her tendency to rock and flap her arms, led to teasing and mockery. The anxieties associated with break times became so great that she began to complain of sickness and headaches each morning, showing increasing reluctance to leave the house. After discussions between her teachers and her parents it was agreed that she would be allowed to remain in the classroom during break, as long as she completed certain chores. Far from resenting this, Carol was delighted at the opportunity to be able to keep the room tidier, and she was soon able to remain in the classroom without supervision. In similar cases, the situation has been greatly improved by allowing children to spend the time in the school library, going home for lunch, or even helping in the school 'snack shop'.

The organisation of teaching materials

No matter how good the overall organisation of the school day, children with autism will generally require much greater supervision and monitoring of their work if improvements are to be made. Many, even amongst the most able, have problems regulating their own progress, or even continuing to work, unless they are continually supervised. Constant attention to the work output of one child is rarely feasible, even in specialist provision where staff ratios are relatively high. Within lesson times, therefore, it may be necessary to attend to the design of work materials in order to ensure that tasks are satisfactorily completed. For constructional tasks, or other relatively simple activities, it is usually preferable to present the student with trays or boxes containing small quantities of material rather than leaving them to select from a larger variety. Once completed, the task can then be placed in another empty container, and returned to a specified 'finished' position. If the amount of material to be worked with is limited, the task requirements clear, and completion marked by the return of equipment to a specific setting, the activity is more likely to be completed without the need for constant prompting. Breaking down a longer task into smaller stages also provides the student with more frequent opportunities for reinforcement. In addition, having a visible 'finishing position' helps the teacher to monitor progress from a distance.

Tasks or exercises for more able children can be broken down in a similar way. Henry, a 15-year-old in mainstream school, had experienced problems when it came to completing course work for his GCSE examinations. Whilst the rest of the class could be left unsupervised to get on with their project work Henry could not cope without continual guidance. His geography teacher provided him with a clockwork timer and placed 'Post-it' labels at intervals in his work book, specifying the work to be done within the time set. At first the timer was set for quite brief intervals, the amount of work to be completed was relatively small, and each time the timer 'pinged' the teacher was reminded to check. As the term progressed, work assignments were made longer and the intervals between checks increased, until he could work consistently for periods of up to 30 minutes at a time. A few other teachers then followed suit, and his independent work improved considerably. Later, his parents provided him with a wrist watch incorporating a timer, so that his need for this additional help became rather less conspicuous.

Comparable procedures worked well for Sally, a 13-year-old in a school for children with learning disabilities. Because of her very demanding behaviour she was provided with one-to-one help for part of each day. However, she would still not work without constant reassurance. Sally had an obsession with 'Happy Eater Faces' and the classroom assistant managed to obtain a large quantity of these. She also stuck a small 'Post-it' label at the end of every work item. When this was completed Sally would take the label to her teacher and be rewarded with a 'Happy Face' sticker. Initially labels were placed in her work book after each work item, then after two items, and then three and so on, gradually increasing the time and the amount of work to be completed before Sally received her reward and reassurance that she had done well. By the end of a term Sally was able to complete a whole page of work at a time before requesting further help.

Homework assignments can be another major problem. Even if pupils with autism manage to take the right books home they are very likely to forget what needs to be done by the time they get there. In many cases, unless the help of parents is enlisted, work tends to be left undone, or the wrong exercises are attempted. From Roger's first days at secondary school his parents and teachers worked together to overcome this difficulty. In his junior school they had found a 'School-Home' book, which travelled between them on a daily basis, invaluable for dealing with problems, and his new form teacher agreed to continue with this. In the first term, with the co-operation of other teachers, homework instructions were written in the book each night, as were details of the books to be taken home. Before Roger left school each evening his form teacher checked that he had the necessary books and his parents ensured that homework was completed before he went to bed each night. Obviously, this arrangement imposed extra work on school staff, so the next stage was to encourage Roger to write down homework instructions for himself. The books used for each subject did not alter much over the term so a general instruction sheet, indicating the books needed for each subject was inserted in his 'School-Home' book. Every night, before leaving school, he ticked off the books that he needed as he packed them. The book list was replaced weekly by his form teacher, but otherwise, by the beginning of the second term, Roger needed little additional help to monitor homework assignments.

Learning the rules

Most children at school develop some sort of sixth sense for understanding what is appropriate, what is not; which games/clothes/pop-stars are 'in' and which are 'out' at any time. How they do so is poorly understood – the important thing is they do it so easily and so well. For autistic children, who have difficulty understanding or following explicit social rules, making any sense of these unwritten and often apparently inexplicable ones is virtually impossible. Matthew, now a 25-year-old, describes his experiences of the first years at secondary school (having previously attended a very small and sheltered primary school) as being like 'those of someone from outer-space'. He generally had no idea what was going on and having finally recognised that a particular 'craze' or sporting activity was in vogue he would belatedly equip himself with the necessary equipment, only to find that it was no longer in fashion. He also failed to follow the other children in other, more important, ways. For example, in his first term, in particular, he suffered extreme teasing from other pupils. Eventually his mother found out that this was because, when he used the urinal, he would pull his pants and trousers down completely instead of just undoing his zip.

Other children get into trouble because, in their desperation to make friends, they will do whatever anyone asks of them – and are unable to recognise the difference between children laughing *at* and laughing *with* them. Tales abound of children, especially in mainstream school, getting into serious trouble for following the instructions of their peers: to call a teacher by an insulting nickname, to remove their clothes in the middle of assembly, or even in one case, to defecate in the school piano (immediately admitting to this when confronted).

The factors governing successful social engagement are so complex that even normal children are unlikely fully to understand them, although they will recognise immediately any minor infringements of the rules (Dodge *et al.*, 1983; Wolfberg, 1995). For the autistic child, however, the most ordinary of social behaviours can cause problems. Darren began to get into trouble at school for laughing every time the teacher spoke. The problem was that, having recognised that the teacher was pleased if the boys laughed at her jokes, he would then guffaw loudly at *everything* she said. He was unable to work out when to laugh and when not to, and so 'to be on the safe side' pretended to be amused by everything.

Because of the complexity of even apparently simple social interactions it is impossible to provide any child with a full understanding of why and how they should behave. Nevertheless, there are some fundamental rules that can help to enhance acceptability in school. Dressing appropriately (which may mean parents keeping a careful look-out for the latest fashions); never removing clothes in public; urinating only in private; never doing things that are known to be 'naughty' or 'silly', however many children ask you to; not correcting teachers, however wrong they may be; not informing teachers about the activities of other children without discussing this first with parents; not commenting on people's physical characteristics; these are all simple guidelines that can make the difference between tolerance and rejection. Learning to wait and watch what other children do can also help. Temple Grandin (1995) notes that although she always had problems understanding social interactions, she would store up memories of how other people had acted, and then, when similar situations arose, would replay the scenes in her imagination like 'tapes in a video' as a guide for what to do. At a simpler level, Darren's inappropriate laughter was modified by instructing him not to laugh *unless other children did so first.* Although his laughter remained somewhat exaggerated, this advice did help to reduce the disruption he caused in class.

As noted in the chapter on social behaviour, there is often little to be gained by offering detailed explanations of *why* certain behaviours are unacceptable. This may have no impact on the behaviour, and may lead to prolonged and futile arguments. At least in the initial stages of dealing with a problem it is often preferable to lay down a simple rule and insist that this is kept. Explanations can then be given when the behaviour is well under control.

Difficulties then arise, of course, because almost no social rules are invariable. Because of Michael's propensity to remove his clothes in primary school his parents and teachers had enforced the rule that no clothes could be removed unless his parents or a teacher from his school gave permission. This worked well, even in senior school, until he broke his leg racing at another school. The sports master there immediately took him to hospital, but neither he nor the doctor in the emergency clinic quite fitted the rule's specifications – he refused to undress until someone from his own school, several miles away, was sent for.

Similarly, staff at Billy's school had become concerned after a number of students had been approached by a man outside the grounds who was offering them trips in his car. Billy's vulnerability, together with his love of cars, clearly made him a potential victim and so the head teacher gave him a long talk on how he must not talk to strangers, and how he must never go in a car unless it was driven by a relative, a close family friend, or someone connected with the school. A few weeks later, when the school bus failed to arrive his mother called a taxi to take him instead. Billy, sticking steadfastly to his teacher's warning, became very agitated and refused to enter it. His parents had to work extremely hard to convince him that taxis were acceptable even though the head had not originally mentioned these.

Nevertheless, despite such potential problems, it is generally better to have even inadequate rules than none at all.

Dealing with change

Despite their dependence on routine, children with autism must learn to tolerate many changes throughout the school years. Very often it is not so much change itself that causes difficulties but the *unpredictability* of that change. Adequate preparation is therefore crucial, although not always easy. Even very able pupils with autism may continue to have problems with abstract or hypothetical concepts, and verbal explanations about what *may* be about to happen are frequently misunderstood. By the time they reach secondary school most normal children have no problems coping with daily variation in the timetable. For children with autism, this variability can be a nightmare. Having a timetable (in a folder or diary) that they can carry around with them, with instructions about *where* lessons will be held and what books or equipment will be needed, can be of considerable help. A simple chart displayed at home can also be a useful reminder of what equipment they need to take to school on a particular day. However, visual reminders alone will not always suffice. Joe, who had just started secondary school, had charts and timetables displayed all over the place, but he still managed to turn up late for most lessons, and without the necessary materials. Only when his parents made up checklists that he had to tick off at appropriate intervals did the situation improve. Initially the checklists were very simple and were just used to ensure that he took (and brought back home) his games equipment on Thursdays. Gradually, they became more sophisticated, covering every day of the week, and over time helped to improve his organisational skills considerably. A similar system worked less well for Fred, another 12-year-old in mainstream school, because he constantly lost any pieces of paper given to him. Laminated pieces of strong card, indicating the lessons and books needed for each day were firmly attached to his rucksack, and this helped to improve things to some extent, although he also lost his rucksack at frequent intervals.

Visual materials can also help less able children to cope with alterations in routine. Fran was a 14-year-old in an autistic unit, who was always extremely upset by changes in staffing. The situation became so bad that if any of the staff's cars were missing from the car park when she arrived at school she would scream and protest loudly, even if the staff member were actually there. Fran's class teacher collected photographs of all the staff in the school and each day she was encouraged to stick up on a board the pictures of those who were 'in'; underneath went the photos of staff who were 'off'. This activity seemed to deflect her agitation over absences, and when it was known in advance that someone would be away, their pictures were placed in the appropriate section before Fran went home for the evening, thereby giving her plenty of warning for the next day.

Peel-on/peel-off pictures can also be used to indicate changes to the regular timetable. For example, if swimming or riding or outings tend to take place at different times of the week or term, photos or drawings of these activities can be used to replace pictures of other, regular activities. 'Picture calendars' (or normal calendars for more able pupils) are invaluable for preparing for major disruptions to the school routine, such as holidays or trips away, and the complexity of these can easily be modified to suit the ability of the children involved.

The need for additional cues or special aids

An important factor, incorporated in many of the programmes outlined above, is the need to make use of alternative, often visual, cues when teaching children with autism. Even the most able are likely to have problems in dealing with complex or abstract information and additional aids to comprehension can make a considerable difference. This is particularly true when it comes to teaching *sequences* of activities. Although children may pick up isolated aspects of the task, they are unlikely to grasp all the stages required. Activities such as cooking or preparing drinks can be easily broken down into their component parts, and these simply illustrated, in the manner indicated in Figure 6.3.

With an appropriate level of prompting, many children should be able to complete tasks of this nature, even if they have difficulties with verbal instructions. Photographs of the *actual* materials to be used or the people involved may be required for less able children, but for others, pictures, sketches, symbols or written instructions may be sufficient. By adapting the system to the individual child a whole range of activities, from putting away play equipment to completing a physics experiment, can be made much easier. Donna Williams (1992) and Temple Grandin (1995), for example, both note that they were unable to cope with maths problems unless every step was first written down.

At an even simpler level, visual cues can help children to dress appropriately, or to keep better track of their belongings. A coloured label discreetly sewn *at the front of* T-shirts or jumpers can help to indicate which way round clothes should go; a red mark inside right

THINGS YOU NEED TO MAKE A CUP OF TEA:

CUP   MILK   TEA-BAG   HOT WATER (FLASK/KETTLE)   SPOON   SUGAR

1. MILK IN CUP

2. TEA-BAG IN CUP

3. HOT WATER IN CUP

4. SUGAR IN CUP

5. STIR IT UP & HAVE A NICE DRINK–BUT BE CAREFUL

Figure 6.3 Stages in preparing a cup of tea (NB: A flask is often safer to use than a kettle; putting milk in first can increase safety; if necessary, liquid can be pre-measured to avoid spills.)
Items in the 'menu' may be ticked off as completed; or they may be in the form of stick-on labels that can be removed after each step.

shoes and a yellow (lemon) mark in the left shoe can avoid consider-able discomfort; a bright identifying mark on bags, sportswear or other belongings can also help reduce losses. Sally's obsession with 'Happy Eater Faces' was used to encourage her to take greater care of her books, bags and clothes, which she was continually losing. Her mother stuck or sewed 'Happy Eater' faces (black outlines drawn on yellow felt) on all her school belongings. These helped to motivate Sally to collect her things before leaving school, and, equally impor-tantly, ensured that her belongings were readily identifiable by all the staff.

Visual cues can help in many other ways. By having work materials set out in a set sequence, or identified by particular colours, the child can be helped to complete tasks with less direct help from adults. A basket placed to the left of the child's desk when he or she begins work in the morning might, for example, contain three different boxes: red, blue and yellow, each containing a different activity. When the blue box is completed the pupil can be taught to replace this on a blue shelf to his right, the red box can go on the red shelf (or the shelf with a red sticker), and so on. In this way it is clear to the child how many tasks need to be completed, and what should be done when they are finished; the teacher too has clear and easily visible information about the rate of progress. (Many other examples of strategies of this kind are to be found in the TEACCH programmes and Jordan and Powell, 1995.)

Visual 'jigs' of the sort used in industrial settings to indicate the correct placements of objects can also be helpful in acquiring new skills. Placing a knife, fork and plate on a plastic mat that has the items already drawn on makes setting a place at table much easier, and if mats are laid out for everyone, a whole table can be set with only minimal prompting. Such cues can also be helpful in ensuring that equipment is put away properly, or even in helping with activities such as dressing. Richard, an adolescent with many physical pro-blems in addition to his autism, was supplied with special orthopaedic shoes to wear at school. Because he had great difficulty putting these on the correct feet, even with colour cues, his teacher drew the outline of each shoe, correctly positioned, on a mat by her desk. Each morning Richard matched his shoes to the outline and then simply stepped into them.

Thought also needs to be given to the materials used when teach-ing new tasks or activities. A flask with a press-button top is much safer for making tea than a kettle for someone who has little under-standing of danger (or a tendency to throw things). Self-tie laces, that automatically wind together make putting on shoes a great deal easier. Food that can be heated in a microwave, rather than laboriously prepared by hand, can motivate even the most reluctant student to try their hand at making a meal.

Finally, the setting in which learning is to take place needs to be given due consideration. Most people find concentration difficult if surrounded by crowds or other distractions, but autistic children are often expected to learn in noisy, open-plan environments. As indicated earlier, Stuart's difficulties in settling in the classroom were greatly helped if he was allowed to have his own table at the back of the room. Other, more active pupils may find it easier to remain still if they are seated in the corner of a room, with their back to the wall and a table in front of them, so that it is less easy for them simply to get up and walk away. Movable screens can also help provide some degree of privacy, or freedom from distraction, when children are engaged in specific teaching tasks. These can also serve as a visual cue for 'on-task' activities, whilst being easily removable at other times.

Using additional resources

Although none of the procedures described above is particularly complex or time-consuming, for teachers who are already hard-pressed, implementing even very simple additional programmes can prove difficult. Again, a few basic guidelines can help.

Firstly, make optimum use of additional professional help whenever possible. Psychologists, psychiatrists, paediatricians, social workers or other professionals with knowledge and experience of working with autistic children may all be able to provide guidelines for action, or suggestions about strategies, even if they have no instant solutions to problems.

Secondly, for those not working in specialist autistic provision, calling on the help of those who do can prove very illuminating. Visiting an autistic unit, or having the staff from one come to visit or advise can be better than reading a hundred books (though hopefully these too will offer some guidance). For teachers already working in special schools, talking to staff from other schools may provide ideas about alternative strategies. The National Autistic Society also provides training, in a variety of different forms, from on-site training to off-site courses, for those working with children with autism.

Thirdly, consider the use of other pupils as possible sources of help. After Stevie's special needs teacher (his route finding difficulties are described earlier) had her request for additional support refused, she enlisted the help of one of the sixth-form students to help him find his way around school. This pupil was hoping to get a place on a psychology course and because her timetable was often free at the start of the day she was keen to use this opportunity to help a pupil with special needs. As noted earlier, several programmes in the USA have utilised peers as therapists with younger children and there is no reason why, with adequate structure, teacher support, and reinforcement for their work, these strategies should not be adapted for use with older students, too.

Fourthly, make use of other people's ideas or strategies. There have been many different programmes published for teachers of young autistic children and although a 'package approach' to education is not necessarily appropriate, modified versions of these can often be a useful adjunct to regular teaching procedures. Studies by Wolfberg (1995) on increasing group play, by Gray (1995) on improving social understanding, and by Dalrymple (1995) on environmental methods for developing flexibility and independence, although focusing on younger children, could be usefully modified to suit older children in a variety of school settings. Recent books by Jordan and Powell (1995) and Schopler and Mesibov (1992) may also offer inspiration.

Fifthly, take note of any advice or information that parents can offer. However expert the teacher, they will know their own child better than anyone else and are also likely to have evolved effective strategies for dealing with or avoiding problems. The example, given above, of Stuart, who had problems finding where to sit in the classroom, indicates how the advice of his mother worked extremely well, at least for those teachers who were willing to listen.

Finally, if problems are to be minimised it is important that staff agree on the ways to approach problems and that they attempt to work together to deal with these. Consistency in management is of crucial importance and disagreements between staff will jeopardise even the best-constructed intervention programmes. Agreement among staff can, however, be difficult to establish in a large school where teachers may have very different educational backgrounds or training. David, a 15-year-old starting a new secondary school, had a tendency to throw his bag and belongings across the floor if upset or confused. The head of special needs at his school discussed this with the other staff, and, on advice from David's previous school, suggested that the best approach was to take little notice, other than quietly and firmly asking him to pick everything up and carry on his way. Whilst some teachers were able to accept this approach, others insisted on taking a more punitive attitude. The resulting variability in teachers' responses led to a rapid escalation in the behaviour and even after several (often ill-tempered) staff meetings it proved very difficult to reach a compromise. Eventually, with the support of the school's educational psychologist, those who did not agree with the approach were persuaded, for a limited period at least, to ignore the throwing and call on the help of another member of staff to deal with it. Thereafter, the problem steadily declined, although if throwing does occur this still tends to be in the presence of the staff members who are most likely to react.

Adopting a flexible approach to teaching

Few of the suggestions made in this chapter are particularly complex or difficult to implement, but they do require greater flexibility on the part of all concerned than is usually the case at secondary-school level. This need for flexibility can also extend to many other aspects of teaching, including the organisation of individual timetables. Few autistic children, even those of above-average intellectual ability, will be able to cope with all the subjects in the curriculum. Sporting activities, with all their demands on social and physical competence, can be a particular source of stress. In such cases, allowing the pupil to avoid activities that are beyond his or her competence can significantly reduce unnecessary confrontation. After all, few schools would insist on children in wheelchairs joining in sports activities, unless they wanted to, yet group games may be just as impossible for a child with autism. Graham, now in his twenties, remembers other children in the school fighting over him at Wednesday afternoon games sessions, because *no-one* wanted to have him in their team! Little is to be gained by further alienating children from their peers in this way, and it does nothing to enhance self-esteem. Allowing the child to spend time in another activity, or even to join in lessons with another class will be much more productive.

Avoiding core curriculum subjects may be more of a problem, but if a child has a particular difficulty in certain topics then the relevant teachers should be made aware of this and helped to modify their teaching and expectations accordingly. Daniel, a 14-year-old in secondary school, developed a surprising talent for French and German and had an excellent vocabulary in both these languages. His ability to cope with English lessons, however, was well below that of other pupils. His English teacher was unable to understand this discrepancy and viewed it as deliberate opposition on Daniel's part. When it was made clear that Daniel's success in French and German was largely dependent on his excellent rote memory, whilst success in English depended on very different skills, his teacher was able to take a rather more sympathetic attitude. He also reduced the demands made on Daniel in lessons and agreed to modify homework assignments in order to help Daniel succeed more frequently, rather than constantly failing.

Flexibility is also important when it comes to developing existing abilities to the highest possible level. If these are in French or German, as above, then the way ahead is fairly clear. Sometimes, however, the skills of someone with autism may have less obvious implications for educational progress. Nevertheless, it is generally much more productive to concentrate on areas of competence rather than deficit. Gemma was a young teenager in a school for children with mild learning disabilities. Although she was intellectually more able than many of the other pupils, her social skills were very impaired. Attempts to increase her social competence had produced little improvement, but she did possess one particular skill which brought her into contact with other children. This was her expertise in computer games, at which she excelled. Although games were prohibited in the classroom, they were deliberately encouraged in other situations because staff recognised that her ability in this area brought her considerable praise and attention from other pupils.

Sometimes special abilities may be highly circumscribed, for example a child may only draw high-rise buildings or may read at an adult level of accuracy but without comprehension. Teachers may argue, with some justification, that such skills are of little value in themselves, and may even try to discourage them. Nevertheless, because they are of such inherent interest they can be very potent in motivating the child with autism to complete a range of other activities. Dan had an obsession with albinoism, and as long as he was allowed to write a paragraph about this topic at the end of his work (no matter how incongruous this was) his written exercises gradually improved. By the time he reached the third form in secondary school the 'albino notes' were restricted to three or four sentences only, and had to be written on a separate sheet of paper, so their intrusion into his regular work was minimal.

For other children, who may, for example, be fascinated with numbers without being able to use them in a practical way, or who can read without understanding, the challenge to the teacher is to make these activities more meaningful, rather than discouraging them. David had somehow taught himself to read, probably by watching adverts on the television, and spent all his free time reading the TV pages of news-papers, most of which he did not understand apart from the names of his favourite programmes. In school, his teacher provided him with sheets of written instructions to follow (involving a variety of social and practical activities), and these had to be completed before he was allowed access to the newspapers. Learning to follow the instructions gradually improved his reading comprehension, and made good use of a previously purposeless activity. With guidance from teachers other children may be helped to use their skills to foster social interactions or to increase their acceptance within the class. Allowing a student who is good at spelling or arithmetic to help other less able pupils can greatly enhance self-esteem, whilst someone with a parti-cular skill in drawing, or extensive knowledge of specific topics, may be a useful contributor to class projects.

Flexibility of provision

Finally, flexibility of provision is also crucial for the appropriate educational placement of children with autism. This applies both to the range of provision on offer and to the ease with which children are able to move from one type of school to another. For some children, early education in specialist provision may be needed to help deal with the behavioural or obsessional problems associated with autism, but transfer to mainstream provision may later be necessary on academic grounds. Other pupils may be able to cope with mainstream school in the primary years but then require more specialist intervention at the secondary-school stage. The transition from one setting to another requires time, patience and careful planning if it is to succeed.

Kelly was a 13-year-old girl who had always attended a school for children with autism, but her teachers felt that they were failing to meet some of her social and academic needs. Because most of the other pupils were boys, she had no female peer group with whom to interact, and she was also academically more able than most of the other students. It was arranged for her to spend some sessions in the local girls' school where she began attending music and home eco-nomics classes with an aide from her own school. Later she was introduced into gym and arts classes and, although she was not able to cope with more academic subjects, by the end of a year she was able to attend the school unaccompanied and clearly profited socially from her time there.

Dominic had attended mainstream school up to the age of 12 but, because of continuing social and behavioural problems, it was agreed that he would not be able to cope in the local secondary school. Instead he transferred to a unit for children with autism in the grounds of a mainstream school, spending part of his day there and attending some lessons in the main school. As time went on his time in mainstream increased and by the fifth year, with the continuing guidance of staff from the unit, he was able to take several GCSE examinations.

In contrast, Ben, who had attended specialist autistic provision when younger, gained a place at a boys' public school when he was 13. Although very academically orientated, the small classes, a vigilant attitude to bullying, and a focus on individual skills rather than weaknesses, made it ideal for him. He excelled at maths and Greek, and the school's willingness to seek outside advice when needed resulted in the placement being very successful. His tendency towards outspokenness and a critical attitude to what he was taught were accepted by most of his teachers, whilst his occasionally outrageous remarks in the middle of assembly rather endeared him to other pupils!

The small size and greater structure offered by private schools may in some cases make them much more appropriate placements than larger state schools. Most parents, of course, are not able to afford this option, but occasionally local authorities can be persuaded to pay the fees if it can be demonstrated that no suitable alternative exists.

Whatever type of schooling is eventually decided upon, a comprehensive Statement of the child's Special Educational Needs is a crucial step in ensuring that the appropriate placement is provided. In order to facilitate these procedures there are now a number of special advice and support groups, such as 'Action 81' which can offer highly informed and practical advice for parents during the 'Statementing' procedure.

However, it is crucial to be aware that the educational needs of a child with autism can fluctuate widely over time. Academic progress at some stages may be much greater than expected; conversely, behavioural, emotional or social difficulties (or changes within the school) may result in disruption to a previously satisfactory placement. Provision may need to be reviewed, and possibly changed, much more often than is the case for other children. A placement that seems appropriate at 5 may be quite wrong by 12 and careful and regular monitoring of the success of placements, for both teachers and other pupils, as well as for the child with autism, is essential.

7 Further educational provision

THE EXPERIENCES OF AUTISTIC PEOPLE IN COLLEGE

Until relatively recently few students with autism were provided with the opportunity to take part in further educational activities of any kind. Many children went immediately from autistic schooling into residential provision, often spending their entire lives with other people with autism. Whilst such a life style ensures consistency and familiarity, it is a long way from the concepts of integration or 'normalisation' espoused in other areas of education or daily living. In their recent follow-up study of young adults with autism, Goode and colleagues (in preparation) found that very few had received any form of further education (see Figure 7.1) and most left school for specialist autistic provision.

However, in the wake of the movement towards integrated schooling, there have developed increasing opportunities for people with special needs to enter further education. Support services are particularly well established in the USA, and although provision in Britain is less advanced there has been a steady growth in colleges for people with learning disabilities together with a rapid expansion of 'Learning Support Units' in mainstream colleges. The Further and Higher Education Act of 1992 now lays an obligation on colleges in England and Wales to 'have regard for students with learning difficulties or disabilities'. The development of courses leading to a wide range of vocational qualifications has also helped to ensure that a much higher proportion of students with special needs has access to courses that suit both their interests and their ability. For example, the system of NVQs (National Vocational Qualifications, or in Scotland SVQs, Scottish Vocational Qualifications) means that there are now many more training courses available on a part- or full-time basis. There are

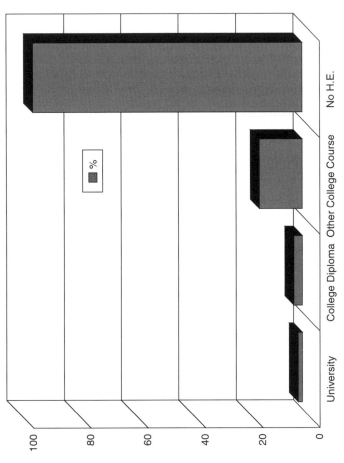

Figure 7.1 Higher educational placements of individuals followed-up by Goode and colleagues

generally five levels of competence within the NVQ framework, from very basic work-related activities which are routine and predictable (Level 1), to much higher levels (Levels 5 or 6) which may be equivalent to degree status or higher and which require complex knowledge and considerable individual autonomy and responsibility. The more basic levels, in particular, are often very appropriate for people with autism, although some may also be able to progress to higher levels.[1]

In principle, this expansion in training should be greatly to the benefit of people with autism, who for a variety of reasons – academic, social or behavioural – may have been unable to obtain any formal qualifications at school. However, as is the case with schooling, the curriculum for students with more general 'special needs' is often not designed to meet the specific needs of those with autism; nor do tutors on such courses necessarily have any specialist knowledge about the condition.

The uneven developmental profile of students with autism, and the problems this poses for teaching, have already been discussed at some length in the previous chapter. Such problems persist well into tertiary education. Thus, most special needs courses are designed to meet the requirements of students who are 'slow learners'. That is, they have no specific deficits in any one area and, although development generally is delayed, their social, communication and academic skills will, on the whole, be at a similar level. This is rarely the case for students with autism, who, almost by definition, will be impaired in certain areas, especially those related to communication and social understanding, but may have much higher levels of academic competence. Other courses may cater for the needs of students with specific learning difficulties, such as dyslexia, but while being academically more appropriate for people with autism these are still unable to cater for their social and emotional needs.

All too frequently, students with autism who manage to find a place in college either become bored at the low level of teaching or frustrated by their lack of ability to cope with the more abstract components of the course. Harry, for example, was an 18-year-old young man with a passionate interest in all things mechanical. He could mend most electrical equipment with ease but although his general intellectual ability was in the normal range he had no formal school qualifications and poor literacy skills. On the recommendation of a Special Careers Adviser, he enrolled in a special needs course at his local college. He was outraged to find that the main purpose of this course was to teach students how to *use* a toaster or washing machine, not how to repair or build them, and he soon left in exasperation.

In contrast, Patrick was accepted on a mechanical engineering course for mainstream students, with the back-up of the Learning Support Unit at college. Following some early problems, it was decided to modify his course so that there was less emphasis on the academic and written aspects and greater focus on his practical abilities. However, because his practical skills were so good, teaching staff had great difficulties in appreciating the depth of his problems in other areas and consistently expected him to achieve at a higher level than was possible. Thus, despite the support that was offered, Patrick became increasingly anxious and depressed over his inability to cope, his tutors became more and more frustrated, and his constant requests for explanations in class steadily alienated his fellow students. Matters came to a head when a group of students confronted him outside college and threatened to 'kill him' if he did not keep quiet in class. Terrified by their threats, Patrick refused to return, and since that time has remained at home, unoccupied and miserable.

Not all attempts at integration, of course, fail so disastrously, but success can require considerable preparation. Ben, who had transferred from an autistic school to a boys' public school at the age of 13, had succeeded well academically and was preparing to go to university to study mathematics. His teachers recognised that his poor social skills would be likely to cause difficulties and were concerned to find him a place at a college that could offer him a high degree of support. As Ben's mathematical expertise was also somewhat esoteric the particular maths syllabus on offer was also carefully examined. In the end, one university was identified that seemed to meet all his requirements. Ben was successful in gaining admission there and throughout his course a special tutor was assigned to monitor his progress. If particular difficulties arose help was also sought from Ben's psychologist, and eventually he obtained a second class degree in maths and computing.

Unfortunately it is not always possible to arrange provision of this kind and for many college students the support systems on which they depended at school disappear entirely. Because of the problems faced by many students with autism in finding or keeping appropriate college places, a number of specialist programmes have been developed specifically for this group.

Specialist autistic schemes

Although no special colleges for people with autism exist (indeed the move towards integration within education would tend to discourage facilities of this kind) there are a number of initiatives to help people with autism acquire the necessary skills to enter college, as well as offering training for college staff who may be involved with students with autism. In America, the support offered by the TEACCH organisation in North Carolina has enabled students to benefit from further education courses. In Britain, another initiative is INTER-ACT (Graham, 1994), a scheme associated with the National Autistic Society which offers teaching in social, communication and problem-solving skills for individuals wishing to enter college. On-site support is also provided in colleges to enable students to follow vocational training courses. Staff from INTERACT will accompany students in classes during the early stages of their course and subsequently can offer ongoing advice and support to the students, and to college staff, as necessary. The LEAP scheme, run under the auspices of the National Autistic Society, is also designed to help students develop the skills they may need to enter college. The focus is on individuals who still need help to develop communication, social, creative and leisure skills as well as to improve self-care and independence. Students may attend there full-time, although some also spend part of their time in Special Education Centres or similar units.[2]

Existing college courses for people with special needs may also help people with autism who find difficulties coping with the social and academic demands of a regular course, and they may prove a helpful stepping stone in learning to cope with the demands of college life. Susanna, for example, had previously failed to complete a word processing course at her local college because of her anxieties and fears at having to cope with large numbers of unfamiliar students and lecturers. A year on a special residential course for students with disabilities gave her the courage to try again, this time successfully. Information about special college courses, many of which are appropriate for people with autism, can be obtained from a number of different directories published by MENCAP.[3] The COPE directory (Compendium of Post-16 Education and Training in Residential Establishments for Young People with Special Needs; Gill and Curbishley, 1994) also provides an extensive list of residential and other college courses.

Links between mainstream and specialist provision

Being able to understand and effectively manage the problems associated with autism is not an easy task. If college staff lack this expertise, then they will need to seek help elsewhere. One way in which this has been done is by specialist autism services forging links with local colleges and offering support for students and staff there. In Nottingham, the Highfield House project was set up in order to integrate 16- to 20-year-old students with autism into the Learning Support Unit of the nearby college of Further Education. Support for students attending the college was provided by staff in the residential unit, and the programme also incorporated training days for the college staff. A similar scheme is organised by Oakfield House, a special unit in Birmingham, which helps students with autism enrol in courses at local colleges. Again, students have a key worker at college and training is provided to improve the college staff's knowledge of and ability to deal with the problems associated with autism (see Morgan, 1996, for further details). Another important initiative, based at Birmingham University, is the distance learning course in autism for staff working in further education settings, which is designed to improve understanding and management skills.

In many cases, however, the links between autistic and non-autistic provision may prove more difficult to establish. Annabel was a 21-year-old woman in a residential home for people with autism. Although at first she had settled well, she soon became bored with the limited day-time programme that the unit could offer. The manager applied for a place on a special needs course at the nearby college but because the home had a reputation for taking on 'challenging' clients, college staff were very reluctant to accept her. In Britain, at least, there are no statutory obligations on Further Education colleges to accept students and careful negotiation is required in cases of this kind. In the end, the college principal agreed to accept Annabel for a trial period of three half-days per week, on condition that the home arranged for her transport and a staff member remained with her at all times. Despite such inauspicious beginnings Annabel thrived; she did well on the practical courses and clearly enjoyed being with more sociable, non-autistic students. Soon the only time that supervision was needed was at break or meal times, mainly because of her outbursts if anyone sneezed or coughed. Eventually a member of the college staff, who had developed a good relationship with her, offered to accompany her at such times, or to arrange for someone else to do so, so that the presence of staff from the home was no longer required.

CHANGING ATTITUDES

Even when support is offered it is evident that many barriers to integration persist. Although integration is more difficult for students who show severely challenging behaviours, problems also arise for those who are relatively mildly affected. These can occur because of lack of understanding, misinterpretation of behaviour, and inflexibility, either on the part of staff or other students, or within the organisational structure.

Even in the Highfield House project, described above, where specialist support was offered, college staff experienced many problems in dealing with the autistic students. Thus, although staff may be used to teaching students with special needs, they may still have difficulties coping with the communication and social impairments that are characteristic of autism. The majority of students in special colleges or Learning Support Units, for example, are unlikely to possess the very specialised knowledge or interests, or memory skills that are typical of students with autism. They are unlikely to correct lecturers' factual knowledge, or to complain about the way in which the course is being run. Many students with autism, however, show no reticence in giving voice to their complaints, nor do they learn to express these in a more diplomatic or effective way. Brian caused total chaos during his first term at college by continually commenting on the tutors' hand-writing. He was particularly concerned if they did not dot the letter 'i', and lectures were constantly disrupted because of this. Such behaviours, understandably, result in students being viewed as rude or as 'trouble-makers'. Rather than recognising their need for *more* help, lecturers whose competence is called into question in this way are likely to become markedly less sympathetic and may even call for the exclusion of such students from their classes.

Rejection may even occur before the student even gets to college. Louis had a first degree in engineering and subsequently applied for and was accepted for a Master's degree at another university. His psychologist and careers officer, who had remained involved since he left school, were aware that he might have problems on a course that depended largely on project work and which required considerable self-discipline and strict adherence to deadlines. Because the university had a Special Needs Department the psychologist, with Louis's permission, contacted them to explain the potential problems and to discuss possible ways of dealing with these. Two days later the psychologist received a letter stating that 'in view of the problems, and limited staff resources, it would be advisable for the candidate to withdraw from the course'!

Other students, too, may need to be given advice or practical support, in order to help them understand the problems and needs of someone with autism. Even at college, problems of teasing, bullying, provocation or rejection can occur. Ben, who was completing a degree in mathematics, was deliberately proposed by other students as a candidate for the President of the Union because his outrageous speeches were a continuing source of amusement to them, and they knew that he was certain to make a complete fool of himself.

Jason, who attended a special college course, was also quickly identified as an 'easy target' by other students. He was desperate to find a girl friend and, recognising this, other students would deliberately lead him into compromising situations (for example, suggesting that he follow women into their changing rooms or toilets) where he was almost certain to be cruelly rebuffed and mocked.

Other students with autism may be taunted for their 'stupidity' if they are unable to cope with more complex or academic components of the course. They may also, as in the case of Harry described earlier, be the source of considerable irritation and disruption to other students because of their constant requests for help, explanation or reassurance.

WAYS OF COPING

Despite the potential problems of coping with college life, whether this be in a mainstream or specialist setting, success at this stage is crucial if the individual with autism is to have any real chance of living and working independently. As with schooling, there are some general procedures that can help to circumvent or minimise difficulties.

Transition from school to college

The move from the relatively supportive environments of home and school to the adult world of college or university is a time of potential upheaval and stress for most young people. However, for most students the social environment and the removal of parental restraints will actively foster personal development and greater maturity. For someone with autism these factors may significantly interfere with their ability to make progress. For them the transition will require much greater help and support.

Transitional programmes, from school to college, or to work, are generally better developed in the USA than in many other countries. Wehman and his colleagues (1988) describe in detail the facilities and programmes that have been used to help individuals with disabilities make the transition from school, stressing the importance of long-term planning and the roles that both teachers and parents can play in preparing students for this significant stage of their lives.

Maintaining links with, and support from schools

A crucial link in the chain of support is the knowledge and guidance of staff in secondary schools. Whether education has been in a mainstream or segregated setting, information from staff who are familiar with the individual's strengths and weakness can be vital for the success of later placements.

Many schools for children with special needs do attempt to prepare pupils for college life as far as they can. They may have an association with a particular college or colleges, so that staff in the different establishments are well known to each other. A planned and gradual introduction into college life during the final years at school is often the most successful form of preparation, for both students and college staff. With a gradual and flexible approach to college entry, potential problems can be identified at an early stage, and staff in the parent school can help to advise on strategies to deal with these. School staff may also be aware of difficulties that may interfere with an individual student's future progress in college. Jeremy's school, for example, recognised that he would not be able to cope alone at times when there were no formal lectures. He had a fascination with electrical equipment and if not otherwise occupied would be likely to roam the campus, looking for things that he could take apart. During his final year at school, a teacher was allotted to accompany him to classes at the local college twice a week. As time went on he was able to remain in class without extra support and efforts were then devoted to finding ways of occupying him during 'free time'. His teacher identified a number of possible activities, including visits to the library, some sessions in the gym, trips to the canteen, and a walk around the grounds, all of which could be used to fill this time. Because Jeremy enjoyed having a set timetable to follow, the college staff, in colla-boration with his teachers, constructed a very detailed weekly time-table for him. No free periods were indicated on this at all; instead, each day was filled by specific activities, many of which, such as a tour around the grounds, Jeremy was soon able to accomplish alone (or with only minimal supervision). In this way, Jeremy was finally able to enter college successfully and with relatively little extra input from college staff.

Collaboration with parents

Just as the advice from school teachers can be an invaluable source of help and intervention, so parents' knowledge of their children may be an essential ingredient in any advanced educational programme. This can sometimes be difficult for staff to accept, since one of the major goals of any college course is to foster independence in their students. However, ignoring information of this kind will almost certainly prove counter-productive. Johnny had attended a school for children with mild learning difficulties throughout his secondary school years and had done quite well there. He himself was of above-average intelligence but his social and communication skills were such that he functioned much better with students of lesser ability. His parents had requested a place, for a one-year preparatory period, in the Learning Support Unit of the local college as they were certain that Johnny would not cope, at least initially, without this help. Because of his relatively high intellectual level and his impressive ability to talk about subjects that were of particular interest to him, the Admissions Tutor felt that his parents were being 'overprotective' and considered that it was time Johnny 'stood on his own feet'. As predicted, the contrast between the protective environment of school and the unstructured world of college proved far too much for him and by the end of the first term Johnny's anxiety and agitation reached such a level that he required psychiatric treatment and had to leave college altogether.

In another case, the parents of Jan, a young woman who had always attended a special school, requested continuing help with transport to college. They felt that she would be able to cope with college when she arrived but doubted her ability to get there alone. However, the local authority argued that she did not need special transport: college was not far away, she had no physical difficulties, and she was intellectually able to cope with the journey. Even though a coach stopped at the end of the road to pick up a more severely handicapped student, Jan was not allowed to travel on this. She became so anxious at the thought of having to walk to college alone, even though she knew the route perfectly well, that she got up earlier and earlier each day in order to make preparations for the journey. Eventually she would hardly go to bed at all and her parents became so concerned for her welfare that they increasingly gave in to her demands to remain at home.

Many parents of children with autism will admit to being 'over-protective' but feel that they have little choice in the matter. Their concerns are not just for the possible physical danger to their children but the emotional trauma, and the widespread effects of this, that can result from inappropriate demands or the failure to meet the needs of a young adult with autism. Clearly, parents and children do need to move apart as time goes on, but few students with autism will have acquired the social competence or the level of independence required to survive when they first enter college. To expect them to be able to cope without support from their families is to deprive them of a vital back-up system, as well as college staff losing a valuable source of information.

Links with Social Service provision

For some students it may not be possible to arrange access to college courses immediately after they leave school. They may need the opportunity to settle first into some other form of day-care or residential provision and only after this has been successfully achieved can plans for their further education be made.

Joe, who was not diagnosed as having autism until his late teens, had been excluded from the local school for children with learning difficulties because of his behavioural problems. He was transferred to boarding provision but was clearly very unhappy there and made several unsuccessful attempts to run away. Finally his parents took him away from school altogether, and he remained at home, looking after himself during the day from the age of 15 to 19. Local Social Services became involved after he was attacked by a group of youngsters in a nearby park. Despite his reluctance to leave home his social worker made a determined attempt to get him into college. The principal agreed to a programme of gradual introduction, with Joe at first just attending art classes, where he was allowed to indulge his obsession of painting the designs from 1960's record covers. His social worker accompanied him initially, but as time went on and more classes were introduced, she gradually faded from the scene, although remaining available for the staff to seek advice from as necessary.

Many Social Education Centres (also known as Adult Training

Centres) which offer day-time provision for people with learning disabilities, will also cater for clients with autism. Frequently, however, the programme within these centres is too unstructured, too noisy and crowded, and too dependent on social interactions to be entirely suitable for someone with autism. The opportunity to attend additional part-time courses at local colleges can therefore be of enormous benefit. Again, this may well require the support of day-care staff. Tessa was a 35-year-old woman attending a day centre, and her previously aggressive behaviours had improved to such an extent that it was felt she could begin to attend a special computer course at the local college. However, because of her reputation, the college was very reluctant to accept her. Considerable negotiation was required and initially she was only accepted if accompanied by staff from the day centre. Gradually it became possible, by ensuring a high degree of structure within the sessions, for her to remain in computer classes with only minimal extra support.

Input from other professional sources

During their childhood many individuals with autism will have had contact with a wide range of professionals. Psychologists may have been involved in assessment or intervention programmes; language therapists may have advised on ways of developing communication skills; occupational or physio-therapists may have provided help with motor or self-help skills; psychiatric help may have been sought for emotional or behavioural problems. Many of these professionals may have valuable advice to offer: on the most appropriate type of courses to follow; on situations that are likely to exacerbate problems or techniques to minimise these; or on ways of developing students' skills in different areas. Unfortunately, just as many students reach college age, access to children's services ceases, so that there is little opportunity for these professionals to offer continuing support. College staff, too, may be reluctant to seek advice from those formerly involved in the *child's* care, believing this is inappropriate for someone on the threshold of adulthood.

   Failure to make use of the knowledge and expertise of those who have known the individual for many years is clearly wasteful and if proper planning for college life is to take place, these resources should not be ignored. Appreciation of the very different strands of information and advice that different professionals can offer, and a willingness to use this in a constructive way, can help to optimise progress and prevent many avoidable problems.

Professional help may also prove useful if unexpected problems arise. The efforts made to ensure that Ben succeeded with his maths course at university are described earlier in this chapter. On the whole, the support offered by his tutors proved very successful but occasionally even their resources were strained. Just before his final exams, for example, Ben announced that conventional notions of algebra were quite unsatisfactory and so he had developed a system of his own. His tutor was rightly concerned that he might fail badly if he went ahead with this, and the psychologist who had been involved with Ben and his family for many years advised that gentle dissuasion was unlikely to work. Instead he was firmly instructed that he could *not* work on his own system until after the exams had been completed. If he did well in these the maths department would then consider his proposals, but until then there was to be no more discussion of the issue. Such advice is hardly in keeping with the desire to foster independent thought in students but from past experience it was clear that if allowed to follow his own ideas as he wished, Ben would become entirely obsessed with them and his output would be totally unproductive.

Joe, who was helped into college through the support of his social worker, also needed further help when it became apparent that other students at college were deliberately provoking him. Groups of young women would approach and ask if he wanted to be their boy friend, or if he would like to kiss them. As soon as he tried to take up their offer, they would scream and rush away, instantly attracting the attention of everyone around. Formal complaints about 'sexual harassment' were made to the college, although Joe's social worker was convinced that these incidents had been deliberately provoked. She ascertained from Joe that the incidents occurred mainly at the bus stop on the way to or from college. Although college staff confronted the women concerned, this had little effect. Instead, arrangements were made for Joe to be escorted to and from college by his social worker or a member of his family. Meanwhile Joe began to attend some social skills sessions to teach him more appropriate ways of responding in such situations; he was also encouraged to inform his social worker whenever the problem arose. Although the problems continued to re-emerge from time to time, the frequency became much less.

The need for structure and consistency

Many problems for students attending college, or for those involved in their care, arise from the behavioural, social or communication difficulties described in earlier chapters. Possible ways of dealing with such problems have already been described in some detail. However, the crucial factor that must be incorporated into college life, whatever the individual student's level of functioning, is the dual combination of structure and consistency. As stressed throughout this volume, it is under conditions of structure and predictability that people with autism function at their best. If they are unsure what should be done, if the situation is unpredictable or if rules vary from time to time, place to place, or individual to individual, then progress will be slow and inappropriate behaviours difficult to change.

Supervisory structure

In most schools the management structure is relatively easy to understand, even by children with severe learning difficulties. In college settings this hierarchy is often less clear. Even in 'Learning Support Units' the student may have to deal with a range of different tutors; contact with personal supervisors may be limited, and if things do begin to go wrong it may be some time before problems are recognised, or appropriate strategies implemented. Unless a student's disabilities are very marked, or his or her behaviour very disturbed, staffing levels often mean that it is impossible to provide all the help needed, even when it is recognised that a student may require additional support. The lack of any systematic monitoring system or the presence of a key worker to turn to at times of stress or confusion can make all the difference between success and failure. It is crucial, therefore, that in planning entry to college, at whatever level, specific agreements be made concerning *who* will be responsible for monitoring progress or ensuring that work assignments are completed satisfactorily; *what strategies* will be implemented if problems occur, and *where* the student should turn to for support. Ideally, for less able students, the number of people involved should be as few as possible, although students in mainstream settings will clearly have to cope with a larger number. Annabel, whose gradual introduction to college was described earlier, soon became well known and accepted there. However, not everyone was aware of what to do if problems occurred, and in particular if she became very upset when someone sneezed or coughed loudly. As all the students had identity badges, Annabel, too, was given one, but under her name was also written the name of the department she was in and the internal phone number of a key worker to contact. As the latter could change from day to day different badges were supplied on different days of the week.

Although her identity label was slightly different from the other students', the variation was not great enough to single her out as being 'different', and indeed it could only be seen by anyone who needed to approach closely.

As is the case for establishing acceptable patterns of work or behaviour in schools it is also essential that staff collaborate in developing rules and that they co-operate in the procedures to be followed if problems occur. Without consistency, even the most sophisticated strategies will be of little use. However, it is important not to underestimate the difficulties of achieving this, hence the need for an agreed and well-established structure that is clear and acceptable to everyone concerned.

Structuring work tasks and timetables

Again, at whatever level the student with autism is functioning, whether it be completing a doctorate or learning basic daily living skills, the task structure and requirements must be clearly specified. The value of the TEACCH programme for less able students, and the need for a high level of cues and checks has already been noted in the chapter on secondary education, and these are all procedures that can readily be incorporated into adult teaching programmes. For more able students this level of guidance will be neither appropriate nor practical but structure is, nevertheless, crucial. Students must know *where* they should be, *what* they should be doing at all times, and *who* they should turn to if problems occur.

Even leisure activities or obsessional behaviours may need to become part of the daily timetable. Gary was a young man who had just begun to attend a Social Education Centre after leaving school. He was delighted to find that he was allowed to drink coffee there at any time, an activity that had always been strictly controlled at home and school. His coffee drinking soon escalated to the level that he was doing almost nothing else. Other students began to be resentful of the fact that he took no part in daily activities, and also because he refused to allow them in the kitchen whenever he was there. If attempts were made to stop his drinking he would become resentful and aggressive. In order to reduce the problem a written timetable was drawn up for him, as shown in Table 7.1.

There was little attempt initially to make any major changes to Gary's day. He would already take part, if somewhat reluctantly, in relaxation and music or dance classes and he loved watching videos. The main alteration in his programme was that these activities, along

Table 7.1 Gary's initial daily timetable

Time	Tutor	Session/Activity
9.30	John	Coffee
10.00	Mary	Coffee
10.30	Sally	Relaxation and Massage
11.00	John	Coffee
11.30	Sally	Music
12.00	Everyone	Lunch
1.30	Mary	Coffee
2.00	Sally	Dance
2.30	Simon	Video session
3.00	John	Coffee
3.30	Everyone	Home

with coffee drinking sessions, were specifically timetabled, as were the staff who were to be involved. Gary enjoyed keeping lists and was happy to have his daily programme laid out in this way. It was made clear that the timetable would be changed as time went on and gradually more and more activities replaced the coffee drinking. The time allotted for each drinks session was also reduced until he was following as full a timetable as most of the other students in the centre and coffee consumption was reduced to a minimum.

Students of higher ability levels will usually be accustomed to following a set timetable but they may need additional help when they are required to complete longer work assignments and, again, the timing of these will need to be precisely specified. Being given a piece of work to complete by the end of the term or year is a recipe for disaster for many students. A few may get into a panic and try to complete it immediately, thus giving the work insufficient attention and preparation; most, however, will find themselves at the end of the year having produced nothing at all. Tutors need to be prepared to break down the task into more manageable units, which then have to be completed within a clearly specified period; they may also need to take on the responsibility for checking progress at each stage.

If necessary, too, the help of other family members may need to be elicited. Dominic was a skilled photographer, trying to obtain an A level in photography at a local college. For his course work he had to prepare a portfolio of photographs, and whenever asked by his tutor how he was getting on would assure him that everything was 'fine'. It was only when his tutor telephoned him at home, just before the final deadline, that it became apparent that *nothing* had been prepared. After a frantic weekend, and considerable expense to get the photos processed by an express service, he did manage to produce some work, but this was of a much lower standard than he was capable of and resulted in his A level results being considerably poorer than they might have been.

Even attendance at college may require careful monitoring. By the time most students enter further education it is generally considered that they should be responsible for their own behaviour and if they fail to attend lectures then that is their concern. However, for some-one with autism, this freedom may be entirely inappropriate. They may begin to attend very erratically, or even, over time, cease to go altogether, drifting gradually into a life of ritual, obsession and solitariness. Self-regulation is unlikely to occur and if the student is to profit from the educational facilities on offer, the requirement of regular, punctual and daily attendance must be imposed from the outset.

Finally, it is essential that tutors are absolutely honest to students about their capabilities, and that they do not allow them to continue with a course that is inappropriate or unlikely to meet their needs. Gareth had enrolled for a wide and disparate range of modules at college in London. It was clear to his family and to his psychologist, who had carried out detailed assessments of his ability, that the work generally was far beyond his capabilities. Moreover, the mix of subjects chosen would never be of any use when it came to finding a job. Year after year he failed most topics, just managing to scrape through a few others. It was evident from his feedback forms that lecturers found his inability to cope very frustrating and that other college students were also irritated by his constant demands on staff time. Nevertheless, as he was paying his own fees, no-one asked him to leave, and attempts by his psychologist to meet college staff were unsuccessful. His mother and psychologist both tried to persuade him to take a more appropriate course but the situation was not helped when he began attending an assertiveness training group. There he was advised that he must manage his own life and not be dictated to by his family. He became progressively more resistant to accepting help, ceased to visit his mother and terminated counselling sessions with the psychologist. Contact was only resumed again after he was admitted to psychiatric hospital suffering from severe depression.

Flexibility of teaching programmes

Somewhat paradoxically, the other crucial ingredient of a successful teaching programme, again at any level, is the need for a flexible approach to the provision of training. Often students with autism are not able to cope with a full day's teaching programme, or cannot cope with the range of subjects offered to other students. Thus, it may be preferable for students to attend on a *planned part-time* basis initially, rather than having them wandering in and out of classes in which they have no interest. Similarly, for more able students, it may prove more successful to encourage them to begin by completing only certain modules of a course, rather than attempting to gain a formal qualification, which may be beyond their capability. If this is successful they may then transfer to a full-time programme in the following years.

Warren's behaviour had become progressively more disruptive after leaving school and as college attendance was clearly out of the question he began attending a Social Education Centre. However, the daily programme there was not adequate to meet his needs and he quickly became bored and frustrated. Negotiations with a local college resulted in his being allowed to attend specified classes there and gradually, as he settled in, the time was expanded. He is still not able to attend for the whole day but the flexibility of the arrangement between the Centre and college has ensured that his week is well structured, without imposing excessive social or cognitive demands.

At the other end of the spectrum was Martin, who had obtained good A level results, but had then suffered a 'breakdown' in his first term at university, mainly because of his social and obsessional problems. He attempted a simple clerical job but again was unable to cope. Eventually he left work and with the help of a very sensitive social worker began to learn basic daily living skills and to overcome some of his obsessions. After a couple of years he was confident enough to do some voluntary work at the local MENCAP centre; this in turn gave him the confidence to take up an Open University course, concentrating on modules in computing, and he has now enrolled for a full-time university degree.

Flexibility is also required in the transitional stage from school to college. Students cannot be expected to cope with this without help and a much longer introductory period is likely to be required than for many other students. An extended preparatory stage may also be required by college staff if they are to develop effective ways of managing problems and encouraging learning. Gradual introductions, over a period of a year or two (or even more), may be necessary if the transition is to be accomplished without difficulty; staff at college may need to be prepared to accept the presence of a support teacher, at least initially, and ideally they will need to undertake some additional training themselves.

This may not be particularly easy to achieve, nor is it cheap; and flexibility is required in attitudes to funding as well as to teaching. For example, current funding in the UK for further education is only for courses leading to a 'recognised qualification'. For individuals with autism, especially those with additional learning difficulties, such qualifications may be unattainable. However, it may be possible for students to gain funding to help develop independent living or communication skills, which will then enable them to enrol on an accredited course. Students can be helped to develop an Independent Living Plan with individually specified goals, but these goals *must* be met if funding is to continue. This has led to concerns that objectives will be set to very low levels in order to avoid any risk of failure (and hence the withdrawal of funding) with the result that the true capabilities of someone with autism may never be adequately tested.

There are also problems in funding when part-time placements in different settings are required. For example, a student may be on roll at a secondary school, whilst spending more and more time at college; or there may be a need to combine funding for attendance at a day centre with funding for college attendance. Many authorities do manage to overcome such complexities but if resources, or motivation, is low, the problems can be made to seem insurmountable. This is in fact rarely the case, but it can involve parents, teachers, tutors or care staff in unnecessary battles to achieve a settled and appropriate educational environment for the individual concerned.

Even with funding, achieving the appropriate environment for individuals with autism in further education is likely to present many challenges. Almost anyone involved in providing services for adults with autism will necessarily be involved in the teaching of basic life skills, no matter what professional role they usually occupy officially. Such teaching will clearly be most effective if it is conducted in the context where those skills will actually be needed. Herein lies the 'Catch-22', in that people with autism may be unable to enter further education if they lack the necessary social, communication, practical or cognitive skills. However, very often, these skills cannot be learned in isolation and will need to be taught in the context of the educational setting.

In summary, further educational opportunities for individuals with autism have improved immeasurably over recent years and soon tertiary education may be expected to be the norm, rather than an exception. A wide range of potential provision is available but in order to gain access to, and profit from this, the special needs of students with autism will require greater recognition, as will the potential costs in terms of money, time and staffing that may be necessary to meet these needs.

NOTES

1 Details about suitable NVQ courses can be obtained from the NVQ adviser at the National Autistic Society.
2 A similar scheme is co-ordinated by the Employment Training Unit, run by Gloucestershire Group Homes, Nailsworth Town Hall, Nailsworth, Glos. GL6 0JF.
3 See, for example the directories of special educational provision published by MENCAP (1990 a and b).

8 Coping with and finding employment[1]

The transition from school to work presents difficulties for most young adults but it is likely to be a period of particular stress for anyone with autism. Support systems that were available in childhood and adolescence tend to disappear once school or college education is complete and for the majority of adults with disabilities there are no specialist employment services. It is estimated that over 70 per cent of people with disabilities remain unemployed and although specific data on unemployment for people with autism are not available, research suggests that even amongst those who are most able, only around 20–25 per cent are likely to be employed. Those who do find jobs also frequently continue to have many difficulties (Goode, Howlin and Rutter, in preparation).

PROBLEMS WITHIN THE WORKPLACE

Inability to communicate effectively or to understand instructions are amongst the most obvious problems faced by someone with autism but other cognitive, social and behavioural difficulties may all have a significant impact on the ability to cope with work. Here, for example, is a graphic illustration from Donna Williams (1992) on the pitfalls of starting a new job.

> I was to begin on the easiest of machines; the button-holer . . . I worked hard and I worked fast. Soon the box of fur coats began to fill up, and the boss passed by, impressed with the speed of my work. He decided to check on the quality.
> A horrified look grew upon his face, and he began to shout . . .
> 'What have you done ?' he screamed over and over. 'Button-holes in the sleeves, button-holes in the collar, button-holes in the back panel. Get the hell out of here.'

'Can I have my money?' I asked shyly.

'No!' he screamed. 'Do you know what you've done? You've cost me thousands of dollars in damage. Get the hell out of here before I kick you out.'

I hadn't realized that button holes were meant to go anywhere in particular.

As the above incident illustrates, failure to understand task requirements can have a major impact on performance, even at the highest level. Further examples, all taken from clinical practice, are noted below and demonstrate how the problems associated with autism can affect the ability to cope with work in many different ways.

Communication difficulties

The inability to communicate effectively affects many aspects of work. Ned, employed as a computer analyst by a major engineering company, was excellent at tracking down the 'bugs' in other people's computer programs. However, he was quite unable to explain to his colleagues, in a coherent way, *what* the errors were, *why* things had gone wrong or *how* the situation could be corrected. Requests to keep written notes were of no help, since no-one could read those either. Whereas his computing skills could have made him a great asset in any team-based work, his problems in reciprocal communication meant that he was only able to function in a solitary, and hence far less effective, capacity.

Failure to appreciate social 'rules'

Stuart, who was on a work experience scheme, constantly made remarks about the sex or colour of people working next to him. Although he had no intention of being offensive, his comments were most distasteful to other staff. Adrian 'drove people mad' by standing too close, touching them, or asking personal questions, whilst Gerald's poor personal hygiene led to other staff in his office demanding that he be given a room to work in by himself.

Inability to work independently

Although people with autism may be able to work well if closely supervised, lack of self-initiative or inability to monitor their own progress can cause considerable difficulties. Randell, a computer programmer, had many problems at work because he would only complete assignments satisfactorily if *every* stage of the task were specified. Without explicit instructions he would do nothing, even if the job were well within his capability. Sean, another young man with considerable skill in computing, was employed to enter data for a large shipping company. Although his work was very precise when supervised, if unmonitored he became very slow and careless, making no attempt to check on the accuracy of his work.

The development of inappropriate work patterns

Rodney, who was responsible for the mail in a small charitable organisation, decided that since all their work was so important, everything had to be sent first class. He paid no heed to instructions to the contrary and, unless closely monitored, would waste large amounts of money in this way.

Leslie worked in an office sorting files and as he appeared to be able to do the filing systematically and without difficulty the initial supervision was rapidly faded. Each evening files were neatly put away but it was only when he was on leave some weeks later that it was realised that he had developed a totally idiosyncratic filing system that no-one else could understand.

David, who also worked for a small company, was very sensitive to noise around him and because he could not concentrate on his work if other people were chatting, he was allowed to listen to his 'Walkman' when the office became very busy. As time went on he spent less and less of the day working and more and more time listening to his tapes. When his manager finally insisted he stop using his 'Walkman' he became very upset and was quite unable to understand why.

Obsessional behaviours and resistance to change in routine

Margaret, although a competent typist, insisted on having her work checked at the end of each page of typing. If a letter ran on to two pages, even by a few lines, she could not proceed until the first page was checked. This behaviour understandably became very irksome for her line manager. Simon, generally a gentle and quiet worker in a library, became very upset if the work routine was disrupted in any way. His insistence that union meetings were held at lunch times or after work rather than in working hours did not endear him to his colleagues, and when he tried to insist that even birthday or Christmas celebrations should be held outside working hours, they became most annoyed. Graham, working in a voluntary capacity in a hospital, also became upset over small changes. One day, without warning, he threw his coffee over the woman who brought around the drinks trolley because she had put the milk into a different container.

Other behaviour problems

Other difficulties may also interfere indirectly with work. Anthony, who eventually managed to find employment after a period of several years, had developed the habit, whilst unemployed, of going to bed extremely late each night (partly because of his many night-time rituals). When he started the new job he made no attempt to change his sleeping habits, with the result that he was usually late and always tired, often falling asleep at work. Jim had an obsession with watching the sun set from a nearby railway bridge. As the year progressed he began to make excuses to leave work earlier and earlier, becoming very disruptive when attempts were made to make him stay.

Coping with promotion

Although this is not a problem that arises for most people with autism, it can give rise to unforeseen difficulties for the few who do manage to succeed in work. Julian was employed as a research worker in a university science department, where his attention to detail and painstaking experimental work was much appreciated. Eventually he was promoted to the post of Senior Lecturer, which required his attendance at meetings and some administrative work. Having worked in a very isolated way for many years, he was quite unable to cope with these demands. Richard, who had a clerical job in a Civil Service department, was put forward for promotion long after his contemporaries. This involved taking on a supervisory role with junior staff but his poor social and management skills resulted in complaints from all concerned.

Mistreatment by others

Because of their difficulties in social interaction and their failure to understand the behaviour of others, people with autism may be very vulnerable to teasing or bullying. Paradoxically, these problems are often greatest for individuals whose impairments are least severe. If someone has a very obvious impairment, it is much easier for outsiders to recognise and, one hopes, show greater sympathy towards this.

Clare, for example, was a 23-year-old woman with autism who also had a marked speech defect. She had a job stacking shelves in the local supermarket where staff were all aware of her disabilities. Moreover, because of her obvious communication problems they tended to leave her to herself, which was just the situation in which she worked best. In contrast, Jeremy, who was of a similar intellectual level to Clare but with good, *superficial* language skills, had a much more miserable time. Although working in a south London warehouse he had a very 'upper-class' way of speaking and a very sophisticated vocabulary. Although his manager was sympathetic and supportive, when he was away several junior staff took a delight in teasing and bullying Jeremy. Eventually, he hit out at one of his attackers, who of course denied having ever hurt him in any way, and because he could not explain the reason for his actions he was dismissed. Jo, a cleaner in a jewellery shop, was so appreciated for his honesty that his employers would sometimes leave him to lock up the night safe. A new night-watchman was quick to recognise Jo's vulnerability, and offered to 'look after the keys' for him. Jo willingly handed these over and when the robbery was discovered the next day he was actually charged with being an accomplice. Although this charge was dropped, his employers reluctantly decided that they could no longer employ him because of his inability to judge other people's motives.

STRATEGIES FOR INTERVENTION IN THE WORKPLACE

Despite the many difficulties that people with autism may face at work, there are a number of basic guidelines which, if followed, can help to improve the situation considerably, for both them and those working with them.

Information for employers

Although some individuals with autism, usually those who are most able, do manage to find employment without help, and indeed may prefer to keep silent about the nature of their disability, in the majority of cases employers will be aware that the individual has 'difficulties' although they may not fully understand what these are. In such cases it is important to be honest with employers about the problems associated with autism, and to provide them with relevant information that might help. The National Autistic Society publishes some basic fact-sheets on the employment of people with autism, which can be helpful in these circumstances (National Autistic Society Publications, London).

The advantages of employing someone with autism

If placement is to be successful, the employer may well need to expend more time and effort, particularly in the early stages of the job, than might be the case with other employees. However, it is also important to stress that there can be distinct advantages in employing someone with autism. As many employers will testify, once the requirements of the job are well established, people with autism often prove to be extremely efficient, competent and reliable workers. Many are happier doing routine, predictable jobs, which other workers may dislike, and they are frequently able to maintain a high level of consistency in such work. Because they do not tend to seek out social interactions with others, they are more likely to work steadily and consistently throughout the day, without taking time off to chat or gossip. Ronnie found a job packing clothing in a small manufacturing company. When assignments arrive he cannot relax until these are all packed and labelled and he will readily work for up to 12 hours at a time (he boasts that his record is 18 hours). His efforts are enhanced by the fact that he does not want the company to take on other employees, as he much prefers to work alone. His work is also very accurate. After packing one assignment of 8,000 shirts he complained to the delivery company that one was missing!

The tendency towards routine can also prove an advantage. Thus, once a work pattern is established, most people with autism will keep firmly to this; they will not take unnecessary breaks; they are rarely absent, and are usually very punctual.

Honesty is another positive feature. Deceit, or the intent to deceive, requires considerable social sophistication, which is usually beyond the competence of someone with autism. There is little danger of dishonesty over expenses, or other infringements of office rules, because of a strict adherence to regulations, and employers often come to place a great deal of trust in employees with autism, whatever their level of functioning. The TEACCH organisation in North Carolina, which has a very successful job programme, reports that large companies turn to them time after time for autistic workers, because of their low absenteeism, trustworthiness and reliability (Mesibov, personal communication).

Making the job requirements explicit

It is essential to recognise that, *almost inevitably,* people with autism will tend to have problems understanding job requirements unless these are made very explicit; they are also likely to be poor at monitoring their own progress or behaviour. If goals are clearly set out many difficulties can be overcome; however, because autism is essentially a disorder of communication, it is also important to be aware that reliance on **verbal** methods of instruction may be inadequate.

Thus, information about the various stages of the job that must be completed, the time scale for these, or the checks that must be instituted, is often best presented in a visual form, either in writing or perhaps in pictures. The sequence in which stages are to be carried out can also be conveyed by these means. Clare's supervisor taught her to prepare a very acceptable cup of tea for other staff in the supermarket in the following way. Firstly, she prepared a display board on which a set of cartoon pictures illustrated the various stages involved in preparation; the board also contained photos of the other staff, indicating how many spoons of sugar each of them took. By taking Clare through these stages on a few occasions, and prompting her to follow the sequence on the board, it was soon possible to leave her alone, without supervision, to prepare drinks.

In the case of Lenny, a young man on work experience as a garage assistant, difficulties arose because of his untidiness with tools. Verbal reminders had little effect but the problem was solved by having a large panel containing hooks and holders fixed to the wall, with the outlines of the most commonly used tools painted upon it. At the end of the day, Lenny simply had to match the tools to their silhouettes. Thereafter, there was no trouble in his putting them away and the procedure also improved the tidiness of other staff members.

Leslie's idiosyncratic filing problems were solved by having him label all files according to a system first agreed between himself and his supervisor. This system was clearly displayed on the office wall as well as on the cabinets. For a short time daily checks on accuracy were made but then random checks (at least weekly) proved sufficient to maintain standards.

Similarly, Sean's inaccuracy and slowness in entering data greatly improved when he was supplied with a simple checklist indicating the number of files he had to work through each day. He was required to tick these off as they were completed and random checks on accuracy were also instituted. As his data entry became more accurate, the daily checklists were replaced by weekly ones, although still with a clear goal for each day. However, an attempt to use monthly check-lists was not successful as his speed rapidly decreased when the goals were made much longer-term.

The need for adequate supervisory and management structures

Because of the rigidity of many people with autism, once poor working practices are established, these can be very difficult to shift. It is crucial to encourage good practice from the outset and a particularly critical element in minimising problems is a clear line-management structure. This is also essential if output is to be adequately monitored; it is important, too, that the individual has a designated person in authority to turn to immediately if problems arise. Initially, supervisors may need to be prepared to monitor progress much more closely than they are used to, if work is to be carried out to the required standard. They may also need to offer greater reassurance. This can obviously become irritating at times, especially if questions seem unnecessary or repetitive. However, once the basic job requirements are well established, direct supervision can be gradually reduced. Visual or written prompts or instructions may then be utilised, further reducing the need for direct contact.

The need for clear feedback

Supervisors also need to be prepared to give direct and honest feedback about an individual's performance. People with autism are not able to pick up subtle cues from others and if not explicitly told that their work or behaviour is unsatisfactory they will tend to presume that their performance is faultless. As an example, Ben had thought that he was doing very well in his clerical job and reported that he was 'getting on fine' with the office staff. His manager had not had the heart to tell him that there were increasing complaints about his behaviour. When Ben went on holiday leave, the women in the office demanded his dismissal on the grounds of 'sexual harassment'. The offences cited included standing too close to them in the lift, spending long periods of time leaning over their desks, constantly talking of his desires for a sexual relationship, and carelessness in the way he dressed (including going around with his shirt open or his trouser zip partially undone). With Ben's permission, the manager contacted his psychologist, who was asked to talk to the staff about the social problems associated with autism and ways in which they could help to deal with these. In collaboration with Ben a 'contract' was drawn up which gave clear guidelines both to him and the other employees about acceptable and non-acceptable behaviours. Ben was asked not to approach closer than within an arm's length of other staff members; if he did so they were to tell him immediately that he was too close. The time spent talking to secretarial staff was limited to official break times only, and, to make this easier, his own desk was partially screened off from the rest of the office. Staff also let Ben know immediately if they considered the content of his conversation to be inappropriate in any way.

Making explicit the 'rules' of behaviour

As the above example illustrates, feedback alone is unlikely to be effective unless it is accompanied by clear rules regarding how behaviours should be changed. Gerald's poor hygiene problems were solved only when his manager decided to address the matter directly. For some time Gerald had been giving increasing offence to colleagues because of his failure to wash either himself or his clothes regularly. Although understandably reluctant to raise such an embarrassing issue, the manager finally decided to act. When questioned, Gerald insisted that he did **change** his clothes on a daily basis, just as his mother had instructed. However, he did not necessarily **wash** them and he regularly recycled soiled shirts and trousers. His manager explained that clothes need to be **washed** regularly as well as changed, and it was made clear that if, at any time in the future, his personal appearance was not satisfactory he would be sent home to change.

Like many other people with autism, Gerald was neither embarrassed nor resentful at being given personal advice of this nature. Temple Grandin (1991) recalls being given a can of deodorant by her boss and told to use it; his secretary was also instructed to take her to buy more suitable clothes. She notes 'This is part of the learning process. I was lucky enough to have people who helped me.' Because of their problems in interpreting subtle messages, or understanding the many unwritten rules by which most people function, clear and direct instructions (even if these refer to intimate topics and might seem somewhat demeaning to other people) are rarely resented. It is *not* being able to understand what to do, *not* being informed if their actions are unacceptable, *not* being told if work is not up to standard, that give rise to problems. Often the person with autism can remain in total ignorance that they have done anything wrong until they are suddenly given a formal warning or even summarily dismissed. The resulting confusion, dismay and loss of self-esteem can be devastating.

Coping with obsessions or resistance to change

Major problems can sometimes occur if obsessional behaviours begin to intrude on normal working activities. Margaret's refusal to type more than one page at a time without being checked was dealt with by the supervisor indicating *on the work to be copied* when a check would be made. Sometimes this was after less than a page, sometimes more. By placing the emphasis on the amount of work to be copied, and by gradually extending the size of task to be completed, it was eventually possible to modify this obsession very successfully.

Dan, a trained accountant, hated change of any sort and stuck doggedly to his daily routines. This could sometimes be an advantage but proved a problem when a new computer system had to be installed. With the help of a social worker who had known him for many years, a detailed programme was carefully introduced to explain to him what would be happening, exactly when the changes would take place, how retraining would be undertaken, and what advantage all this would offer. Because his social worker, in whom he had great trust, worked closely with his managers, reinforcing their decisions at every stage, Dan was able to accept what, for him, was a momentous change in his working practices.

Over time, and with such support, staff working with Dan have become very skilled in helping him to cope with change and gradually to accept more and more responsibility within the firm. Because of an increase in work load at certain times of the year, the company needs to employ a number of temporary workers. Initially, Dan had considerable difficulties in working with new staff, but as several 'temps' were employed on a regular basis, his managers tried to ensure that this was the group with whom he was asked to work. Despite his complaints, he grew used to the annual changes in staffing and is now able to supervise temporary workers very satisfactorily. Gradual changes to his physical environment have also been implemented. To begin with, he could not concentrate in a large, open-plan office and needed to work in a room alone. This was then replaced by a screened-off area in the corner of the main office. Gradually his desk was moved to a more central section and he is now able to work successfully in a busy and public area.

Offering personal support

Because of the vulnerability of people with autism, employers may need to be prepared to offer more personal support than is normally expected. They may also need to ensure the co-operation of other employees and possibly, too, offer protection against exploitation, teasing or bullying.

In Ben's case, there is no doubt that the direct involvement of other staff was crucial. In particular, explanations of *why* Ben acted in the way he did, and advice on how staff might help him, had a dramatic effect on their attitudes. Sympathy, however, is unlikely to last in the absence of practical advice and hence the additional 'contract', indicating what behaviours were or were not acceptable, was also needed. Ben is still at work with the same company after 8 years.

Clare's position in the supermarket was greatly helped by her supervisor, whose own daughter had a hearing impairment, and hence she was generally sympathetic towards the problems of people with communication difficulties. She kept a close watch on Clare's ability to cope with the demands of the job, so that problems could be detected at an early stage. She was also very vigilant against teasing or bullying by other members of staff. At one stage, when Clare became depressed, she was quick to recognise the early symptoms of this and to ensure that she received appropriate help. Although Clare was then off work for some time, her general reliability and accuracy were such an asset that the job was willingly kept open for her.

Making use of additional professional involvement

Although, as the examples above illustrate, many problems can be solved by relatively simple means, employing someone with autism does place unusual demands on employers, supervisors and often other employees. For this reason, it may well be helpful to elicit the support of other professionals. Especially if they were diagnosed as children, people with autism may have access to other support networks and if this help can be appropriately utilised, the risk of job failure can be considerably reduced. Often, it is not that the advice needed is particularly sophisticated or complex, but straightforward guidance from someone who understands the problems associated with autism can be surprisingly effective. Psychologists, social workers or psychiatrists who know the individual well may be able to supply quick and simple advice on overcoming or avoiding problems, or they may be able to offer additional help themselves. Laurie's sleeping patterns were improved after his support worker offered to ring him at 10 o'clock every evening and warn him to get ready for bed. This helped him to get to sleep earlier, to get to work on time, and to stay awake while he was there!

Professionals who are knowledgeable about autism can also give valuable advice, even before the job starts, about how best to structure the working environment; how to break down the different stages of the job; how to make instructions clear and explicit; how to deal with unacceptable social behaviours, the tendency to adhere to fixed rituals or routines, or problems in accepting change.

Professional advice may be helpful, too, when any major changes to working practice are envisaged. As noted earlier, a particular problem for some autistic people is that once they acquire job skills, promotion to a higher level may be recommended. Unfortunately, promotion often results in increases in responsibility with which they are unable to cope. Julian was quite unable to deal with the administrative and social demands of becoming a Senior Lecturer and eventually required psychiatric help because of his anxiety. With his psychiatrist's support, the university agreed to change his position to an 'honorary' one, which meant that he could maintain his status, whilst avoiding the organisational responsibilities of the post. Professional guidance may also be needed to reassure worried employers. Graham had attacked the 'tea lady' when she brought his milk in the *wrong* container and, despite his previously gentle character, his employers were worried lest this incident might herald the onset of other aggressive outbursts. The psychologist involved in supporting him was able to point out that the most probable cause of the incident was the disruption of his normal routine and that such behaviour was most unlikely to recur as long as he was warned in advance about possible changes. This prediction proved true and Graham is still at work.

Finally, the occasional involvement of outside support agencies can prove helpful in ensuring the *continuation* of good working practices. Otherwise, with time, or with changes in staffing, successful strategies originally used to minimise difficulties may be forgotten. When first employed in a computing company, Neil's difficulties in coping with change were fully recognised and every attempt was made to explain events to him well in advance. So successful was this strategy that after he had been there for over two years his problems in this area were almost forgotten. In consequence, no-one thought to discuss with him the fact that his immediate manager was to be replaced.

When the new manager appeared Neil responded by threatening to bite him! Attempts to repair the relationship were not successful, and eventually Neil was once more made 'redundant'.

The right to personal dignity and confidentiality

Although liaison between professional counsellors and employers, or between management and other employees, may be crucial in minimising or avoiding problems, discussions must always be conducted in a way that is acceptable to the person with autism. If work charts or behaviour 'contracts' are drawn up these should not be displayed in a way that is demeaning or derogatory. This will apply to all individuals, whether they are in open employment or in a more sheltered setting. If information about autism is made available to other employees this must be done with respect to personal dignity and with the individual's consent. As noted earlier, people with autism tend to react positively to advice about their actions or appearance, rather than showing embarrassment or resentment, but this does not mean that such guidance should be given without careful thought and planning. The balance lies between offering a high level of support (which clearly goes beyond the boundaries of normal working practices and might be viewed as unduly stigmatising) and doing nothing. However, the latter approach is unlikely to prevent others becoming aware of the disability, and in the absence of support, personal and work-related problems will almost inevitably result in social isolation or rejection and, all too often, the loss of employment.

GETTING A JOB

So far, discussion has focused on the problems that are likely to arise once an individual is actually in work. However, for many people with autism, even for those who have succeeded at college or university, the preliminary stages of applying for work, filling in forms, making telephone enquiries, preparing for or attending an interview, may prove to be hurdles that they are unable to overcome.

Justin, for example, having obtained a second class degree in chemistry from university, sent out application forms for numerous jobs. Not one led to the offer of an interview and finally his mother realised that in the 'health problems' section of every application form he had written lengthy descriptions of all the illnesses he had had since childhood, including every episode of flu he could remember and occasional infestations of head lice or threadworms. When she suggested that this information was not needed he became very upset, pointing out that it could be an offence to withhold relevant information. The problem was that he had no way of discerning what was or was not relevant.

Clive, who had a higher degree in electronics, was helped to prepare an impressive c.v., which attracted the attention of a number of prestigious companies. None of his interviews, however, led to the offer of a job. Although he insisted that he got on well in the interviews, his parents suspected that he probably 'got hooked' on irrelevant topics or details of his family life. These traits, together with his poor eye-contact and poorly modulated tone of voice were, they felt, unlikely to create the right impression. However, other than trying to give him some advice on how to act, they were unable to do anything to improve the situation.

Developing links between employers and specialist schools

Schools can play a vital role in fostering a successful transition to work and, in many specialist autistic schools, training in job-related tasks and the social skills required to accompany these are a central part of the curriculum. Links with employers, via job experience schemes, are also important so that students can familiarise themselves with different types of work environment. Indeed, much of the success of the TEACCH supported employment schemes is attributed to the emphasis on vocational training that is at the core of their educational curriculum.

Practice sessions within the school, structured by teachers who are familiar with the tasks involved, can be of great benefit, whilst the skills needed for interviews can be developed through role-play and practice. Video recordings are valuable for giving direct feedback and allowing individuals to correct mistakes or develop more appropriate skills, and people with autism often show very little, if any, reticence or embarrassment at being recorded in this way.

Wehman and his colleagues (1988) describe in detail the facilities and programmes that have been used to help individuals with severe disabilities make the transition from school to employment in the USA. They stress the importance of long-term planning, the development of employment options and potential placements, the roles that teachers and parents can play in vocational training, and local state or federal initiatives that have been crucial in improving employment prospects for individuals in North America.

Support from colleges

Although specialist schools are often able to facilitate direct links with potential employers, not all children with autism are in special schools. More able children, in particular, are likely to be in integrated provision, and, as most mainstream pupils now go on to further education of some kind, direct links between teachers, who know the children well, and potential employers are much less common. The amount of help and understanding received at college is very variable and whilst some colleges are extremely supportive of students with autism, others show far less understanding of their complex social, behavioural and educational needs. The organisation INTERACT (Graham, 1994), described in the previous chapter, provides training in vocational skills such as accuracy, timekeeping and meeting deadlines and can offer sheltered work opportunities to help students develop appropriate work skills.

A similar scheme is co-ordinated by the Employment Training Unit, run by Gloucestershire Group Homes (Matthews, 1996). Other, more general, college courses for people with special needs may also help people with autism to obtain the necessary qualifications and skills. Again, information about special job preparation courses can be obtained from MENCAP's various directories.[2]

APPLYING FOR WORK

Anyone with a disability is at a disadvantage when it comes to seeking work and, whatever their level of functioning, a well-presented c.v. can be crucial. Appropriate help in preparing a c.v. or application forms can be obtained from staff at colleges, Job Centres or Job Seekers Clubs. It also helps to find out as much about the particular job in question as possible, perhaps by speaking with someone in the company, talking to someone who has done a similar job, or finding out where the company's main interests or markets lie.

It is essential, too, to be honest in completing application forms or c.v.'s. Some people with autism understandably feel that they should keep secret the fact that they have a disability, have attended special school, been out of work for prolonged periods, been made redundant, or even dismissed from previous jobs. Attempts to cover up such information are rarely successful. Donald, who had experienced several extended periods of unemployment and had been dismissed from two previous jobs, tried to disguise these facts on his c.v. by changing the dates of his times in work. This led to obvious inconsistencies in chronology and his ineffectual attempts to explain these simply caused increasing difficulties.

If the autistic problems are relatively mild and not easily detectable by outsiders, then of course it is up to the individual to decide how open to be about his or her disability. However, as it is quite likely that problems will be detected at some stage, experience suggests that it may be wiser to indicate that there have been developmental difficulties in the past. Some adults with autism tend to explain the problems in terms of having (or having had) a communication disorder rather than autism, which is true, if not exactly precise. Other people prefer to use the term 'Asperger syndrome'. They feel, quite rightly, that many people, if they know about autism at all, will have rather stereotyped and misguided notions of what the disorder entails and that this alternative label may be less of a barrier to employment. Whatever the choice, it is essential to be able to give a brief, but clear and honest explanation of what the difficulties are and, if relevant, how they might have an impact on the job in question.

Preparation for interviews

Attending job interviews is a stressful experience for anyone. Interviews demand the ability to cope with unfamiliar settings and people; they require high levels of social and communication skills, the ability to think rapidly and under pressure, and to weigh up the underlying meaning behind questions, as well as to formulate appropriate answers. For anyone with autism it would be difficult to envisage a more stressful experience! In a later section the advantages and possible drawbacks of being formally registered as 'disabled' are discussed. However, one advantage is that entry into a job may not necessarily be on the usual, highly competitive, interview basis. Moreover, being aware of the fact that an applicant has a disability may lead to the interviewers being more sympathetic, allowing more time to answer questions, being clearer in their own questioning and avoiding asking any 'trick' questions. If applicants are registered as disabled it may also be possible for them to be accompanied by someone who can provide additional support during the interview or help clarify questions. Even if help is available, or the interview is conducted under special circumstances, applicants still need to invest time and effort in preparation. Studies show that, with appropriate training, people with autism can be helped to improve the skills needed in applying for a job (Howlin and Yates, 1995). Figure 8.1 shows how adults attending a social skills group were able to improve

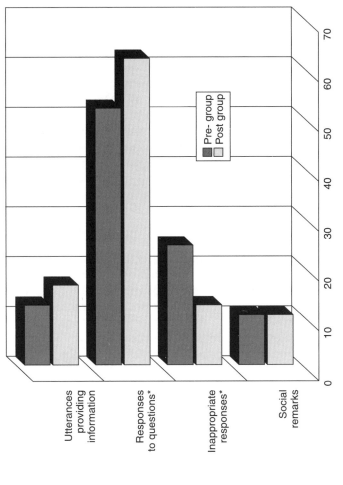

Figure 8.1 Changes in telephone conversation following attendance at a social skills group

Note: * Significant change between assessments ($p < 0.05$)

their 'telephone techniques' (to enquire about job vacancies), after advice and practice in the correct ways to answer questions or request relevant information.

If specialist help of this kind is not available, role-play with family members or friends can help to familiarise the applicant with basic interview procedures. Video recordings can be invaluable in demonstrating how the interviewee looks and sounds, the appropriateness of eye-contact or 'body language', and his or her responses to questions. The potential candidate also needs to pay attention to the requirements of the particular job and to the more general aims of the company involved, so that replies can be appropriately structured around this knowledge. Most firms will arrange for candidates to speak informally with staff in the company prior to the interview and this opportunity should be made use of whenever possible.

If relevant, the candidate must also be prepared to give a concise reply to questions about the nature of the disability, why special schooling was needed or why there is a history of previous unemployment or redundancy. It is important, too, to be able to explain how aspects of the disorder may have an impact on the job (both negative and positive) and what efforts have been made to overcome problems. Interviewers are likely to be much more sympathetic to a candidate who recognises his or her difficulties and has taken active steps to deal with these.

If the candidate wants to *ask* questions at the end of the interview, a note pad with a brief, readily visible and easy-to-read *aide-mémoire* can be useful. Again, questions should be checked with a sympathetic listener beforehand to make sure they are appropriate and neither irrelevant nor rambling.

Finally, attention should be given to general appearance and to the need to turn up on time! A dummy run, to check that the journey can be made in plenty of time, is well worth the effort.

SUPPORTED EMPLOYMENT SCHEMES

The move towards supported employment, offering 'real pay for real jobs' for people with disabilities, began in the late 1970's in the US, where it is now financed by relatively generous state and federal funding. Such schemes offer support in the workplace for individuals who for a variety of reasons are unable to compete in the open job market. Once an appropriate placement has been found (often, in the US, through collaboration between specialist employment agencies and voluntary support groups) a job coach is employed to work alongside the client in order to ensure that <u>all</u> the components of the job (including the social and personal aspects) can be carried out satisfactorily. The amount of support required depends on the skills and abilities of the individual employee but Marcia Smith (1990) describes how even severely disabled people with autism have been helped into jobs through these schemes. Of 55 adults supported by Maryland Community Services for people with autism, all were in supported employment of some kind. Many had little or no language, and most had severe to moderate intellectual handicaps. They also showed many of the problems characteristic of autism, including withdrawal, aggression and self-injury, and ritualistic or obsessional behaviours. Despite this, many were in full-time work and earning above the average wage for the state. Table 8.1 summarises the outcome of this project, which is reviewed in Howlin (1991).

Similar results have been reported for the supported employment scheme run by Gary Mesibov and his colleagues at TEACCH, in

Table 8.1 Characteristics of 55 adults with autism attending a supported employment scheme in Maryland, USA

Language level	%
None	33
Words only	5
Phrases	9
Fluent speech	53
IQ level	%
< 30	25
30–49	15
50–70	29
> 70	31
Behaviour problems	%
Aggression/self-injury	80
Ritualistic	25
Withdrawn	96
Job outcome – hours worked per week	%
< 20	18
20–30	56
> 30	25
Wages received	%
< minimum wage	47
> minimum wage	53

North Carolina. There the majority of clients work between 30 and 40 hours per week and are paid at least the basic minimum wage (most receiving considerably more). Although most placements are in unskilled jobs, even individuals with severe intellectual impairments can be successfully supported.

A comparison of young people with autism living in Britain, carried out at the Institute of Psychiatry in London (Goode, Howlin and Rutter in preparation), revealed a far less favourable outcome. In a follow-up study of 75 adults, aged between 21 and 42, just under 23 per cent were in independent paid employment; and around 8 per cent were in sheltered employment of some kind. The vast majority, well over two-thirds, were in special centres, with little or no opportunity for developing competitive employment skills. Despite the fact that 20 per cent of the group had obtained some formal qualifications (9 per cent had A level qualifications or higher and several had university or college degrees) the occupational levels of most of those in employment were low and unskilled, and few had received any specialist help in work. (See Figure 8.2 for a summary of these findings.)

Even amongst those in jobs involving computing or accountancy, the level at which they functioned was often lower than their educational attainments would have predicted. Probably only three or four individuals were employed at a level fully appropriate to their qualifications; these were a cartographer, a scientific analyst for an oil company, and two computer programmers (see Table 8.2).

Similar levels of employment, again with most individuals being in poorly paid and unskilled jobs, are reported in other follow-up studies. Nevertheless, the development of supported employment schemes in the USA has begun to result in higher levels of job retention and job satisfaction for individuals with learning disabilities more generally (Moon *et al.*, 1990). In the three years between 1986 and 1989, for example, more than 1,400 programmes were authorised by state agencies, with an increase of 157 per cent in the number of individuals participating in supported schemes over this period (Shafer *et al.*, 1990). This model appears to be much more effective than other special work schemes. McCaughrin and colleagues (1993) have conducted a detailed analysis of the cost-effectiveness of supported employment schemes and conclude that, compared with sheltered employment, such schemes resulted in a better quality of life and considerable economic benefits for those involved. Although initial costs can be high, if the wages earned and the cost of unemployment benefits are taken into account, the necessary funding can usually be recouped over a five-year period.

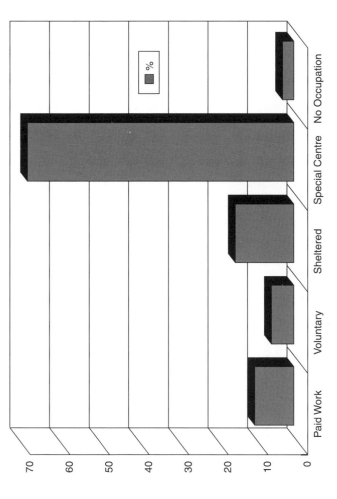

Figure 8.2 Employment levels of subjects followed-up by Goode and colleagues (percentage in different placements)

Table 8.2 Educational and occupational levels of individuals who were in work followed-up by Goode and colleagues

Subject age	Formal qualifications	Job descriptions
28	HND	Admin. assistant, HMSO
40	Accountancy diploma	Clerical/book keeping
24	None	Grave digger
28	None	Part-time washing up
40	City & Guilds	Semi-skilled factory worker
26	HND	Computer programmer
39	None	Factory worker
34	MSc degree	Computer programmer
29	College diploma	Postal assistant
37	A levels	Part-time book-keeping
42	None	Trolley collector, supermarket
30	None	Factory work
21	MSc degree	Oil analyst, North Sea rig
29	BSc degree	Trainee cartographer
29	None	Farm labourer (parents' farm)
21	None	Decorator (father's firm)
23	None	Factory worker, disability scheme
22	College	Sheltered factory work
39	None	Factory work, manual
30	CSEs	Fabric designer
26	None	Electrical work
25	CSEs	Charcoal burner
24	None	Office work, family business

Although there are some supported employment schemes in operation for people with special needs in the UK (Wertheimer, 1992), provision is limited and funding 'sporadic . . . piecemeal and fragile' (Pozner and Hammond, 1993). Only 80 agencies were involved in supported schemes in Great Britain in 1992 and none of these focused specifically on the needs of people with autism. Most initiatives have been developed for individuals with mild to moderate learning difficulties and the jobs involved have largely been routine, low-level, unskilled and low-paid. In a recent review of supported employment, Pozner and Hammond (1993) analysed ten such schemes operating in Great Britain. Although job retention was found to be high, almost all employment was in the cleaning and catering industries; the majority of jobs were part-time and many clients earned only between £1 and £2 per hour. There have been no schemes designed to meet the needs of more able individuals, some of whom may be highly educated and perhaps hold university degrees. Moreover, such schemes are not adapted to deal with the complex social, emotional and communication difficulties that are faced by people with autism. In their case the necessary *job* skills may often be acquired relatively easily, or with only minimal training. However, it is these associated problems which, if not adequately understood or managed, can rapidly lead to job breakdown.

Recently, a new scheme has been set up in conjunction between the National Autistic Society and the Department of Employment to explore the value of supported employment specifically for more able individuals with autism (Howlin and Peacock, 1994). This project has the following unique features.

Firstly, the emphasis is on training for skilled, well-paid employment and jobs are organised largely through major international companies involved in banking, transport, telecommunications and food retail, who have offered their support through the Employers' Forum on Disability. This should enable candidates to circumvent the usual competitive system of applications and interviews, which so severely disadvantages people with autism. If, over the first few months with support, candidates are able to demonstrate competence in the job itself, more permanent placements will be offered.

Funding for job coaches and for the initial stages of job training is provided through *existing funding* from the Department of Employment's Access to Work and Rehabilitation schemes. This means that the scheme does not require additional (and therefore usually temporary) funding. Close liaison with local Ability Development Centres, PACTs and occupational psychologists should also help to ensure that, if successful, the scheme can be readily assimilated into ongoing Employment Services.

The highly specialised knowledge required for supporting people with autism in the workplace is provided by staff from the National Autistic Society. Unlike other supported employment schemes, the main focus of the project is not on direct, job-related skills (as the individuals concerned should already possess a relatively high level of competence in these areas) but on ways of improving the social and emotional deficits which so often prove to be the main barrier to successful employment for people with autism.

This collaboration between employers, the Department of Employment and the National Autistic Society will be the first 'compact' of its kind in the UK and, if successful, should serve as a model for new approaches to training and employment.

Specialist centres for people with autism have also begun to offer training in job skills and support within the workplace, although with the focus generally being on less able individuals. Gloucestershire Group Homes (Matthews, 1996), for example, provide an employment training unit for adults with autism or Asperger syndrome in the Gloucestershire area, working closely with local employers and the Employment Service. Details of other support schemes, some of which may be suitable for people with autism, can be obtained from MENCAP's register of job opportunities for people with disabilities (MENCAP, 1990a, b).

Charitable organisations

Support, and sometimes additional funding, may also be obtained from other agencies working with people with disabilities. The Shaw Trust[3] offers subsidies to employers to enable them to offer jobs to individuals who, for any reason, are unable to work at the same pace or at the same level as other employees. Sheila was a 25-year-old woman with autism, working as a hotel chambermaid. Because of her obsessional tendencies her work was extremely thorough and careful but also very slow, and occupational assessments estimated that her output was approximately 60 per cent that of other workers. The Trust was able to provide her employers with a subsidy to cover this.

The Pathway Employment Services, run by MENCAP, can also offer short-term financial support as well as a 'foster worker' to help people with disabilities enter the work market. Currently, Pathway operates in around thirty local authority areas in England. Publications by MENCAP are invaluable for finding out about other schemes and their directories of 'Opportunities in Employment for People with Learning Difficulties' contain much that can be useful for people with autism (MENCAP, 1989).

Specialist employment agencies

There is a small, but growing number of employment agencies whose specific brief is to help people with disabilities find work. National employment agencies, such as Brook Street Bureau, also have a particular interest in helping clients with disabilities. Most of these agencies will have relatively little experience of people with autism, particularly those of high intellectual ability, but some have developed a particular interest in this group of clients.[4] Many offer detailed assessments and systematic instruction, help with job training and interview techniques, and may also involve supported employment.

Groups such as Remploy can also offer training and sheltered work-shop experience. Again, details of agencies with an interest in helping disabled clients can be found in the MENCAP directories of employment opportunities (MENCAP, 1989).

REGISTER AS DISABLED?

Disability Employment Advisers (DEAs)[5] can provide useful advice and contacts in the search for work. They will help to make links with employers who have an interest in taking on workers with disabilities, can advise about relevant training schemes (such as those organised by Training and Enterprise Councils or 'TECs'), and can organise formal work assessments. However, few DEAs will have had much experience of the skills and needs of people with autism and the range of jobs to which they have access can be quite restricted. Thus, placing individuals with higher-level qualifications in jobs of an appropriate level often raises considerable problems. Moreover, links with the DEA inevitably raise the question of whether someone with autism, no matter how mild or 'invisible' their disability, should register as disabled. There are a number of reasons why this option should at least be considered. Firstly, certain specialist schemes (such as those organised by Remploy) require applicants to be on the Disability Register.

Secondly, registering may make it easier to apply for benefits such as the Severe Disablement Allowance or the Disability Living Allowance, and is also more likely to help individuals 'pass' the government's 'Assessment of Incapacity' test. If the criteria for this assessment are not met existing benefits may be lost and there may be increased pressures on individuals actively to seek work, or to accept inappropriate employment. 'Rehabilitation' or 'Access to Work' funding may also result in additional financial support (currently up to £20,000 per individual over 5 years in England and Wales) to enable people with disabilities find and keep employment. This may be easier to obtain if an individual is on the Disability Register (although the crucial point is that one should at least be *eligible* to register).

Thirdly, the Disabled Persons (Employment) Acts (1944, 1958), place an obligation on any firm with over 20 employees to employ at least 3 per cent of people with disabilities in their workforce. Although this is rarely complied with, if a company does wish to fulfil its quota it may be prepared to view candidates with disabilities in a more favourable light, or to employ them under different conditions.

Certain jobs may be 'earmarked' as particularly appropriate for people with disabilities or some form of positive discrimination may operate. George, for example, worked as a computer analyst in a large construction company. As the recession progressed, the company was forced to make more and more of its workers redundant. George had always resisted being registered as disabled, although the company was well aware of his difficulties. However, as external pressures on the firm increased, the directors decided that the only way in which they could offer him protection from redundancy was for him to register as disabled.

Like George, many able people with autism feel that to register as disabled can lead to unnecessary stigma and misunderstanding. They may be reluctant to 'advertise' their disability in this way and fear that this could be detrimental when seeking work. The choice is obviously up to the individual concerned and to the particular circumstances of the job, but as restrictions on those claiming disability benefits are steadily increased, the disadvantages of *not registering* are becoming more evident. Moreover, it is not necessary to remain on the Disability Register for ever and if the employment situation does improve there is nothing to stop individuals from de-registering.

OBTAINING ADVICE ON BENEFITS

One of the hurdles that anyone who is unemployed will have to overcome is the 'benefits maze'. This – like Alice in Wonderland – has a tendency to change suddenly and dramatically, and alterations can have a major impact on those already claiming benefits, as well as on potential claimants. Benefits may be available for those looking for work, those needing special provision within the workplace, people on low earnings or those still involved in training. However, who can claim, what can be claimed, and whether or not it is actually beneficial to make a claim (in either the long or the short term), are all highly complex issues. Individual advice on benefits can be obtained from Citizens' Advice Bureaux. Staff will need detailed information on personal and financial backgrounds in order to help, but their guidance is usually extremely competent and valuable. Nevertheless, they will almost certainly need extra information about the needs of people with autism.

Application forms for benefits tend to focus on easily recognisable handicaps, such as physical or sensory impairments, or on psychiatric illnesses, and it may prove difficult to complete the necessary forms in a way that accurately reflects the needs of someone with autism. If forms are not filled in correctly this can easily lead to benefits being refused or stopped; hence accurate, professional advice is *CRUCIAL* before any formal documents are completed. The National Autistic Society (*Claiming What's Yours* – 1995) provides information on welfare benefits; the criteria required for obtaining these; current methods of assessing disability, or the capacity to work; advice on completing forms, dealing with the assessment process; and how to appeal against decisions. The NAS is also able to offer some advice on a personal basis.

Support from a GP, another medical adviser or a social worker may be needed when making claims, and it is always worth letting them know in advance if their help is likely to be needed. (For a brief summary of possible benefits see Table 8.3.)

FINDING OUT ABOUT POSSIBLE WORK OR JOB OPPORTUNITIES

Voluntary work is often an important first step on the employment ladder and can help overcome the 'Catch-22' problem, faced by many people with autism, of not being able to get a job without experience and not being able to get the experience without a job. A substantial number of people with autism have eventually managed to find permanent employment in this way. Large charitable organisations such as Oxfam have the advantage, by virtue of their size, of being able to offer volunteers a wide range of possible activities. However, they may prove rather daunting for many people and for some, smaller, local charities may offer better opportunities. Community care schemes often need voluntary workers to help with the very frail, elderly or disabled and some people with autism have proved to be very patient and devoted in work of this kind. Jonathon had maintained a number of voluntary posts since leaving college, including one that involved pushing wheelchairs for people in a hospital for the terminally ill. Because of his patience and good humour and his ability to find his way through the labyrinthine mazes of the extensive Victorian site, the hospital management eventually offered him a part-time job. Stuart, who managed to find voluntary work with a major charity, was taken on to the permanent pay-roll there as an accounts clerk on a full-time basis, after being with them for two years.

Again, MENCAP may be able to offer advice about possible voluntary work opportunities, although it is also advisable to approach individual charities in the local area.

Table 8.3 Summary of benefits that may be available to people with autism (April 1995)

Name of benefit	Who can claim	Criteria	Approximate amount per week
Income Support	These on low or no income	Working less than 16 hours per week	£46.50
Severe Disablement Allowance	Those incapable of working	Must pass government's new 'Incapacity Assessment'	From £35+
Disability Living Allowance	Those needing additional care at home, even if in well-paid job	Individuals with specified 'care and mobility needs'	From £12
Disability Working Allowance	Those needing 'top-up' to existing salary	Individuals who have been in receipt of a disability benefit *prior* to starting work	Maximum £46, but can result in loss of other benefits
Therapeutic Earnings	Those needing work for 'therapeutic' purposes, e.g. to build up confidence/self-esteem	Individuals earning less than £44 per week, and working under medical supervision	Up to £44
Incapacity Benefit	Replaces 'Sickness Benefit' and 'Invalidity Benefit'	Must have paid sufficient National Insurance Contributions prior to incapacity; after 28 weeks will need to pass new 'Incapacity Test'	£44 to £58

Note: This table gives only a very brief account of possible benefits. Further details should be obtained from the National Autistic Society *before* any claims are made.

Thirty years ago there was almost no specialist provision for young children with autism but the combined efforts of professionals and parents have resulted in the development of widespread, varied and effective educational programmes. Today the need is for a similar expansion in vocational training and occupational provision for adults with autism, especially those for whom modifications within the normal working environment could offer far greater opportunities for social integration and personal development.

NOTES

1 A substantial part of the material for this chapter was initially prepared as a teaching module for the Distance Learning Course for professionals working with adults with autism. Birmingham University, School of Education.
2 MENCAP (1990a, b).
3 The Shaw Trust offers training and financial support to help individuals with learning difficulties into work. Addresses of local branches can be obtained from Special Careers Officers or MENCAP.
4 Two schemes within the London area are the Status Employment Agency, which offers job finding and supported employment for people with disabilities, and Lambeth Accord, which offers training in job skills.
5 DEAs may be contacted through the local Job Centre or Placement, Advisory and Counselling Team (PACT).

9 Psychiatric disturbances in adulthood

A PERSONAL VIEW

Therese Jolliffe, a young woman with autism, writes movingly (Jolliffe *et al.*, 1992) about the difficulties that she and others like her may face on a daily basis:

> Most people find that they can at least share their physical suffering with others, but no-one really understands what the emotional suffering of a person with autism is like, and there is no pain killer, injection or operation that can get rid of it or even . . . relieve it a little. Autism affects everything all the time [even] your dreams . . . People with autism get very angry because the frustration of not being able to understand the world properly is so terrible – sometimes it gets too much, then people say they are surprised when I get angry. Life is such a struggle; indecision over things that other people refer to as trivial results in an awful lot of distress . . . if someone says 'We may go shopping tomorrow' or 'We will see what happens' they do not seem to realise that the uncertainty causes a lot of inner distress . . . I constantly labour, in a cognitive sense, over what may or may not occur . . . It is the confusion that results from not being able to understand the world around me which I think causes all the fear. This fear then brings a need to withdraw. Anything which helps reduce the confusion has the effect of reducing the fear and ultimately reduces the isolation and despair, thus making life a bit more bearable to live in'.

Being forced constantly to confront such problems, often with little help and support, it is hardly surprising that people with autism may also suffer additional psychiatric difficulties as they grow older. However, for a number of reasons, the nature of the association between autism and other disorders, particularly schizophrenia, is often misunderstood.

HISTORICAL BACKGROUND

The terms 'early childhood schizophrenia' and 'infantile psychosis' were originally used as alternative labels for autism (Creak, 1963; Eisenberg, 1972), and for many years there was ambiguity as to whether autism was, in fact, a psychotic disorder. Kanner himself initially considered that autism would probably turn out to be an early manifestation of schizophrenia, writing in 1949: 'I do not believe that there is any likelihood that early infantile autism will at any future time have to be separated from the schizophrenias'.

In 1972, however, Michael Rutter wrote an important paper documenting many crucial differences between autism and schizophrenia. These included: age of onset; the pattern and course of the disorders; family history and intellectual functioning. Although subsequent diagnostic classification systems (such as ICD–10 or DSM IV) have made clear that the two conditions are distinct, there continue to be reports suggesting an association between autism and schizophrenia. Such accounts may understandably provoke considerable anxiety amongst families and people with autism and hence need to be considered with great care.

STUDIES OF THE ASSOCIATION BETWEEN AUTISM AND SCHIZOPHRENIA

A follow-up study by Bender and Faetra in 1972 suggested that as many as 90 per cent of a group of children diagnosed as autistic were considered to have developed schizophrenia in adulthood. Dahl, in a later study (1976), quoted figures of 50 per cent. Watkins and colleagues in 1988 found that 39 per cent of children with a diagnosis of schizophrenia (assessed on a number of separate scales as well as by clinical interview) had shown 'autistic symptoms' when younger. More recently, work by Sula Wolff and colleagues in Edinburgh has stressed the link between Asperger syndrome and schizoid disorders, again suggesting that this group may be more at risk of developing schizophrenia in adult life (Wolff and McGuire, 1995; Wolff and Chick, 1980).

Lorna Wing has criticised such claims on the grounds that they are 'distressing without being constructive' (Wing, 1986), and certainly the diagnostic criteria employed in these studies are often questionable. Thus, it is not always clear that all cases fulfilled criteria for autism in childhood and, in particular, Ghaziuddin and colleagues have raised concerns about the diagnosis of 'Asperger syndrome' (Ghaziuddin, Tsai and Ghaziuddin, 1992a). Werry also discusses in some detail the problems inherent in making a diagnosis of early onset schizophrenia or of schizotypal/schizoid disorders (Werry, 1992).

Despite these caveats, there continues to be a small number of reports of the later development of schizophrenic illness in cases with autism or Asperger syndrome. Wolff and McGuire, in a 1995 follow-up study, found that 2 out of 17 females and 2 out of 32 males with a *possible* diagnosis of Asperger syndrome (they were initially diagnosed as 'schizoid') later developed schizophrenia. Clarke and colleagues (1989) report on one case of schizophrenia in a group of 5 young men with autism who later developed psychiatric disturbances (Clarke *et al.*, 1989). Lorna Wing (1981), in a study of 18 individuals with Asperger syndrome, notes one case with an unconfirmed diagnosis of schizophrenia. Petty *et al.* (1984) describe 3 cases in whom early onset schizophrenia seems to have been preceded by autism. There are also occasional single-case reports of the association between autism and later schizophrenia (Szatmari *et al.*, 1986; Sverd, Montero and Gurevich, 1993).

Because of the small size of many of these studies, or the retrospective focus on individuals with psychiatric problems in adulthood, it is important to be extremely cautious of claims indicating 'an excess of schizophrenia in later life' (Wolff and McGuire, 1995). Larger follow-up studies of children and adolescents certainly do not support such statements. Ghaziuddin and colleagues found no cases of schizophrenia in a sample of 68 autistic children under the age of 18 (Ghaziuddin, Tsai and Ghaziuddin, 1992b). There were none in Volkmar and Cohen's sample of 163 cases (reported by Werry, 1992) nor were any reported in Chung's follow-up of 87 Hong Kong children (Chung, Luk and Lee, 1990).

Adult studies generally suggest similar findings. None of the cases followed up by Kanner over a period of 40 years was reported as showing delusions or hallucinations, although Kanner's use of terms such as 'psychosis' or 'schizoid' illnesses for individuals who still maintain many autistic features is confusing at times.

Rumsey, Rapoport and Sceery (1985), in a detailed psychiatric study of 14 young adults with autism, found no cases of positive schizophrenic symptoms (hallucinations or delusions) and concluded: 'These findings would suggest that autistic children do not generally, with any great frequency, develop schizophrenia or other adult psychiatric disorders, but rather display continuing, less severe symptoms of their original autism which significantly limit their social and economic independence'.

Goode and her colleagues in England followed up 74 adults with autism who were over the age of 21, none of whom had developed a schizophrenic illness (Goode, Howlin and Rutter, in preparation). Although the large-scale study in Japan of 201 young adults notes that 4 were placed in psychiatric hospitals, the reasons for this are not given (Kobayashi, Murata and Yashinaga, 1992).

Rates of schizophrenia also appear to be relatively low in studies of more able individuals or those with Asperger syndrome. Asperger noted that only 1 out of his 200 cases developed schizophrenia: 'In all other cases, some of which I have observed for twenty years or longer, I have not seen a transition of autistic personality disorder into genuine schizophrenia' (Asperger, in Frith, 1991). Tantam (1991) diagnosed 3 cases of schizophrenia in 83 individuals with Asperger syndrome but notes that this figure is likely to be higher than in an unselected sample because these were all psychiatric referrals. One individual in the Szatmari study of 16 high-functioning adults was receiving treatment for chronic schizophrenia (Szatmari *et al.*, 1989b). None of the 19 relatively able subjects in the study by Mawhood (1995b) had a schizophrenic disorder (although interestingly 2 out of the comparison group of individuals with a severe developmental language disorder did so).

A number of other cases are reported of individuals showing a mixture of psychotic symptoms, including paranoid and occasionally delusional thoughts. One young man described by Lorna Wing (1981) could not be deterred from his conviction that someday Batman was going to come and take him away as his assistant. Clarke *et al.*, (1989) report on another case of delusional disorder and one with an unspecified psychosis. The Szatmari study notes several cases of paranoid thinking or possible hallucinations whilst Tantam reports four additional cases with hallucinations, one case with epileptic psychosis, and two with obsessive compulsive disorders. Szatmari and Rumsey also describe a number of cases of obsessional or compulsive disorder in their studies of more able individuals, although, as Szatmari notes, 'We found it very difficult . . . to distinguish between obsessive ideation and the bizarre preoccupations so commonly seen in autistic individuals'.

In summary, although being autistic does not offer protection against schizophrenia or related disorders, there is no evidence that the incidence is any higher than in the general population.

AUTISM AND OTHER PSYCHOTIC DISORDERS

By far the most prevalent psychiatric disturbances reported, in either single-case or follow-up studies, are those related to anxiety and depression. As early as 1970, Rutter noted the risk of depressive episodes occurring in adolescents or older individuals with autism (Rutter, 1970). Other authors have also reported a high frequency of affective disorders (see Review by Lainhart and Folstein, 1994 and Table 9.1)

Amongst the larger-scale of these studies, Tantam reported a rate of 12 per cent for affective psychosis in a group of adults with Asperger syndrome. He also noted that in several cases the illness incorporated a delusional content, often linked with the individual's autistic preoccupations. One man, for example, had thrown himself into the Thames because the government refused to abolish British Summer Time and he believed that watches were damaged by the necessity of being altered twice a year.

In addition to the cases with a psychotic disorder, a further 8 per cent suffered from other problems related to depression or anxiety. Similar figures are reported by Wing (1981) who found that 23 per cent of her group of 18 individuals with Asperger syndrome showed signs of an affective disorder. Two had attempted suicide and one other had talked about doing so although their attempts had not been successful. One young man, who had become very distressed by minor changes in his work routine, tried to drown himself but failed because he was a good swimmer. When he tried to strangle himself the attempt also failed because, as he said, 'I am not a very practical person'. Wolff and McGuire (1995) also report that death from suicide was greater in their sample of 'schizoid' men and women, several of whom were probably suffering from Asperger syndrome, than in the general population (10 out of 17 women and 17 out of 32 men had attempted suicide).

In Rumsey's follow-up of 14 relatively high-functioning individuals, generalised anxiety problems were found in half the sample. Six individuals also showed occasional outbursts of temper, aggression or destructiveness, usually triggered when they were under pressure, but also for trivial occurrences (such as a lack of soap in the bathroom).

Because none of these investigations claims to be based on representative samples, the resulting figures for the prevalence of psychiatric disturbance must be treated with caution. A preliminary study by Abramson and colleagues (1992) suggests that the rates of affective disorder may be as high as 33 per cent. Tantam's findings indicate overall rates for mania of 9 per cent, 15 per cent for depression and 7 per cent for clinically significant anxiety disorders, whilst the rates for schizophrenia are much less, at around 3.5 per cent. In the absence of larger-scale studies, such statistics must remain tentative, but it has become increasingly clear that problems related to depression and anxiety are a significant risk for people with autism as they grow older.

PROBLEMS OF DIAGNOSIS

Diagnosing schizophrenia in people with autism

One of the difficulties in reaching consensus about the frequency of psychotic illness lies in the unusual patterns of communication and social behaviour found in autism. Because of this the application of conventional diagnostic systems can lead to considerable problems. Dykens and colleagues (Dykens, Volkmar and Glick, 1991), in a study of thought disorder in intellectually able people with autism, found that many gave abnormal responses on the Thought, Language and Communication Disorder scale (Andreasen, 1979). 'Poverty of speech' was particularly marked, but Rorschach responses were also odd, with many idiosyncratic and unusual expressions occurring. For example, when describing what the inkblot looked like, one subject reported: 'just the human heart in black and white'. Dykens and colleagues note that thought disorder is generally considered to be a first-rank symptom of schizophrenia and diagnosis is often made on the basis of this. If the unusual language of individuals with autism makes them *appear as if they have thought disorder* then there is a serious risk of misdiagnosis.

Misinterpretation of this kind might well explain the high rates of schizophrenia reported in some studies. Lorna Wing (1986) suggests that individuals with autism or Asperger syndrome may be incorrectly diagnosed as having a psychotic illness because of the way in which they respond to questions about their mental state. Thus, responses may be very slow, and often tangential to the question asked. However, although unusual, concrete and pedantic, they do not show the vague woolliness of schizophrenic thought. Wing quotes the answer of one young man to a general-knowledge question about charities:

Table 9.1 Reports of affective disorder in adolescents and adults with autism or Asperger syndrome

Author	Age	Sex	Total/N	Initial diagnosis	Psychiatric disorder
Darr and Worden 1951	33	F	1	Autism	Low mood; delusions
Reid 1976	32	F	1	Autism	Depression
Wolff and Chick 1980	17+	M	22	'Schizoid'/Asperger	2 Depression 1 Mood swings 5 Attempted suicide
Wing 1981	16+	M	18	Asperger	4 Affective disorder
Komoto et al. 1984	13 13	F M	2	Autism	Depression Bipolar illness
Rumsey et al. 1985	18+	M	14	Autism	7 Generalised anxiety disorder
Gillberg	14	M	1	Asperger	Manic depression
Akuffo et al. 1986	40	F	1	Autism	Manic depression
Steingard and Biederman 1987	24	M	1	Autism	Manic episodes
Linter 1987	15	M	1	Autistic-like	Manic depression

Study	Age	Sex	N	Diagnosis	Psychiatric diagnosis
Kerbeshian and Burd 1987	13	M	1	Atypical autism	Major depression
Sovner 1988a, b	25 26	F	2	Autism PDD	Depression " "
Sovner 1989	31 24	M F	1 1	Autistic	Depression Manic depression
Clarke et al. 1989	23	M	5	Autistic	1 Major depression
Szatmari et al. 1989b	?	M+F	16	Autistic	4 'Anxiety disorder'
Kerbeshian et al. 1990	33	M	1	Autistic + SLD	Bipolar
Ghaziuddin et al. 1991a, b	17 16	M F	2	Autistic + Down's Autistic	Depression "
Tantam 1991	18+	M	46	Asperger	4 Mania 4 Bipolar 2 Depression 11 Non-psychotic anxiety/depression
Kurita and Nakayasu 1994	1	M	21	Autism + MR	SADS

'They provide wheelchairs, stilts and round shoes for people with no feet'. She also notes that people may well answer 'Yes' to any question asked, simply to cut short the conversation, or they may pick up and repeat phrases used by other patients on the ward (particularly unusual ones) which can further complicate diagnosis.

The literal interpretation of questions may also lead to problems. If someone with autism is asked a standard diagnostic question, such as 'Do you ever hear voices when no-one is in the room?', most will answer 'Yes', for of course we all hear voices when people are not actually in the same room. If asked 'Do you ever think people are talking about you?', the majority of people with autism are likely to answer in the affirmative, since people have probably been talking about them for as long as they can remember! This failure to interpret the underlying meaning of the question is likely to lead to a positive response by someone with autism, even though there is no real evidence of delusions or hallucinations.

Other problems can arise from individuals' concrete use of language or their inability to describe abstract or emotional concepts. Danny, a 19-year-old student who had just started college, developed symptoms of severe anxiety, including headaches, stomach aches, and a variety of other signs. When referred to a psychiatrist he insisted that his stomach pains were caused by a 'shark in his insides'. This explanation was interpreted as a delusional symptom; he was admitted to hospital and placed on long-term medication for schizophrenia. However, his mother explained that as a young boy he had a favourite book where illnesses were described in this way: such as a crocodile in the head giving people headaches, a mouse chewing at the root of a tooth causing toothaches, or a monkey with a hammer producing pains in the ear. In his attempts to explain his physical symptoms he had reverted to these childish symbols, with little understanding of the impact that this could have.

Diagnosing affective disorders.

The inability of people with autism to communicate feelings of disturbance, anxiety or distress can also mean that it is often very difficult to diagnose depressive or anxiety states, particularly for clinicians who have little knowledge or understanding of developmental disorders. Even parents may explain changes in behaviour as being 'just a phase' that their son or daughter is going through, especially if they have experienced previous periods of withdrawal, slowness or 'odd' behaviours in childhood. In many cases it is only when the illness becomes very marked that the severity of the disorder is recognised. By this time the individual may have become very withdrawn, often refusing to leave the house, giving up work or other activities, and failing to care for themselves adequately. Martin, a 21-year-old living by himself, was not recognised as being ill until a visit from his brother revealed that he had no food in the house, had not eaten for days, had not paid rent for weeks, and had been failing to collect his welfare benefits.

Jonah's mother knew that he had been having difficulties at work but she was not aware of any major problems. He continued to visit on a regular basis and kept to all his other set routines. She was distraught to receive a rather formal note informing her that he intended to commit suicide the next week. He added 'I am sending you this note because I did not want you to go around to the flat and be upset if I had left it in a mess' (there was no recognition that she would be devastated by finding him dead). Diana's mother had assumed that her growing reluctance to leave the house was just another of her obsessional phases and it was only when she became increasingly tearful and withdrawn that psychiatric help was sought. Steven, a young man in his early twenties, was referred for behavioural treatment because of his increasing 'obsessions'; he could not bear to be touched, refused to let anyone close to him and became virtually mute. Although a behavioural programme was attempted this had little effect and it was only when anti-depressant mediation was introduced that his behaviours slowly began to improve.

The diagnostic process may also be complicated by the fact that stress and depression can sometimes manifest themselves as aggressive or even paranoid behaviours. Douglas, who is also described in the next chapter, had become increasingly upset by the pressures of work. He had no-one to talk to except his elderly mother and, finally, when she failed to respond to his pleas for help, he attacked and injured her. It was only then that the need for psychiatric help became apparent, although he himself continued to deny any need for this.

The inability of individuals to talk about feelings or emotions is also a major problem for clinicians. Diagnosis and treatment for mental disorders relies heavily on the individual's ability to describe feelings; if this ability is lacking it can be very difficult to offer appropriate help. Stuart's parents were convinced that he was becoming very withdrawn and depressed, but when they eventually managed to obtain a referral to a psychiatrist Stuart sat with a fixed grin on his face, repeating 'Everything is fine'. His parents were dismissed as over-anxious and intrusive and it was only when he became very disturbed that their concerns were finally taken seriously.

Moreover, as noted above, even if a diagnostic assessment is attempted, the very concrete and unusual way in which people with autism talk about their feelings can easily lead to errors and misunderstandings. Elaine was a 30-year-old woman whose daily life had been severely disrupted by the death of a favourite careworker. Initially she showed little response to this but progressively became more and more distressed. When asked what the matter was she could only repeat 'The cabbage was burnt on Tuesday'. Cabbage, particularly if burned, was a particular hate of hers but her inability to talk about emotional distress in any other way very much hindered attempts to assess her mental state.

Understandably, many psychiatrists working in the field of adult mental health know relatively little of the problems of people with autism. It is crucial, therefore, when carrying out a diagnostic assessment, that the physician involved is fully informed about the individual's usual style of communication, both verbal and non-verbal, so that symptoms are neither overlooked nor misinterpreted. Many parents, especially of more able individuals, report that they are often discouraged or prevented from speaking to the professionals concerned in the treatment of their son or daughter. Whilst respecting the right of the person with autism to be treated like an adult, it is also vital that the information received is reliable. Szatmari and colleagues (1989b), for example, in their study of high-functioning adults with autism found that the history given by parents indicated the presence of psychiatric disturbance much more frequently than information based on the individual's own reports. Communication deficits are so central to autism that it will almost always be necessary to seek help in 'interpreting' what is said from someone who knows the individual well. The need for an 'interpreter' may be just as great as for someone who is deaf, yet access to such assistance is often denied.

Diagnosing psychiatric disturbance in less able individuals

In many of the studies reported above, the diagnosis of psychiatric disturbance has been made in individuals who are relatively high-functioning. Few studies, with the exception of those of Kerbeshian and colleagues (1987, 1990), have diagnosed psychiatric disorders in people with autism and severe mental retardation. Indeed, the diagnosis of psychiatric disturbance in individuals with severe to profound learning disabilities poses a major problem to clinicians working in this field and although attempts have been made to adapt current diagnostic systems to meet the needs of this group the situation remains far from satisfactory. (See Bregman, 1991 and Bernal, 1994 for helpful discussions of these issues.)

Because individuals with autism are often so immersed in their routines, certain aspects of their daily functioning may remain apparently intact even when they are disturbed or depressed. Parents often report a determined insistence on carrying out daily rituals or routines, and the characteristic symptoms of depression, such as changes in eating or sleeping, may be slow to emerge because of this. Instead, important indicators are increases in aggression to self or others, unprovoked attacks on people or property, agitation, withdrawal, or an increase in obsessional and ritualistic behaviours. Behaviours of this kind are, understandably, frequently perceived as inappropriate and maladaptive by carers, but may be the individual's *only* means of communicating disturbance or distress. Rather than attempting to modify such behaviours directly, by using 'time out', or ignoring, or similar procedures, it is essential to try to establish the true nature of the problem. Particular heed should be taken if the emergence of such behaviours is associated with loss or major change. However, depressive and other illness may not necessarily be related solely to external factors, and even if an external explanation cannot be found this does not rule out the possibility of a psychotic illness. Detailed assessment and observation of the individual and his or her environment may well be required if the correct diagnosis and consequent appropriate treatment procedures are to be formulated.

TREATMENT

Just as the recognition of mental illness in people with autism can present many problems, so, too, can the provision of appropriate help and intervention.

Medication

Although there are some useful reviews of the drugs that can be used in the treatment of behaviour problems in autism (Coleman, 1992; Campbell and Cueva, 1995) there has been relatively little study of medical treatments for psychiatric disturbances. In a recent survey of drug treatments, parents reported a bewildering variety of interventions and an equally wide range of drug effects (Rimland, 1994a).

The failure to understand the nature of the individual's illness (for example, confusing concrete language with a delusional thought system) clearly has major implications for intervention. Thus, careful diagnostic assessment, based on information from all relevant sources, including the patient and carers, is essential if treatment is to be effective. Clarke (1996) presents a balanced and informative account of pharmacological interventions for psychiatric disturbances in people with autism and it is clear from this that, although in the past there have been claims for the overwhelming effectiveness of certain drugs, there is little to substantiate such assertions.

Recently, for example, fenfluramine was widely recommended as a treatment for many different problems associated with autism, but such claims would appear to have little foundation (Duker *et al.*, 1991). As with all medical treatments, drugs may have very different effects on different individuals and need to be carefully monitored. The wide spread of ability in people with autism, and the presence of associated problems, such as epilepsy, can mean that their response to medication may be even more variable than that in the general population. Paradoxical responses to medication (becoming very over-active and agitated when prescribed a tranquilliser for example) are an additional risk. Certain drugs, such as neuroleptics, which may be helpful in the treatment of schizophrenic disorders, may also have untoward effects. Some, for instance, may reduce facial expressiveness and therefore contribute to the social difficulties of someone who already has impairments in this area (Tantam, 1991).

In the case of marked psychiatric disturbance, however, delays in prescribing appropriate medication can have serious effects. If it is decided that pharmacological treatments are to be employed, carers should be fully informed about possible side-effects so that signs of any negative reactions can be dealt with quickly and effectively. Clear guidelines should be agreed *in advance* as to how progress will be monitored, how long the drug will be given before its efficacy is assessed, and how long medication should continue before the drug is discontinued, recommended for longer use, or gradually withdrawn.

All too frequently one comes across cases of individuals with autism who have been on the same drug, or cocktail of drugs, for many years, with little obvious benefit. Often medication continues because carers are frightened about what will happen if it is withdrawn, whether or not there is any evidence that it is or ever has been effective. Other individuals, particularly those in long-stay hospitals or institutions, are simply prescribed one drug after another, in the apparent hope that eventually 'something' might work. The result is often to make their lives even more impoverished than they were initially, without providing any obvious benefits.

Some individuals with autism may refuse to take medication at all because they are convinced this will be damaging to their health and a great deal of persuasion may be required to overcome this resistance. Others who suffer unwanted or expected side-effects may discontinue treatment, no matter how essential this is. Sarah, a young woman in her mid-twenties, had been prescribed medication for severe depression for several years. This had little apparent effect, other than an increase in weight. Her mother requested a review of the medication, in order to explore possible alternatives, but she was told that this was unnecessary. However, Sarah had always had an obsession with her appearance and when strict dieting had no impact on her weight she stopped taking the medication overnight, without her doctor's knowledge, and after a short time had to be admitted as an emergency to her local psychiatric hospital.

It is essential to predict possible side-effects, as far as possible, for if the individual is prepared for these he or she may be able to tolerate them more willingly. If they are not tolerable, for whatever reason, then unnecessary delay in seeking an alternative may result in total refusal to accept further treatment.

Avoiding the development of further behavioural disturbance

A particular problem that arises in treating people with autism stems from their adherence to routine. Once they become set in a particular pattern of behaviour it can be very difficult to shift this. Hence, if unwanted behaviours become established during the course of a psychiatric illness it can prove almost impossible to change these later, even when mental health has significantly improved.

Steven, whose withdrawal and muteness are described in an earlier chapter, was not recognised as having a depressive illness for many months. A behavioural programme was implemented to reduce his 'obsessional' behaviours, but this proved both ineffective and inappropriate. Finally, he was placed on anti-depressant medication and showed slow but steady improvement. However, even when he seemed much recovered he still refused to let anyone approach him and remained virtually mute. A subsequent behavioural programme, carried out at home and at his day centre, has helped gradually to increase his tolerance of being touched but he continues to avoid speaking if possible and his preferred mode of communication is through writing. He has never returned to the full range of activities he enjoyed before his illness and over-zealous attempts to encourage these result in marked resistance.

James, now in his thirties, became very housebound during his late teens, when he was depressed. By the time his parents sought help, his reclusiveness was well entrenched, and although his mood state is now much improved he is still resistant to leaving the house. If he does go out this is only for a short walk with his mother and he is far more dependent on his parents than he was when younger. Moreover, because of his dependence on them, the quality of life for the entire family has greatly deteriorated.

Psychological approaches to intervention

This tendency for 'ill' behaviours to persist, even when the disorder is in remission, makes early diagnosis and treatment particularly crucial. It also means that psychological treatments, to re-establish appropriate behaviour patterns, should be employed as an adjunct to pharmacological interventions as early in the recovery stage as possible.

Prior to a brief period of inpatient treatment for depression, Sally had developed many obsessional behaviours, refusing to leave the house or to talk to anyone outside. On her return home, a careful programme was planned in order gradually to encourage a wider range of activities. Initially the demands were very limited: one walk with the dog in a week and one visit to the hospital hydrotherapy pool (she enjoyed swimming but could not cope with the crowds in the local leisure centre). Her mother took time off work to be with her at such times, and, gradually, with help from Social Services, the frequency of outings was increased. She is still unable to go out unaccompanied, but at least no longer spends all her time in bed, as she had done before her admission.

Psychological therapies, particularly those using a cognitive-behavioural approach (Sheldon, 1995; Haddock and Slade, 1995; Beck, 1976) may be used to repair the loss of confidence and self-esteem which often follows illnesses of this kind. However, because such strategies traditionally focus on internal cognitions, or emotional states and feelings, they will need some modifications. Encouraging someone with autism to *write down* positive things that have happened is obviously more helpful than simply instructing them to restructure negative thoughts. Following a short depressive illness Damien remained convinced that his life was one of great deprivation and misery. In fact, because he had a small legacy from his parents, he had far more opportunities than many other young men of his age. In counselling sessions he would always concentrate on his inability to find a job (which he did not really need) or a girl friend (with whom he could never have coped). Although allowing some time for his complaints the therapist began to insist that he kept lists of 'good things' that had happened between sessions. Initially he had difficulties finding even one positive event to report, but as time went on he was encouraged to produce increasingly longer lists, which then became the focus of therapeutic work.

When working with less severe problems, or with individuals of lower ability, more direct behavioural strategies can be very effective. Relaxation and distraction techniques, such as thought stopping, have been described in some detail in the chapter on obsessional behaviours and are often particularly successful in dealing with anxiety-related problems. (See also Clements, 1987 for methods of working with more severely disabled adults.) However, it may be necessary to address environmental factors too. George, for example, had a marked fear of dogs, which at one stage almost prevented his leaving the house. A desensitisation programme, which aimed gradually to reduce his fear of dogs, was implemented and his anxieties slowly reduced. He also learned to avoid certain places, such as the local park, where dogs were likely to appear without warning. However, problems arose again when he started work and had to pass a factory where guard dogs roamed the grounds. His anxiety increased rapidly to the stage where he could not go to work unless accompanied by his mother. His mother learned that the dogs' barking was also upsetting other residents, and in the end they campaigned to have the dogs better restrained and kept well away from the road. Once this was accomplished she began systematically to reduce the distance she accompanied him, until he was eventually able to walk to work alone as long as she stood and watched until he passed the factory gates.

Sometimes behavioural approaches alone cannot be implemented, particularly if anxiety or agitation is very severe. In such cases anxiety-reducing medication may improve the response to psychological intervention, or encourage the individual concerned to attempt alternative strategies for dealing with difficulties.

Responses to loss

Grief reactions, following loss of a relative, a favourite staff member or another resident, often prove particularly difficult to recognise or to treat. The person with autism may seem apparently unconcerned, even by the death of someone very close, and if they do mention it are likely to concentrate on tangential, even seemingly callous issues, such as how much they may have been left in the will. Even if asked directly they will often deny any upset. Maria, a woman of 40, with superficially good communication skills, when asked if she was sad about the death of her father insisted she was 'glad he's gone to heaven and is out of pain'. However, at the same time she began to embark on bizarre monologues about punishment and pain, murder and the police, and was clearly extremely disturbed. It proved very difficult to help her work through her feelings of grief (and probably anger) because of this denial. Although reflective methods were tried, suggesting how other people would feel in these circumstances, it was doubtful that these sessions meant very much to her, and usually they ended with long discussions about her obsession with the weather. In the end she did emerge from this period of disturbance, but this seemed to be in the absence of any real support. In contrast, Colin, who in many ways was less able, was helped to talk more constructively about the death of his father. His mother was anxious that explanations should be kept as concrete as possible, since once, when he was a child, she had made the mistake of pointing upwards and telling him that his grandad had 'gone to heaven'. For many months afterwards he would persistently try to get into the attics of houses, apparently under the impression that that was where heaven was. On this occasion she used booklets specially designed for people with learning disabilities, which illustrate clearly the events surrounding a parent's death, and how people react and feel (Hollins and Sireling, 1994). How much he really understood was never clear but he seemed to enjoy 'reading' these books (they have no words) and discussing how and why those left behind reacted as they did. Although such materials are not specifically written for people with autism, because of their directness and clarity they can be a useful aid to carers in their attempts to offer comfort and support. Other books in this series can also be used to help people deal with reactions to rejection, abuse, and major life changes such as leaving home (Hollins and Roth, 1994; Hollins and Hutchinson, 1993)

Psychotherapy and counselling

Counselling to deal with the impact of trauma or bereavement may be an important adjunct to therapy, particularly for older or more able individuals. Although there is little experimental validation of these techniques, experience suggests that such intervention also needs to incorporate direct, practical advice about strategies for change. Introspection alone, even for very able clients, is rarely effective, and may well prove counter-productive. Douglas was an 18-year-old who had received analytically based psychotherapy for some years. Early sessions had focused on his relationship with his mother and the role this may have played in his subsequent problems. Douglas became obsessed with this 'explanation' and was convinced that his mother was entirely responsible for all his difficulties, including his late development of language and occasional seizures. Because of this he made no attempts to modify his own behaviour, and even when he got into trouble with the police for following young women, he insisted that his was all his mother's fault.

Inpatient hospital treatment

Many families, and individuals themselves, may be resistant to inpatient hospital treatment. There are understandable fears that the person with autism may be misunderstood or become even more distressed by this major upheaval; there may be concerns, too, about the use of prolonged or inappropriate medication. Thus, it is essential that those dealing with patients with autism are aware of the implications of this condition for diagnosis, assessment and treatment. If professionals themselves are inexperienced it is vital that they consult with and take advice from others who do have expertise in this area. However, it is also crucial that if hospitalisation is required this is not avoided because of lack of knowledge or understanding. Janie was a young woman whose autism had not been diagnosed until she was in her twenties. She then suffered a period of severe depression, constantly talking about her wish to die and making several unsuccessful suicide attempts. Because she was unable to talk about her feelings, and because she always had a determined smile on her face, local psychiatric services dismissed her problems as 'hysterical and attention-seeking'. Her mother recognised the severity of her depression, but at the same time was convinced that if Janie went into hospital 'she might never come out again'. Over several months Janie became progressively more withdrawn, reclusive and paranoid. Finally, she stopped eating and sleeping and became so disturbed that she was admitted to hospital. By this time the severity of her problems was such that it required many months of treatment and medication before any improvement occurred. Delays in receiving hospital treatment, should this become necessary, also increase the risk of developing maladaptive behaviour patterns (such as never leaving the house, or sleeping only during the day and playing records all night long) which will later prove very difficult to modify.

The treatment of epilepsy

Epilepsy, of course, is not a psychiatric disorder as such (although occasional cases of epileptic psychosis have been reported; Tantam, 1991), but epilepsy may require treatment by psychiatrists or neurologists in adulthood, and hence is included here. It is estimated that around one-third of individuals with autism develop epilepsy, with onset often occurring in adolescence or early adulthood. The incidence tends to be greater in individuals of lower IQ, with the rates being highest in those with severe to profound learning difficulties. If these groups are excluded, the overall rate seems to be around 18 to 20 per cent (Goode, Rutter and Howlin, 1994; Tantam, 1991), with there being little difference between those of normal IQ and those with moderate learning disabilities. Gillberg (1992) suggests that the most common form of seizure disorder is complex-partial (psychomotor) epilepsy.

Treatment will clearly be determined by the nature and frequency of the seizures, and there is no evidence to suggest that successful control is particularly difficult to achieve for people with autism. However, because individuals are unlikely to report unwanted side-effects themselves, careful monitoring of their response to treatment, and readiness to change medication if necessary, is particularly important. Otherwise, physical or behavioural difficulties may escalate. Or, in the case of more able individuals, they may refuse to continue with medication.

Some adolescents or young adults may have one or two isolated fits, but no more, and because of the disadvantages of giving unnecessary medication, drugs are often not prescribed in these cases unless there is evidence of more frequent attacks.

THE NEED TO BE AWARE OF BEHAVIOURAL CHANGE

Although much remains to be understood about the nature and treatment of psychiatric illness in people with autism, it is apparent that the risks of disturbance, particularly related to anxiety and depression, are substantial. For those who are more able, and hence more aware of their difficulties, such responses are hardly surprising. They may fully recognise their limitations, and acknowledge the many differences between themselves and their peers, yet have virtually no means of altering this situation.

Even these individuals are unlikely to communicate their distress, or express their need for help in an effective way, and for the less able this may be almost impossible. Thus the early detection of mood disorders, and hence the provision of appropriate treatment, may depend heavily on the vigilance of carers. Sudden changes in behaviour, a loss of interest in previously enjoyed activities, swings of mood, unexplained outbursts of rage or anger, aggressive or self-injurious attacks, increasing withdrawal, can all be indicators of emotional stress. Undiagnosed physical or medical problems, such as infections, or inappropriate medication, may also be a cause of behavioural disturbance. It is crucial always to take these signs seriously, to explore why such changes have occurred, and to examine possible physical, emotional and environmental factors (especially those related to loss or change) as thoroughly as possible. In this way it may be possible at least to minimise the impact of psychiatric disturbance on individuals who already have to contend with the burden of their autism.

10 Legal issues

IS THERE A LINK BETWEEN AUTISM AND CRIMINALITY?

Although there is little evidence of any significant association between autism and criminal offending, occasional and sometimes lurid publicity has led to suggestions that there may be an excess of violent crimes amongst more able people with autism, particularly those diagnosed as having Asperger syndrome. Certainly, tragic events do sometimes occur. In the UK in 1994, for example, a 13-year-old boy diagnosed as having Asperger syndrome murdered an 85-year-old woman on her way to church without any motivation. A small number of other reports have also appeared in the literature from time to time. In her original account of people with Asperger syndrome Lorna Wing describes the case of one individual, out of a total of 34, who had injured another boy, apparently because of his obsession with chemical experiments.

Mawson and colleagues (1985) report on a 44-year-old man with Asperger syndrome who was committed to Broadmoor Special Hospital after attacking a baby. This followed a series of other attacks, including stabbing, on young women or children which had begun in his teens. The attacks seemed to be related to his obsession with getting a girl friend, his dislike of certain styles of dress, and his dislike of the noise of crying. He also had a fascination with poisons. Simon Baron-Cohen (1988) describes the strange case of a 21-year-old man who had, over a period of several years, violently assaulted his 71-year-old 'girl friend'.

In another report, Chesterman and Rutter (1994) describe a young man with Asperger syndrome who had been charged with a number of sexual offences. However, these seemed to relate mainly to his obsession with washing machines and women's nightdresses. The case was complicated by the fact that he struck the interviewing police officer when it was suggested that he might also have been contemplating burglary; as far as he was concerned 'he was merely intending to make use of the occupant's washing machine'.

Everall and Le Couteur (1990) describe a case of fire-setting in an adolescent boy with Asperger syndrome and Digby Tantam (1991) mentions five cases of fire-setting, four of which occurred when other people were in the building. He also cites another case in which someone had killed his schoolmate 'probably as an experiment'. Nevertheless, he also adds that violence, in a fight, in an explosion of rage or in sexual excitement is rare. Amongst the men with Asperger's syndrome he studied, sexual offending, too, was unusual, although some got into trouble for indecent exposure. Property offences were also rare except as the 'side-effects of the pursuit of a special interest'.

There are a number of other, largely anecdotal reports of offending by people with autism or Asperger syndrome. Inappropriate social responses, especially to strangers, may result in police involvement, and crimes may also be linked to obsessional interests. Because of this, offending may well be of an unusual or even bizarre nature, such as attempting to drive away an unattended railway engine because of an obsession with trains or causing explosions and fires because of an obsessional interest in chemical reactions (Wing, 1986).

Estimates of offending by people with autism or Asperger syndrome

On the basis of their single-case report, Mawson and colleagues suggest that many people who come to the attention of secure units because of violent offences may have Asperger syndrome. In fact, evidence in support of such a statement is extremely limited. Scragg and Shah (1994) assessed the entire male population of Broadmoor Special Hospital, using case notes to identify possible autistic cases. Then, by means of the Handicap, Behaviour and Skills schedule (Wing and Gould, 1978) and personal interviews, they identified 3 cases with autism and 6 with Asperger syndrome, using Gillberg and Gillberg's criteria (1989). Out of a total of 392 patients this represented a prevalence rate of just over 2 per cent. Although the numbers are small, this is clearly a much higher figure than the rates for autism or Asperger syndrome in the general population, which are about 0.04 per cent for the former and 0.55 per cent for the latter (Ehlers and Gillberg, 1993). The offences committed included violence or threats of violence (5 cases), unlawful killing (3 cases, including 1 of matricide) and fire-setting (1 case). Solitariness or lack of empathy was noted in each case. Six of the cases had a fascination for topics such as poisons, weapons, murder books or combat. Because the prevalence of Asperger syndrome in this special hospital setting was higher than predicted Scragg and Shah also conclude that there is an association between Asperger syndrome and violence. Nevertheless, as Ghaziuddin points out, the number of reports of violence or offences by people with autism or Asperger syndrome is actually very small. In 1991 he reviewed accounts of offending by people with Asperger syndrome (Ghaziuddin, Tsai and Ghaziuddin, 1991b). Out of a total of 132 cases, only 3 had a clear history of violent behaviour (these are the cases described by Wing, 1981, Baron-Cohen, 1988 and Mawson *et al.*, 1985, noted above). The low incidence of violence found by Ghaziuddin is compared with a rate of 7 per cent of violent crimes (rape, robbery and assault) in the 20–24-year age group in the United States (US Bureau of Justice Statistics, 1987).

As Scragg and Shah (1994) suggest, there may well be more people with autism in prisons or secure accommodation than is realised, and it is clearly important that such individuals are correctly identified and treated. However, estimates of the prevalence of violence in this group can only be made on the basis of community studies. Until then, speculation on the alleged links between violence and autism or Asperger syndrome is only likely to increase the stigma and distress of sufferers and their families. Currently, there is no reason to suppose that people with autism are more prone to committing offences than anyone else; indeed, because of the very rigid way in which many tend to keep to rules and regulations, they may well be more law-abiding than the general population.

CAUSES OF OFFENDING

Although it has been suggested that lack of empathy may be a significant factor in violent attacks by people with autism or Asperger syndrome, other significant variables include their lack of social understanding, the pursuit of obsessional interests, and a failure to recognise the implications of their behaviour, either for themselves or others. Rigid adherence to rules may also give rise to problems. Occasionally, too, crimes may be unwittingly, or unwillingly, committed at the instigation of others. Very often, of course, a combination of these factors is involved, but rarely does there appear to be deliberate intention to hurt or harm others.

Failure to recognise the impact of behaviours on others

Douglas was a man in his forties who, despite numerous problems since childhood, had not previously been diagnosed as autistic. He was arrested after attacking his 80-year-old mother. Apparently he had been under considerable stress at work, and had tried, he said, to make his mother understand his problems. Finally, in desperation he had hit out at her. He insisted that 'she was not badly hurt . . . nothing broken . . . just a bit bruised', and that he had 'only shaken her about a bit'. He expected their lives to return to normal after her return from hospital and could not understand why it had been necessary for the police to be involved. His apparent lack of remorse led to criminal proceedings, his placement in a bail hostel, where he was very badly treated, and subsequently probation, which he greatly resented. He continues to believe that his mother will return to live with him, despite her removal into Social Services care many miles away, and remains bitter that so much should have been made of 'such a trivial incident'.

Obsessional pursuits

Sandy, a young woman who since a child had had an obsession with matches, had spent many years in a residential school. Staff there were well aware of the potential dangers of her obsession and ensured that matches were never available. Throughout school no problems occurred and eventually, in her late teens, she left to live with a foster family who cared for a number of other disabled people. After only a few days she found a box of matches, and set fire to the bed of another resident while he slept. Serious damage was caused and it was only with luck that no lives were lost. Sandy showed no remorse for her actions, and it was felt by all concerned that if she had access to matches on other occasions the same behaviour would occur. The only alternative was to remove her from the foster home to a unit where much greater supervision could be guaranteed but where access to 'normal living' was far more restricted.

Max, a boy in his mid-teens, became fascinated with reading accounts of death and destruction, and the Bible and stories of the holocaust in Nazi Germany occupied almost all his time. One night his parents awoke to the smell of gas and found the oven full on. He admitted he had done it 'to see what happened to people if they were gassed', but showed no intent to harm or any realisation that what he had done could cause death.

Obsessional pursuits also seem to have been involved in the case described by Mawson and colleagues. In his teens he is described as becoming 'girl-mad' and would carry around pictures of naked females, openly and without embarrassment. He once tried to strangle a girl 'because he had lost control of himself' and he developed 'a frank sexual interest in a female teacher', following her about and getting close to her at every possible opportunity. He was eventually admitted to Broadmoor.

Lack of social understanding

Louis, a young teenager, had great difficulties understanding facial expressions, particularly those of children. He would try to touch the faces of young children and if he felt a facial expression 'was not friendly', he was likely to become quite aggressive. Attempts to help him appreciate the danger of this behaviour, both for himself and others, failed, and after an attack on a young girl he was eventually placed in secure hospital care.

Eric, a youth of 18, tended to be badly teased by youngsters in his nearby town and would get very upset by this. His parents had grown used to him coming home and kicking doors and furniture when this happened. However, one night when they were not in he decided to kick the neighbour's car instead. This he did in full view of the owner, who was a policeman and who immediately arrested him.

Misuse by others

A particularly sad case was that of Darren, who had been thrown out of his home by his father at the age of 16 after being used by a local gang of youths as an unwitting agent in various petty thefts. He was placed in a Social Services hostel, where he seems to have suffered prolonged sexual abuse from other residents. On one occasion he ended up in hospital having been forcibly injected with drugs. Eventually he was arrested by the police following a robbery in which he had been made to drive the stolen goods away in a 'getaway vehicle' whilst the others disappeared. He was initially picked up because the car he was driving had no tax disc, no lights and *no bonnet*, but he was quite unaware that these deficits were bound to bring him to the attention of the police. Fortunately, one of the arresting officers, who had a relative with autism, suggested that he might be autistic, and psychiatric services were called. After the diagnosis of autism was made the case was dropped and Darren was finally returned home to his family.

Another example of the autistic person being vulnerable to abuse is also given in the chapter on employment. Jo was a young man who had worked in a jeweller's shop for some time and who was often trusted to lock up the safe at night. A new night-watchman, recognising Jo's innocence, simply asked him to hand over the keys one night. The resulting robbery led to his arrest as an 'accomplice' and although this charge was dropped he inevitably lost his job.

Rigid interpretation of rules

Jonathan, who had been working in an office for several years, lost his job after attacking a cloakroom attendant with his umbrella. She had given him the wrong ticket and he believed himself to be perfectly justified in acting in this manner as 'she was not doing her job properly'. Had he shown any remorse it is possible that he would have been given a formal warning but allowed to stay on. However, he was adamant that it was she who had 'broken the rules' and like many autistic people he was not able to recognise that even if he felt no remorse it might be useful at least to pretend.

APPROACHES TO INTERVENTION

The way in which dangerous or potentially criminal behaviours are dealt with will depend on individual circumstances and the underlying causes of the behaviour. If obsessional, social or communication deficits are at the root of the problems then these will need to be addressed in the manner suggested in earlier chapters. However, again, a few basic guidelines need to be remembered.

Begin early

In the discussion of obsessional and social problems in earlier chapters, emphasis was placed on the need to be aware of the possibility that behaviours that seem innocuous, innocent or even charming in young children may take on a very different perspective when adulthood is reached. Although figures are not available, clinical and anecdotal evidence suggests that many of the actions that lead people into trouble as they grow older are not new, but are simply developments of behaviours established in childhood.

Christopher was fascinated with copying words and pictures as a child. He became accomplished at copying other people's handwriting and his parents were quite proud of the way in which he could copy their signatures. By the age of 14 he had managed to open several bank and building society accounts in the local town and would cash money by forging his parents' signatures on cheques. He obtained several hundred pounds in this way, which, in turn, he used to feed his other obsession with railways and travelling. By the age of 15 he was totally beyond the control of his gentle but ineffective parents, and by 17 had been arrested on forgery charges.

Joey, mentioned in the chapter on obsessions, had had a fixation with washing machines since he was tiny. Having become used to wandering in and out of neighbours' houses he later widened his horizons and would enter any house where he heard a washing machine in action. The sight of a well-built, silent young stranger sitting on the kitchen floor on returning home is not one that most people expect, and after the police became involved his family had to try to keep him within sight as much as they could. This proved an almost impossible task for them, and greatly frustrating for him, and it was many months before the behaviour could be brought under control.

Inappropriate sexualised behaviours, resulting from obsessional interests, can also give rise to problems. Although many of these, such as touching women's tights or breasts, may be perceived as innocent enough in a 3-year-old, they may be viewed very differently in a 13-year-old, and could result in placement in prison or a special hospital by the age of 30.

Establish consistent rules

Awareness among carers of the potential dangers of such behaviours, and the imposition of appropriate limitations from an early age, could often prevent serious difficulties later. Without help, the autistic person will not be aware of the possible implications of his or her actions, nor their impact on other people, and, even with help, understanding may remain very limited. Prevention is by far the most effective strategy and instilling the basic rules of social behaviour from an early age is crucial. Teaching children to say 'No' if asked to do anything that they know is wrong is also important.

Although, as pointed out in previous chapters, rules do have their problems, it is generally better to establish firm rules in early childhood, which can then be relaxed, if appropriate, later. The imposition of new or stricter guidelines on adults is likely to prove very difficult and will almost certainly be much resented.

Social skills training

In some instances, additional training in social awareness may also offer help. In the case of the young man with an obsession with faces, described earlier, attempts were made to improve his ability to interpret facial expressions more accurately, and thereby to reduce his aggressive outbursts. Baron-Cohen (1988), in his account of the young man who regularly beat up his 71-year-old partner, also suggests that a social-cognitive approach to intervention may be of value.

While such suggestions seem promising, there are no long-term evaluations of the effectiveness of this approach and in some cases the profundity of the social impairment is such that attempts to improve social understanding are almost certain to be of limited effectiveness. Indeed, in some cases it may be necessary to ensure that the individual is no longer exposed to the situation in which the problems occur or that others are protected from the risk of danger – decisions that may have profound effects on personal liberty.

THE RESPONSE FROM THE CRIMINAL JUSTICE SYSTEM

A further important issue is the way in which serious or dangerous behaviours are handled by the police and the courts. Although individuals with mild learning difficulties are known to be a particularly vulnerable group (Clare and Gudjonsson, 1993), personal experience suggests that the judicial system is frequently very lenient towards those with obvious disabilities. Police responses to dangerous or illegal behaviours may be quite gentle and friendly, thereby inadvertently giving the message that the behaviour is not particularly serious. Indeed, a lift home in a police car following a misdemeanour may well prove a considerable incentive to repeat the action. If it is necessary for the police to be involved, perhaps following an aggressive attack on staff or peers, it is essential that the matter is dealt with formally and sternly, so that the individual concerned fully recognises the seriousness of his or her actions and is discouraged, as far as possible, from repeating these.

If court action is required, it is important that all involved are fully aware of the social and communication deficits of the individual with autism, and that an expert assessment is carried out to determine the extent of their problems, and the implications of these for management. The accused individual must also be given every help to understand what is happening as well as to appreciate the seriousness of their actions. The series of books written by Sheila Hollins can help prepare everyone involved for what will happen (Hollins, 1994; Hollins *et al.*, 1996). Very often an expert assessment will avoid the case coming to court, or will help to evade punitive action. However, in certain circumstances such assessments may conclude that, because of the lack of social awareness or the severity of obsessional behaviours (or a combination of the two), individuals are of such risk to themselves or others that a custodial sentence is deemed necessary.

Custodial treatment

Although custodial sentences are rare, if they should be considered necessary then, once again, it is crucial that all those involved in management are fully aware of the needs of someone with autism. Lack of social understanding, isolation, vulnerability to abuse, inappropriate behaviour, due either to failures of comprehension or obsessional tendencies, are all likely to single out the person with autism from other clients. For some, the set daily routine of secure establishments may well have benefits, but if treatment or therapy is offered they may be unable to make use of this. When Andrew was placed in a secure unit for 'sexual offending' (continually exposing himself in public, despite warnings), staff learned that he had been previously abused as a child. Group therapy, with similar victims, was arranged, but Andrew was unable to contribute to the group and was frequently disruptive. Another therapist realised that he was most willing to talk about his problems when alone in woodwork sessions and she had begun to make some progress with him. However, woodwork was considered a privilege, privileges were withdrawn because of his disruptiveness in the group, and hence his one opportunity to take advantage of therapy was effectively denied.

Unless an informed and flexible approach to management can be developed, what is meant to be, at least partly, a therapeutic regime can be highly punitive, and completely unproductive as far as someone with autism is concerned.

11 Problems with sexual relationships

The earlier chapter on social functioning explores the general difficulties that people with autism face in making social contacts. Failure to understand the nature of relationships, the skills required for developing these, or the rules governing interactions, can all cause difficulties, even in the most superficial of contacts. When sexual relationships are involved the problems may be even more profound.

FACTORS ASSOCIATED WITH SEXUAL PROBLEMS

Wanting to be like everyone else

Very naturally, for many adolescents and young adults, the desire for a sexual partner is extremely strong. These desires can be further heightened by the belief that 'everybody has a boy/girl friend' and that not to have one will make them appear even more unusual and unacceptable.

Gerald, a 22-year-old with mild learning difficulties, is constantly telling everyone how much he needs a girl friend as he has decided he has to get married by the age of 25 and 'time is running out'. He has little perception of his own role in this process, nor of the impact his problems are likely to have. His main concern is that his brother was married at 25, and he does not want to be 'outdone by him'.

The firm belief that everyone else has successful relationships, finds girl friends and gets married can lead to considerable dissatisfaction and frustration. It can be extremely difficult to convince young adults with autism that other people do manage to find fulfilment without intimate relationships; their view of everyone else living 'happily ever after' also proves remarkably resilient to factual information.

Even when individuals are more aware of their own limitations, the need to be loved and accepted is a very powerful force and there may well be a conflict between the desire for the comforts of intimacy and recognition of the problems that a close relationship would entail. Marion, a young woman in her twenties, had been very close to her mother and was devastated when her parents made the decision to move abroad for health reasons. She greatly misses the comfort that her mother had always provided, but at the same time admits that she could not cope with an intimate relationship with anyone else. She says, very seriously, 'I'd really like to find a gay man to be my friend, someone who I could talk to and cuddle sometimes, but without any risk of demands for a sexual relationship'.

Other individuals, such as Temple Grandin, have deliberately avoided intimate or sexual relationships because they find them far too confusing.

> She was celibate. Nor had she ever dated. She found such inter-actions completely baffling, and too complex to deal with.
> 'Have you cared for somebody else?', I asked her.
> She hesitated for a moment before answering, ' I think lots of times there are things that are missing from my life'.
>
> (Sacks, 1993)

Lack of social understanding

In autism, the complex skills required for developing and maintaining social, emotional or sexual relationships are often lacking. Because of this failure of understanding, attempts to acquire a partner are often extremely primitive and can sometimes lead to serious problems.

For example, it is not uncommon for young men with autism to get into trouble because of their tendency to approach any young women they see and ask if they would like to go out with them. In other cases approaches may be even less subtle. David, who had been attending a special college course, was sent home by the principal after a few weeks because he had begun exposing himself to female students. He had done this quite openly in front of a member of staff, with apparently no realisation that it was in any way likely to cause offence. Julian, who had recently left his all-boys school to attend college, was also suspended after he and a female student had been found having intercourse during the lunch break. Neither he nor the young woman concerned (who had quite severe learning disabilities) had made any attempt to stay hidden, much to the amusement of the other students. Knowing of his social difficulties, the principal warned him that such activities could not be tolerated, and that he would have to leave if he were found in similar circumstances again. The very same afternoon he was spotted with another female student, having apparently little understanding that the embargo applied to *all* females, not just the one he had met that morning.

Lack of emotional understanding

For other individuals it is not so much their lack of social under-standing that is the primary problem but their inability to cope with the emotional demands of a close relationship. Again, in his interview with Temple Grandin, Oliver Sacks questions her about love and sex:

'What do you imagine *falling in love* is like?', I asked.
'May be its like swooning – if not I don't know . . . I've never fallen in love . . . I don't know what it's like to rapturously fall in love . . . When I started holding the cattle I thought 'What's happening to me? Wondered if that was what love is . . . it wasn't intellectual any more.'
She is wistful about love, in a sense, but cannot imagine how it might be to feel passion for another person.

(Sacks, 1993)

Obsessions and infatuations

Even if overt sexual behaviours are not involved, other attempts to develop relationships can give rise to difficulties. Oliver, a young man of 20, became obsessed with the daughter of his father's company director. He began to follow her everywhere, telephoned her con-stantly and lay in wait for her outside her home whenever he had any free time. The police were called on several occasions and eventually a legal injunction was sought against him. Oliver refused to accept this, believing that, since the young woman used to speak to him kindly, she wanted a more intimate relationship with him. Because he refused to comply with the injunction, and showed absolutely no understanding of the serious nature of this offence, he was eventually admitted, on a compulsory Section, to a psychiatric hospital.

Social naivety

Problems can also arise if the person with autism is treated with particular sympathy or kindness. Roland, who was visiting his family in America, was delighted to find a young female cousin in California who was very demonstrative towards him. Feeling rather sorry for him, she would cuddle him and sit on his knee, telling him how sweet he was. The situation changed suddenly when her fiancé came home and her attentions were directed elsewhere. Roland continued to seek kisses and cuddles and in the end, because of the fiancé's displeasure, it was 'suggested' that he move on to visit another branch of the family. This he did, somewhat puzzled, but on his return to England was still convinced of her affection towards him. He wrote endless letters, most of which went unanswered. He was convinced that she would soon ask him to return and became increasingly despondent when she did not.

Because Anthony, a first-year university student, was recognised as having special problems, a female student was asked to 'befriend' him and offer help or support as necessary. Totally misinterpreting the motives behind her kindness, Anthony became convinced that she was in love with him and pursued her relentlessly, until staff were forced to intervene, much to his resentment and incomprehension.

This naivety can at times be exploited by other people. Daniel, working in a computer office, was told by other staff that the boss's daughter 'really fancied him'. They persuaded him that if he telephoned her several times a day she would eventually admit to her feelings. After a few phone calls of this kind Daniel found himself in serious trouble and it was only through his manager's intervention that he managed to keep his job.

Sexual vulnerability

In the case of many women with autism the problems often seem to be rather different in nature. Few attempt to pursue members of the opposite sex in the same way as men, but they can find themselves in unexpected difficulties because of their failure 'to read' the necessary social cues. Judy, a woman in her thirties, had a tendency to pour her heart out to anyone who would listen, giving intimate details of her past emotional, social and sexual life. On several occasions she had been happy to have men accompany her home in order that she could continue with her tales, but was then horrified if they made any sexual approaches. They, in turn, could become very unpleasant if they believed she had simply been 'leading them on'. No matter how she tried, she said, she could not work out whether people were trying to be sympathetic or wanting to exploit her, and she had reached the conclusion that it would be best for her never to talk to strangers again – a decision that would severely limit her social activities.

Janice, another young woman, was an expert swimmer and had absolutely no embarrassment about stripping off in public and in her rush to get into the swimming pool was quite likely to change into her costume with little attempt at modesty. Moreover, even if she were fully dressed, she had no hesitation in showing people her underwear or demonstrating bruises or marks anywhere on her body. Because she was physically attractive, such behaviours often gave very misleading signals to her instructors or other people using the pool.

Donna Williams (1992) also recounts the time when she had met a young man at the skating rink. After being walked home by him a few times he had kissed her and told her 'he wanted me to come and live with him one day'. Being rather tired of living at home, she piled her belongings into a taxi and arrived at his house.

'What!', he exclaimed in disbelief.
'You said you wanted me to live with you', I explained.
'One day, I said', he stressed.
Nevertheless I was there and that was that.'

Such naivety, of course, is not confined to women. Marcus, a man in his thirties, horrified his parents when he told them that he always went to a certain city pub after he left work, as the people there were so friendly. The pub was a well-known meeting place for gay men, but although there was no indication that he had been abused in any way, his parents insisted that he stopped going.

Sandy, a man in his thirties, was given a great deal of support from his cousin, who was homosexual. The cousin had never exploited this relationship in any way but on one occasion a friend of his made sexual advances towards Sandy, who complied with these. Later Sandy admitted that he had not wanted to do what was asked, nor had he found it a pleasant experience, but he had not liked to say 'No' for fear of upsetting his cousin.

Other unacceptable behaviours

In the case of less able people with autism it is often very difficult for carers to be fully aware of their sexual needs. Problems in this group are often related to behaviours such as masturbation in public, taking off clothes, touching others in an unacceptable way, or developing fierce attachments to particular members of staff. If not dealt with appropriately, behaviours of this kind can lead to exclusion from a wide range of activities; there may also be repercussions for other clients. Josh, for example, would go through phases when he seemed to masturbate almost constantly. After an incident at the local swimming pool, when he removed his pants in full view of a mothers' and toddlers' club, all the clients at his day unit were banned from using the pool. Paul had had a fascination with female breasts since he was tiny, and as a grown man he still continued to try to stroke any 'well-endowed' women. On a day trip to the beach he had wandered up to a couple of elderly women in swimming costumes and caused such a furore that the whole group had to leave rapidly.

Infatuations with particular individuals can also give rise to problems. Jenny, a young woman in her late teens, developed a marked attachment for one of her male careworkers at the centre. If he were not there for any reason, she would become extremely distressed and whenever she saw him would rush up and embrace him, attacking anyone who tried to remove her.

DEALING WITH PROBLEMS OF RELATIONSHIPS

Self-awareness

Despite the many difficulties that may be encountered, some autistic individuals, particularly those who are more able, do manage to develop effective coping strategies. However, these often involve *avoidance* of potential problems, rather than attempts to deal with them directly. Kanner, in his follow-up study, describes the types of rationalisations made by individuals to explain their lack of close relations. Activities such as dating were said to 'cost too much' or be 'a waste of money'. Another man said he felt that perhaps he 'ought to get married but can't waste money on a girl who is not serious'. Kanner notes, too, that many seemed to feel frightened by any intimacy and that there was a 'sense of relief' in being able to excuse themselves in this way. Oliver Sacks also describes Temple Grandin as choosing to avoid close relationships, rather than to deal with the confusion they would inevitably bring (Sacks, 1993).

Donna Williams's precipitate move into her boy friend's house led to both physical and sexual abuse and later she avoided sexual relationships. However, she was then horrified when close friendships, which to her had no sexual component, became more serious. Describing the point at which her friendship with a boy called Tim suddenly becomes much more intense on his part she writes: 'It was like a slap in the face . . . he had killed off the sense of security I had found in him in one fell swoop'.

Extending social contacts.

For individuals who are less aware, or less able to take control of their own lives, the most effective approaches to dealing with problems of a sexual nature are similar to those described in the chapter on more general social problems.

One important way of reducing feelings of isolation and rejection is to try to improve outside social contacts as far as possible. For many individuals, the opportunity to mix with people in their own age group, particularly if they include the opposite sex, can defuse the urgency for a close relationship. This focus on the opportunities to make *contacts* with other people, rather than directly on *relationships*, offers a much greater chance of enriching the quality of people's lives. Often the apparently overwhelming desire for 'a girl friend' can be substantially diminished as long as the individual concerned has contact with more people generally, and is encouraged to fill his time as usefully as possible. Social skills or self-help groups, such as 'Asperger's United' also play an important role here, in that even if the individuals concerned have few other contacts, they can at least relate to a small number of other people with similar problems and interests.

Avoiding potential problems in childhood

From the very earliest years avoidance of behaviours *that may give rise to later problems* is essential. Behaviours that in adults are regarded as sexually inappropriate or threatening, such as taking off clothes in public, or touching women's legs or breasts, may well have been condoned or encouraged when the child was young. Later these behaviours may continue, either because the child or adolescent has no perception of their social unacceptability or, conversely, because they become aware of the attention that inevitably ensues. It can be difficult to find a more effective way of getting attention, for example, than marching up to an elderly woman on the bus and fondling her breasts!

Firm and consistent limitations on behaviours of this kind in childhood are the most effective way of avoiding problems in future. Clear and unambiguous policies on dressing or undressing in public, topics that should not be discussed with strangers, rules on when and where to masturbate, should all be introduced as early as is appropriate for the individual concerned.

Sex education

This is often an aspect of growing up that tends to be overlooked for teenagers with autism. They are likely to learn little or nothing from their peer group (the source of most children's sexual knowledge) and parents tend to be occupied with too many other problems to devote time to this one. Nevertheless, because of their deficiencies in social understanding, sex education may be even more important for them than for other children. The problem is that the instructional methods or materials that are appropriate for normal youngsters may be worse than useless for children with autism. Many mothers, for example, can recount tales of their autistic child divulging the contents of a 'sex lesson' loudly and publicly in the middle of a crowded store or bus. Melone and Lettick (1983) describe a useful, straightforward and, above all, practical programme of sex education that has been used effectively with moderate to more severely impaired clients in a residential setting in America. This focuses on obvious topics such as the identification of body parts, dealing with menstruation and masturbation, aspects of personal hygiene, and appropriate social behaviours, ranging from how to relate to strangers and familiar adults to dressing appropriately or using public lavatories. The programme also covers issues such as physical examinations, so that if routine health checks, for example, are required, the student knows what is expected and how to cope.

For those with greater independence, some of the sex education programmes that have been developed for use with people with more general learning disabilities may be used or adapted to meet the needs of the autistic individual. Many different books and resource packs are available and individual choice will determine which are used. Most attempt to teach students to recognise when behaviours are acceptable or not, when they might be in a vulnerable situation and need to say 'no', as well as basic information about preventing disease or unwanted pregnancy. A potentially useful package is that developed by Ann Craft and members of the Nottingham Severe Learning disability sex education project (1985). *Sexuality and Mental Handicap* by Hilary Dixon is another useful source of teaching ideas and strategies (1990). The topics covered in these manuals include recognition and awareness of body parts, menstruation and the menopause, masturbation, sexual relationships (including how to say 'No'), and sexual health, using contraceptives, and avoiding the risk of AIDs and other infections. Most importantly, however, the manuals are set firmly within the context of developing other social skills, such as improving self-esteem, making decisions, understanding social roles, making friends, and dealing with emotional feelings generally. They are accompanied by video and photographic aids and include helpful exercises involving role-play, group discussions, practical advice and problem-solving, many of which could well be suitable for people with autism. They also provide detailed and useful bibliographies.

However, when working with people with autism it will also be necessary to help them develop awareness of areas with which non-autistic students of similar intellectual levels usually have relatively little difficulty. *Why* certain behaviours, such as following people or removing clothes in public, may offend or frighten others; *what* other people will think of them if they do; *what* unwanted consequences may follow; all these will need to be made clear and explicit.

Teaching of this kind should, ideally, be offered on an individual basis but it is also crucial that the fundamental rules be endorsed by everyone involved. If parents, staff and other carers keep consistently to the same guidelines, then it will be much easier for the person with autism to learn what is required, and what behaviours are or are not acceptable.

It is also necessary to ensure that the rules *continue* to be reinforced. A single lesson or even a course of 'sex education' is unlikely to have a significant impact on future behaviours. Instead rules must continue to be made explicit whenever the situation warrants. It is important, too, to expect that mistakes will occur from time to time. Instead of despairing when this happens, such occasions can be used as practical teaching sessions. Indeed, these may prove much more effective than abstract instructions. For example, after Josh was barred from the swimming pool for masturbating, he became much more aware of the likely consequences of this in the future and the problem showed some reduction. Geraldine, a young teenager with a tendency to strip off all her clothes, also showed a reduction in the frequency of this behaviour when it resulted in her being temporarily banned from her favourite activity, horse riding.

Improving the general quality of life

As is the case in dealing with many other social difficulties, a crucial aspect of any intervention programme is to improve the quality of life generally. Explaining to an adolescent youth that sexual relationships are not necessary for happiness and that many people live fulfilled and happy celibate lives is not likely to have a great impact, unless satisfaction can be gained in other ways. As well as making rules and regulations, it is important to increase alternative leisure activities as far as possible, especially those that offer the opportunity for meeting other people. Clubs for people with disabilities, as well as mainstream activities suited to the individual's own special skills or interests, can prove remarkably helpful. Rupert, a man in his early forties, eventfully joined a silverwork class, and found he had a real gift in this area. He says he finds the activity 'far more therapeutic than going to see a psychiatrist' and because of the attention he gets from the rest of the class his oft-stated wish 'to find a good woman who will look after me' now seems to have subsided. John, a teenager whose pursuit of female companions led to his exclusion from a number of local clubs, eventually enrolled in karate classes in which he did extremely well. Again, the admiration he obtained from other members of the group seemed to diffuse his previously over-riding goal of 'getting a girl friend'.

For less able individuals, too, attention to the daily programme may have far greater impact on the frequency of unacceptable behaviours than any attempts at direct intervention. Observational studies, even of highly specialist and well-staffed units, often reveal that life for those attending or living in them is remarkably bleak (Murphy and Clare, 1991). Under these conditions of deprivation it is not surprising that behaviours such as masturbation, tearing or stripping off clothing, or even sexual harassment of others occurs. An individually designed timetable, with attention to the structure of each part of every day, can be a crucial factor in reducing difficulties. Focus needs to be placed on the whole life of the individual, not on specific 'undesirable' behaviours, which may well be indicators of deprivation and understimulation.

DEALING WITH SEXUAL ABUSE

It is generally acknowledged that there is an increased risk of sexual abuse towards individuals with disabilities of any kind (Tharinger, Horton and Millea, 1990). People with autism, who may look perfectly normal but are lacking in the most rudimentary understanding of social interactions, may be particularly vulnerable. The strategies described in this chapter and elsewhere, of developing appropriate 'rules' of social behaviour from an early age, and teaching individuals to 'say no' to suggestions they know to be wrong, can help to reduce these risks a little. However, if abuse does occur, it may be very difficult for someone with autism to explain what has happened, or to prevent its re-occurrence, and even more difficult for them to talk about their feelings of distress. Often the only indication that abuse has occurred may be a sudden or marked deterioration in the individual's behaviour or mood. Establishing exactly what has happened or who the perpetrator might be can pose almost insurmountable problems. Howlin and Clements (1995) discuss ways in which the trauma resulting from abuse (physical as well as sexual) may be better recognised, but even if abuse is suspected it may be almost impossible to prove. The picture books designed by Sheila Hollins for people with learning disabilities can be helpful in exploring some of the practical and emotional issues surrounding abuse, but professional help should always be sought in such circumstances. If abuse has occurred, counselling techniques developed for people with learning disabilities may help to minimise the inevitable confusion and distress. If, as is often the case, firm evidence is lacking, efforts may have to concentrate instead on ensuring that the environment is as safe and secure as possible. Because the person with autism may be unable to tell what has happened, or to prevent it happening again, the onus of protection lies entirely in the hands of carers, and this responsibility should never be treated lightly.

12 Fostering independence

VARIABILITY OF OUTCOME

As discussed in the initial chapters of this book, the outcome for people with autism or Asperger syndrome is extremely variable. Some may spend all their lives in educational and residential accommodation with other autistic individuals. Others may go through university, find jobs and even marry. Innate linguistic and cognitive skills are major factors in influencing outcome, with good intellectual and language skills being the most important predictors of outcome. However, these alone are not enough. In order to optimise potential abilities, continuing help will be needed in order to minimise the impact of social and communication deficits, to reduce the negative impact of ritualistic behaviours, and to maximise the value of obsessional interests or special skills. Previous chapters have indicated the strategies that can be used to improve functioning in these areas and suggested ways in which occupational and educational facilities can be modified to enhance skills and modify deficits.

There are a number of other aspects, not previously addressed, that are also important for outcome.

CHANGING EXPECTATIONS AND ATTITUDES

Jim Sinclair, a man with autism, writing in the book *High Functioning Individuals with Autism* (Schopler and Mesibov, 1992), notes: 'In May of 1989, I drove 1,200 miles to the 10th annual TEACCH conference, where I learned that autistic people can't drive'. Although well aware of his own deficits he describes how people with autism may be held back by the mistaken expectations and assumptions of others – 'assumptions [that] are usually much more resistant to learning than my ignorance'.

Whilst it is important to avoid excessive demands, or to have unrealistic expectations of what people with autism can achieve, undervaluing their potential ability can do equal damage. Donna Williams, now a successful writer, and Temple Grandin, a psychologist with an international reputation, both recall that as children they were considered as 'crazy' or 'stupid'. Given the right help and support, and encouragement to use their particular gifts, both eventually flourished, although for Donna, who received much less understanding from family and teachers, the journey was far more slow and painful.

The balance between under- and over-pressurising can be a difficult one to achieve, but can be helped by thorough assessments of the individual's skills and deficits. Language and IQ tests alone are not sufficient (although they may be crucial in changing approaches to individuals who have been mistakenly regarded as 'backward' or 'retarded') and it is important to be aware that different tests may produce very different estimates of ability. Temple Grandin (1992), for instance, describes how although she scored at the ceiling of certain tasks, she performed at only average levels or below on those requiring speed of processing or symbolic functioning. Assessments of social functioning and levels of behavioural disturbance are also required before any conclusions about potential abilities or appropriate placements can be made.

LACK OF SELF-DRIVE AND INITIATIVE

At a recent meeting for people with Asperger syndrome in London, organised by the National Autistic Society, it was suggested that some of the individuals there might make their own arrangements to meet on a regular basis, without the facilitation of Society staff. The suggestion was greeted with much incredulity. 'You should know', said one young man, a university student who had contributed actively to the day, 'that you might as well ask us to go to the moon'.

This might sound over-dramatic and exaggerated, but in fact problems of drive and self-motivation characterise many people with autism, and in some cases can severely limit progress. Even Temple Grandin describes how dependent she was on her mother and governess for developing her early abilities and on gifted and experienced teachers for teaching her to make the best use of her skills in school and college. 'Passive approaches', she asserts, 'don't work'!

Again, whilst it is important to avoid over-dependence on parents or teachers, unless the push for action, for achievement, for success comes from other people it is unlikely to emerge spontaneously. Just as those who are least able will, if left to themselves, spend their time in stereotyped and ritualistic activities, so those who are more gifted will do little to utilise their gifts unless directed how to do so.

It is important to recognise that this somewhat didactic approach sits rather uneasily within the current philosophy of care for people with disabilities. Normalisation principles of 'choice' and 'self-direction' may help many individuals with learning difficulties to mature and flourish. For someone with autism they may prove a major handicap. Clara Park (1992) describes how her daughter made no use of her exceptional drawing skills for many years. Only when she was given small amounts of money for each picture did her interest revive. It was not even that the money meant much to her, 'but numbers did, and she liked to see them rise in her checkbook'.

In order to be able to exercise choice, individuals must have access to several options; in the case of people with autism it may well be necessary for families or carers to help them experience, first, what these options are.

FLEXIBILITY OF PROVISION

The need for flexible and individualised teaching arrangements in order to maximise opportunities in later life has been discussed in earlier chapters. Flexibility of living arrangements in adulthood is also important if individuals are to be given the chance to mature at their own pace. The follow-up studies described in Chapter 2 indicate how few young adults are ready to leave home and live independently as soon as they finish school or college, and even the most able will need some years of continuing support before they are able to cope alone. In the London-based study (Goode, Howlin and Rutter, in preparation) of 74 adults over the age of 21, only 4 lived independently and 4 in semi-sheltered accommodation. One-third continued to live with their parents, whilst 50 per cent were in residential care of some kind (see Figure 12.1).

The following scenarios give examples of different types of provision and the success or failure of these, depending on the ability of the individuals concerned and the amount of support offered.

Autistic communities

In the 1960's and 1970's autistic communities offered the chance of a new life for many young adults who, otherwise, would have had little

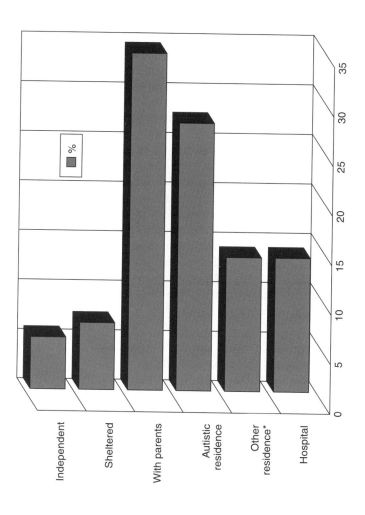

Figure 12.1 Living arrangements followed-up by Goode and colleagues (percentage in different placements)
Note: 'Other residence' includes communities such as Steiner or Home Farm Trust.

option but to go into hospital care. Such provision proved invaluable for many individuals and their families, offering for the first time environments that were uniquely able to cater for the needs of people with autism. The focus was on structured environments that could enable the young adult to continue to grow socially and emotionally, whilst at the same time minimising behavioural disturbance. Generally there would be a few houses on one site, with up to 30 or 40 autistic residents in total. Many were sited in extensive grounds in the countryside, offering opportunities for working in quiet horticultural settings. Examples are Somerset Court in southern England, some of the TEACCH centres in North Carolina, Benhaven in Massachusetts, and Bittersweet Farms in Ohio. (See the special issue of *Journal of Autism and Developmental Disorders*, volume 20, number 3, 1990 for more details.)

In recent years, however, there has been a swing away from facilities of this kind – partly because of their size but mostly because of their isolation from ordinary community life. The possible disruption of family ties is also an issue. Gregory was a young man who had lived all his life in a small inner-city apartment with his mother and sister. On leaving his school for autistic children he moved to a community for autistic adults almost two hundred miles away, in the middle of the countryside. His parents have no car and little money for the trains and taxis required to visit him. Although they remain devoted to their son, as they have grown older visits have become more and more difficult and can now take place only two or three times a year.

Small group homes for people with autism

Because of such problems, the next logical move was to provide specialist housing for people with autism, but in normal community settings, with opportunities to develop links with local work and leisure facilities and to maintain family ties. Again, the TEACCH organisation in North Carolina was at the forefront of such developments, which have now spread to other states and to Europe.

For a significant number of people with autism they offer many advantages and a great sense of security, as well as enabling them to develop new contacts outside. Even so, they are not without their difficulties. Because of their small size staffing can be a problem; the organisational structure may be too loose to allow the development of consistent management strategies; and staff may lack the skills to deal with more complex problems. Anthony, a young man with a degree in mathematics, was admitted to a new group home for people with Asperger syndrome. The staff there had all previously worked with autistic clients, but were not particularly familiar with the needs of this more able group. Anthony, who had previously lived with his father, resented attempts to direct his activities and there were also tensions between him and another resident. She would deliberately provoke him when no-one was around and he would respond by smashing crockery. Although no-one was ever hurt, and despite the fact that his outbursts only occurred when he was distressed, he was warned that no further incidents would be tolerated. Some months later, goaded beyond endurance, he smashed another cup and was immediately told to leave.

With adequate training and support for staff, and access to a wide range of educational, occupational and leisure facilities within the community, problems of this kind need not arise, and for many people with autism such provision offers the best opportunities for continuing development. However, because facilities of this kind are relatively expensive, places remain limited and are currently available to only a minority of people with autism.

'Mixed' communities or group homes

The criticism that people with autism are unlikely to provide each other with the opportunities needed to foster social development seems, on the surface, reasonable enough. However, there is little evidence to support the view that simply mixing with non-autistic disabled individuals will enhance social functioning. Nevertheless, there is often considerable pressure from social services to 'integrate' people with autism into small group homes. This is obviously a much cheaper option than providing specialist autistic provision, but the lack of structure, poor understanding by staff, emphasis on group activities, inadequate or inappropriate daily programmes and often lack of space can result in major problems.

Occasionally, however, even this type of provision may meet the needs of someone with autism. Brendan was a young man who had became very disturbed in a large unit for people with learning disabilities. He had been transferred to a small group home and, although staff knew little about autism, they recognised his need for isolation and routine. His day, although not particularly well structured, was at least predictable, and he was 'befriended' in the house by two middle-aged women residents who took it upon themselves to look after him, checked that he did some routine chores and were not in the least disturbed by his obsessional behaviours. The lack of pressure resulted in a marked reduction in stress and anxiety and after a while Brendan was able to regain some of the skills he had formerly lost.

Larger communities such as those run by the Home Farm Trust, Camp Hill, or other Steiner organisations may also be able to offer a supportive environment for some people with autism. The calm atmosphere, variety of activities, and sense of space can be very beneficial and, because residents have a mixture of different disabilities, there may be more opportunity for social interactions.

On the whole, however, residential placements of this kind will work well only if staff take seriously the need to understand the special problems of people with autism, are willing to adapt the environment to meet these needs, and can offer an appropriate degree of support and structure. It is also important to be aware that positive relationships with other residents rarely develop spontaneously, although, with time and effort, these can be gradually fostered.

Living at home

Because of lack of, or dissatisfaction with, available provision, many adults with autism continue to be dependent on their parents long after most young people would have left home. Although such arrangements may have short-term advantages, in the long term they can prove destructive for all concerned. Over-dependency can foster resentment and numerous relationship problems. It may restrict family life to an unacceptable degree. And, even if the arrangement is successful, it will not be possible for this to continue for ever.

George was a man in his forties whose attempts to move into sheltered accommodation had always terminated after a few weeks. At the slightest problem his parents would suggest he move back home again, but once he was there all would resume their chronic pattern of arguments, nagging and manipulation.

In contrast, Jenny lived happily with her 75-year-old mother, and they were a mutual source of companionship to each other. Although Jenny had a part-time job, her mother did all the cooking and housework, and at the age of 35 Jenny could neither make a cup of tea nor use a washing machine. Tragically her mother died suddenly of a heart attack, leaving her daughter entirely alone and unable to cope. Social Services, who had had no previous contact with the family, had to try to find her somewhere to live but without any knowledge of her special needs, organising a suitable placement proved extremely difficult.

Susie's parents had refused to let her go away from home after a brief and disastrous stay in a residential unit at the age of 20. As the years went on she became more and more obsessional; self-stimulatory and self-injurious behaviours increased and it was impossible to leave her alone at any time. Although Social Services offered some financial support, her parents have only a few hours of help a week at home and, as the years go by, although they are virtually housebound and becoming increasingly anxious about what will happen when they die, they still cannot bear to let her go.

Brien also lived with his elderly mother after his father died. His father had always insisted that Brien 'would never go into a home' and that his brothers or sisters would ultimately take care of him, a wish that none of them dared to contradict. However, his mother was much more realistic and began to arrange for brief periods of respite care in a nearby group home. Brien began to enjoy his weekends away, and gradually spent longer periods there each week. As his mother became more infirm he was able to move into the new home without distress, developing a close relationship with several staff. When his mother eventually died, not only was Brien well settled, but he was surrounded by people whom he knew and trusted and who could offer him the consolation and counselling he needed.

Independent living

This does not necessarily mean living entirely alone, and indeed many people with autism may never be able to cope without some degree of help and support. However, a range of possible options are available. Matthew lived with his widowed mother until he was in his thirties but she then decided that he must become more independent. She bought him a small flat a few streets away, where, initially, he just spent his weekends. As time went on he began to sleep there during the week, and gradually started to eat a few meals alone. His mother has built up a network of 'friends' and supporters for him locally, and although she continues to be very involved, she now feels that if she were to die he would be able to cope with this additional support. Gerald's parents knew that they would have to leave London because of health problems, but before they left they worked together with their son and local services to find him somewhere to live. Accommodation was provided by an organisation that supports people needing rehabilitation (for example, after a psychiatric illness). Although he has an independent apartment, a warden is available to check that all is well, and if problems arise these can be quickly dealt with. Gerald's parents remained living close by for a year or two after he moved, but were then able to move to the country without further difficulty.

Daniel, a 30-year-old clerk, was not felt capable of living in a flat of his own, but a charitable organisation run by the church provided a bed-sitter in a house for residents with other disabilities. Residents are taught to cook and care for themselves, as well as to co-operate in necessary group activities, such as cleaning and shopping. A 'support tenant' lives on-site to provide help if necessary. After ten years here Daniel is now looking for a flat of his own.

Although *gradually* increasing independence by such means is desirable, this may not always be possible. Although she was highly intelligent, Anna had always lived at home with her mother and was very dependent on her for all her needs. When her mother died suddenly Social Services became involved, although they had never previously been aware of her needs. They found her a tiny flat, helped her to furnish this, and taught her basic cooking, shopping and cleaning. Surprisingly she coped very well but as they became aware of her social isolation and vulnerability, a key worker was allotted to 'call in' every few days and keep a check on possible problems. This degree of supervision was neither expensive nor time-consuming but, because it was offered *before* problems arose, has undoubtedly helped to prevent major difficulties.

The road to independence can also be helped by recently developed 'supported living' schemes. These are designed to allow people with disabilities to choose where and with whom they will live, and, with help, to negotiate the package of support they will need in order to achieve independence. This may involve help with finances, shopping, domestic arrangements or travel; access to work, training or leisure opportunities; counselling or emotional support. Financial support is provided through statutory benefits and a number of agencies can now offer assistance with supported living schemes of this kind. A summary of such a scheme is provided by Bob Lowndes (1994) and further details can be obtained from local Social Services. Morgan (1996) also describes plans for an out-reach scheme to enable people with autism to live in homes of their own.

LETTING GO

As the above examples indicate, there is no one ideal form of provision for people with autism. Different environments will be needed to suit different needs; not only is there a need for a wide range of provision but it should also be possible for individuals to change their living environments as their needs or skills change.

A few basic guidelines can help to ensure that the transition from home to other accommodation is accomplished as smoothly and with as little disturbance as possible.

- Plans for adult life should be made as early as possible, preferably by the mid-late teens. In order to help the transition from home, respite provision should be provided, if appropriate, from an early age. This will enable the individual and his or her family to get used to separations, as well as providing a welcome break.
- There should be NO expectations that other family members will take on the role of caring for the person with autism when parents die. No matter how willing they may be when younger, changing circumstances can make this impossible as they grow older; and expectations of this kind will only generate unnecessary guilt, and possibly resentment.
- Social Services MUST be made aware of the individual's potential need for care from an early stage. Usually this is not a problem in the case of those who are more handicapped and have always needed special provision. However, if someone has been through mainstream education, perhaps gone to university and had a job, it can be very difficult to persuade hard-pressed Social Services that, in their mid-twenties, they suddenly need special support or accommodation. Thus, even if there seems to be little reason to request help in the foreseeable future, it is important that the *potential need* is formally recognised.
- Develop additional support networks. Somewhat paradoxically it is often most difficult to provide very able people with the help they need. Specialist provision is rarely appropriate, but living alone they are at risk of being very isolated, and may be vulnerable to abuse, and prone to depression. If parents are alive and well they will generally be able to help out if problems occur. If they are not available this role will need to be taken on by others. Again, Social Services support should be enlisted well before problems emerge. Charitable or religious groups, or other family members, may also be able to offer ongoing help, as long as the basic support systems are already well established. Encouraging activities and interests outside the home can also help to ensure against loneliness and isolation.

MARRIAGE AND CHILDREN

Problems related to marriage or having children will not apply to most people with autism. However, some do develop long-term relationships and a few get married. Often such relationships develop through family contacts, or via religious groups, but as with any relationship, having common interests is clearly an essential ingredient. Unintrusive support from families can also help, especially when there are practical problems.

Jonas met his wife at the church group they both attended, and other members were keen to foster the relationship between two people who clearly had mild disabilities. Jonas's mother, however, was always critical of his wife's family and when their marriage finally broke down, Jonas admitted that this constant criticism, and the fact that his wife had been unable to share in his love of music in any way, were amongst the major reasons for the breakdown.

There is little information on how many people with autism do get married, or how often such marriages are successful. Because of the genetic nature of the disorder, it is not unusual for mothers of autistic children to describe very similar characteristics in their own partners. Often the extent of difficulties is not recognised until well into the marriage, and problems generally arise because of obsessionality or lack of emotional attachment or understanding. In many such cases the women were often attracted by the man's intelligence or gentleness. One woman admitted to marrying because her partner's *lack* of emotionality was such a relief after the tempestuous emotional characteristics of her own father and brothers.

There are few accounts of people with autism having children, but when this does happen grandparents tend to play a major role in ensuring all goes well. Again, the genetic nature of autism means there is clearly an increased risk that a parent with this condition may well have an affected child. What the exact risks are are unclear, but in fact those adults who do contemplate having children tend to be discouraged more by the practical problems involved; child-rearing is difficult at the best of times, but for someone with the social, communication and obsessional problems associated with autism the difficulties may be insurmountable. If counselling is sought on this matter, the practical and genetic implications of such a decision will need to be given equal weight.

DEVELOPING OTHER SOCIAL NETWORKS

For most individuals with autism marriage will not be a feasible option but that does not mean that life should be lonely and without interests. Sport and other leisure activities can be an important source of interpersonal contacts, and social interactions often develop more easily if built around specific activities that require co-operation and sharing. More able people with autism can be encouraged to make use of local sports clubs or special-interest groups; for those who are less able, sporting activities may need to be carefully modified, but can lead to impressive gains in independence and social interactions. (See Evans, 1995 for programmes especially adapted to meet the needs of people with autism.)

For many, church or religious groups can also provide much-needed support and social contacts. They offer the opportunity to be with other people, but in a relatively structured, protective and predictable environment, with a common source of interest. More able adults often express their relief at feeling they can trust people within the church group in a way they cannot do outside and clearly feel much more at ease in these surroundings. For those who are less able, church groups may also prove more tolerant than society as a whole. Diana's constant chanting was quite accepted by the Jehovah's Witness congregation, which she attended each week, and in her calmer moments they would also invite her to play the piano, much to her and her parents' delight.

However, it is also important to be aware of the potential vulnerability of someone with autism to the blandishments of more obscure sects. Unscrupulous use by extreme pressure groups can also be a risk. Janice, who loved animals, became involved in a local anti-vivisectionist organisation and was so distressed by their propaganda that she began to give them all her money. Despite the fact that she rapidly got into serious debt, it proved very difficult for her family to persuade her to discontinue her membership. The family was also very concerned that she might become involved in the violent protests that tended to be the hallmark of this group.

FINANCIAL SUPPORT

Finally, whatever plans for living, daily occupation or leisure are formulated, the one sure thing is that these will require financial support. For anyone with a disability, resources are likely to be very limited and this may well restrict their opportunities to make use of the facilities that are available. Again, Social Services can be a crucial source of information about the various benefits that may be available. Citizens' Advice Bureaux are also invaluable sources of advice. Among the benefits that may be available are those listed in the chapter on employment. Other potential sources of finance may come from the Invalid Care Allowance, Housing Benefit, Council Tax Benefit, the Social Fund (financed by the Rowntrees organisation) and help for those with severe mobility problems. Further details can be obtained from the National Autistic Society booklet *Claiming What's Yours* (1995). The Society can also advise those wishing to draw up wills or trust documents in order to protect the financial interests of someone with autism.

CONCLUSIONS

Although, in the course of this book, much has been written about the problems faced by individuals with autism and those caring for them, it is also clear that such difficulties are not necessarily insurmountable. Despite sometimes overwhelming odds, many individuals with autism have managed to achieve a great deal in their lives. In far too many cases, however, these achievements have been attained with very little professional support or guidance. In recent years experimental and research studies have greatly increased our understanding of the 'enigma' that is autism. If, in the future, such knowledge can be used to influence practice more widely, then the outlook for all those affected by this condition may be more positive. Thus, growing awareness of the communication and social deficits of young children with autism should result in the development of more appropriate and relevant teaching strategies. In particular, recognition of the need to encourage *functional* communication skills, at whatever level of competence is appropriate, may help to reduce the myriad of problems that result from impairments in understanding and communication. Early training in social skills, and in the ability to understand how others think, feel or believe, may also have a long-term impact on individuals' acceptance into society. Also, support and advice for families, *from the earliest years*, on how to minimise the impact of obsessional and ritualistic behaviours, may avoid the development of seriously disruptive behaviour patterns later.

However, in order to implement such strategies there needs to be much greater acknowledgement of the need to make professional and educational support available *before* problems become apparent. Once disruptive or inappropriate patterns of functioning are established, they can become extremely difficult to change. Thus, intervention in early childhood, to prevent or minimise the emergence of difficulties resulting from social, communication and ritualistic problems, may have a major impact on the quality of life in later years. Financial support for early prevention is, in the long term, likely to prove far more cost-effective than crisis management in later life, and certainly, as far as autism is concerned, a focus on the prevention of problems will undoubtedly be more productive than fruitless searches for cures.

References

Abramson, R.K., Wright, H.H., Cuccara, M.L., Lawrence, L.G., Babb, S., Pencarinha, D., Marstella, F., and Harris E.C. (1992). Biological liability in families with autism. *Journal of the American Academy of Child and Adolescent Psychiatry*, 31, 370–371.

Akuffo E., MacSweeney D. A. and Gajwani A. K. (1986). Multiple pathology in a mentally handicapped individual. *British Journal of Psychiatry*, 149, 377–378.

Alvin J. and Warwick A. (1991). *Music Therapy for the Autistic Child*, 2nd edn. New York. Oxford University Press.

American Psychiatric Association (1980). *Diagnostic and Statistical Manual of Mental Disorders (DSM-III)*, 3rd edn. Washington DC. APA.

American Psychiatric Association (1994). *Diagnostic and Statistical Manual of Mental Disorders (DSM-IV)*, 4th edn. Washington DC. APA.

Andreasen N. C. (1979). The scale for the assessment of negative symptoms (SANS): conceptual and historical foundations. *British Journal of Psychiatry*, 155 (Suppl. 7), 59–62.

Asperger H. (1944). Autistic psychopathy in childhood. Translated and annotated by U. Frith (Ed.), in *Autism and Asperger Syndrome* (1991), Cambridge. Cambridge University Press.

Attwood T., Frith U. and Hermelin B. (1988). The understanding and use of interpersonal gestures by autistic and Down's syndrome children. *Journal of Autism and Developmental Disorders*, 18, 241–257.

Autisme Europe (1988). *Proceedings of the International Conference on Autism*. Hamburg.

Ayres J.A. (1979). *Sensory Integration and the Child*. Los Angeles. Western Psychology Service.

Baron-Cohen S. (1988). Assessment of violence in a young man with Asperger's Syndrome. *Journal of Child Psychology and Psychiatry*, 29, 351–360.

Baron-Cohen S. (1995). *Mindblindness: An Essay on Autism and Theory of Mind*. Cambridge, Massachusetts. The MIT Press.

Baron-Cohen S. and Howlin P. (1993). The theory of mind deficit in autism: Some questions for teaching and diagnosis. In S. Baron-Cohen., H. Tager-Flusberg and D. J. Cohen (Eds.), *Understanding Other Minds: Perspectives from Autism*, (pp.466–481). Oxford. Oxford University Press.

Baron-Cohen S., Tager-Flusberg H. and Cohen D. J. (Eds.) (1993). *Understanding Other Minds: Perspectives from Autism.* Oxford. Oxford University Press.

Bartak L. and Rutter M. (1978). Differences between mentally retarded and normally intelligent autistic children. *Journal of Autism and Childhood Schizophrenia*, 6, 109–120.

Beck A. T. (1976). *Cognitive Therapy and the Emotional Disorders.* New York. International Universities Press.

Bemporad J. R. (1979). Adult recollections of a formerly autistic child. *Journal of Autism and Developmental Disorders*, 9, 179–197.

Bender L. and Faetra G. (1972). The relationship between childhood and adult schizophrenia. In A. R. Kaplin (Ed.), *Genetic Factors in Schizophrenia*, Springfield, Illinois. C. C. Thomas.

Bernal J. (1994). Psychiatric illness in learning disability (unpublished article St George's Hospital Medical School), London University.

Biersdorff K. (1994). Incidence of significantly altered pain experience among individuals with developmental disabilities. *American Journal on Mental Retardation*, 98, 619–631.

Biklen D. (1990). Communication unbound: autism and praxis. *Harvard Educational Review*, 60, 291–315.

Bishop D.V.M. (1994). Developmental disorders of speech and language. In M. Rutter, E. Taylor and L. Hersov (Eds.), *Child and Adolescent Psychiatry: Modern Approaches*, Oxford: Blackwell.

Bolton P., Macdonald H., Pickles A., Rios P., Goode S., Crowson M., Bailey A. and Rutter M. (1994). A case-controlled family history study of autism. *Journal of Child Psychology and Psychiatry*, 35, 877–900.

Bondy A. and Frost L. (1995). Educational approaches in pre-school: Behavior techniques in a public school setting. In E. Schopler and G. B. Mesibov (Eds.), *Learning and Cognition in Autism*, Current Issues in Autism. New York. Plenum Press.

Bowler D. M., Stromm E. and Urquhart L. (1993). Elicitation of first order 'theory of mind' in children with autism. Unpublished ms, Department of Psychology, City University, London.

Brady M. P., Shores R. E., McEvoy M.A., Ellis D. and Fox J. J. (1987). Increasing social interactions of severely handicapped autistic children. *Journal of Autism and Developmental Disorders*, 17, 375–390.

Bregman J. D. (1991). Current developments in the understanding of mental retardation. Part II: Psychopathology. *Journal of the American Academy of Child and Adolescent Psychiatry*, 30, 861–872.

Brown W. H. and Odom S. L. (1991). Strategies and tactics for promoting generalization and maintenance of young children's social behaviour. *Research in Developmental Disabilities*, 12, 99–118.

Campbell M. and Cueva J. E. (1995). Psychopharmacology in child and adolescent psychiatry. A review of the past seven years. Part I. *Journal of the American Academy of Child and Adolescent Psychiatry*, 34, 1124–1132.

Cesaroni L. and Garber M. (1991). Exploring the experience of autism through first-hand accounts. *Journal of Autism and Developmental Disorders*, 21, 303–314.

Chesterman P. and Rutter S. C. (1994). A case report: Asperger's syndrome and sexual offending. *Journal of Forensic Psychiatry*, 4, 555–562.

Chock P. N. and Glahn T. J. (1983). Learning and self-stimulation in mute and echolalic children. *Journal of Autism and Developmental Disorders*, 14, 365–381.

Chung S. Y., Luk, F. L. and Lee E. W. H. (1990). A follow-up study of infantile autism in Hong Kong. *Journal of Autism and Developmental Disorders*, 20, 221–232.

Clare I. C. G. and Gudjonsson G. H. (1993). Interrogative suggestibility, confabulation, and acquiesence in people with mild learning disabilities (mental handicap): implications for reliability during police interrogations. *British Journal of Clinical Psychology*, 32, 295–301.

Clarke D. J. (1996). Psychiatric and behavioural problems and pharmacological treatments. In H. Morgan *Adults with Autism*. Cambridge. Cambridge University Press.

Clarke D. J., Littlejohns C. S., Corbett J. A. and Joseph S. (1989). Pervasive developmental disorders and psychoses in adult life. *British Journal of Psychiatry*, 155, 692–699.

Clements J. (1987). *Severe Learning Disability and Psychological Handicap*. Chichester. John Wiley and Sons.

Coleman M. (1992). Pharmacological therapies. In C. Gillberg (Ed.), *Diagnosis and Treatment of Autism* (pp. 257–270). New York. Plenum Press.

Craft A. (1985). *Living Your Life: A Sex Education and Personal Development Programme for Students with Severe Learning Disabilities*. Cambridge. Learning Development Aids.

Creak M. (1963). Childhood psychosis: A review of 100 cases. *British Journal of Psychiatry*, 109, 84–89.

Dahl B. (1976). A follow-up study of a child psychiatric clientele with special regard to the diagnosis of psychosis. *Acta Psychiatrica Scandinavica*, 54, 106–112.

Dalrymple N. J. (1995). Environmental support to develop flexibility and independence. In K.A. Quill (Ed.), *Teaching Children with Autism: Strategies to Enhance Communication and Socialization* (pp. 219–242). New York. Delmar.

Darr G. C. and Worden F. G. (1951). Case report twenty-eight years after an infantile autistic disorder. *American Journal of Orthopsychiatry*, 21, 559–569.

DeMyer M. K., Barton S., DeMyer W. E., Norton J. A., Allan J. and Steele R. (1973). Prognosis in autism: A follow-up study. *Journal of Autism and Childhood Schizophrenia*, 3, 199–246.

Dewey M. (1991). Living with Asperger's syndrome. In U. Frith (Ed.), *Autism and Asperger Syndrome* (pp. 184–206). Cambridge. Cambridge University Press.

Disabled Persons (Employment) Acts (1944, 1958); Employers' Obligations: Notes for Guidance. Employment Service, London.

Dixon H. (1990). *Sexuality and Mental Handicap: An Educator's Resource Book*. Cambridge. Learning Development Aids.

Dodge K., Schlundt D., Schocken I. and Delugach J. (1983). Competence and children's sociometric status: The role of peer group entries. *Merrill-Palmer Quarterly*, 29, 309–316.

Duker P. C., Welles K. A., Seys D., Rensen H., Vis A. and van der Berg G. (1991). Brief report: Effects of fenfluramine on communicative, stereotypic, and inappropriate behaviours of autistic-type mentally handicapped individuals. *Journal of Autism and Developmental Disorders*, 21, 355–364.

Durand B. M. (1990). *Severe Behavior Problems: A Functional Communication Approach*. New York. Guilford Press

Durand B. M. and Carr E. G. (1991). Functional communication training to reduce challenging behavior: Maintenance and application in new settings. *Journal of Applied Behavior Analysis*, 24, 251–254.

Durand B. M. and Crimmins D. B. (1988). Identifying the variables maintaining self-injurious behavior. *Journal of Autism and Developmental Disorders*, 18, 99–117.

Durand B. M. and Crimmins D. B. (1991). Teaching functionally equivalent responses as an intervention for challenging behaviour. In B. Remington (Ed.), *The Challenge of Severe Mental Handicap: A Behaviour Analytic Approach* (pp. 71–96). Chichester. Wiley.

Dykens E., Volkmar F. and Glick M. (1991). Thought disorder in high-functioning autistic adults. *Journal of Autism and Developmental Disorders*, 21, 303–314.

Egel A. L., Koegel R. L. and Schreibman L. (1980). Review of educational treatment procedures for autistic children. In L. Mann and D. Sabatino (Eds.), *Fourth Review of Special Education* (pp. 109–149). New York. Grune and Stratton.

Ehlers S. and Gillberg C. (1993). The epidemiology of Asperger Syndrome: A total population study. *Journal of Child Psychology and Psychiatry*, 34, 1327–1350.

Eisenberg L. (1956). The autistic child in adolescence. *American Journal of Psychiatry*, 1112, 607–612.

Eisenberg L. (1972). The classification of childhood psychosis reconsidered. *Journal of Autism and Childhood Schizophrenia*, 2, 338–342.

Evans G. (1995). Leisure activities for people with autism. In P. Howlin, R. Jordan and G. Evans, *Life Skills for People with Autism*. Distance Learning Course, University of Birmingham School of Education.

Everall I. P. and Le Couteur A. (1990). Fire-setting in an adolescent boy with Asperger's syndrome. *British Journal of Psychiatry*, 157, 284–287.

Foxx R. M., Kyle M. S., Faw G. D. and Bittle R. G. (1989). Problem solving skills training: Social validation and generalization. *Behavioral Residential Treatment*, 4, 269–287.

Frankel R. M., Leary M. and Kilman B. (1987). Building social skills through pragmatic analysis: Assessment and treatment implications for children with autism. In D. J. Cohen and A. M. Donnellan (Eds.), *Handbook of Autism and Developmental Disorders*. New York. Wiley.

Frith C. (1995). Brain mechanism for 'Having a Theory of Mind'. In J. Deakin (Ed.), *The Psychopharmacology of Social Communication and its Disorders*. Oxford. Oxford University Press.

Frith U. (1989). *Autism: Explaining the Enigma*. Oxford. Blackwell.

Frith U. (1991). *Autism and Asperger Syndrome*. Cambridge. Cambridge University Press.

Gabeney P. (1993). *Coping with Challenging Behaviour*. Unpublished m.s. Portfield School, Hampshire.

Ghaziuddin M., Tsai L. Y. and Ghaziuddin N. (1991). Depression in autistic disorder. *British Journal of Psychiatry*, 159, 721–723.

Ghaziuddin M., Tsai L. Y. and Ghaziuddin N. (1991a). Fluoxentine in autism with depression. *Journal of the American Academy of Child and Adolescent Psychiatry*, 30, 508–509.

Ghaziuddin M., Tsai L. Y. and Ghaziuddin N. (1991b). Brief report. Violence in Asperger Syndrome: A critique. *Journal of Autism and Developmental Disorders*, 21, 349–354.

Ghaziuddin M., Tsai L. Y. and Ghaziuddin N. (1992a). Brief report: A comparison of the diagnostic criteria for Asperger's Syndrome. *Journal of Autism and Developmental Disorders*, 22, 643–651.

Ghaziuddin M., Tsai L. Y. and Ghaziuddin N. (1992b). Co-morbidity of autistic disorder in children and adolescents. *European Journal of Child and Adolescent Psychiatry*, 1, 209–213.

Ghaziuddin M., Butler E., Tsai L. Y. and Ghaziuddin N. (1994). Is clumsiness a marker for Asperger's syndrome? *Journal of Intellectual Disability Research*, 38, 519–527.

Gilby K., Jones G. E. and Newson E. (1988). Autistic children in ordinary mainstream schools. Report to the Department of Health and DES (Report available from the Child Development Research Unit, Nottingham University).

Gill L. and Curbishley, L. (1994). COPE (*Compendium of post-16 education and training in residential establishments for young people with special needs*). Wiltshire Careers Service, Support Services Unit, County Hall, Trowbridge, Wiltshire.

Gillberg C. (1984). Infantile autism and other childhood psychoses in a Swedish urban region: Epidemiological aspects. *Journal of Child Psychology and Psychiatry*, 25, 35–43.

Gillberg C. (1985). Asperger's syndrome and recurrent psychosis – a case study. *Journal of Autism and Developmental Disorders*, 15, 389–397.

Gillberg C. (1992). Epilepsy. In C. Gillberg and M. Coleman (Eds.), *The Biology of the Autistic Syndromes*, 2nd Edition (pp. 60–73). Oxford. MacKeith Press.

Gillberg C. and Gillberg C. (1989). Asperger's syndrome: Some epidemiological considerations: A research note. *Journal of Child Psychology and Psychiatry*, 30, 631–638.

Gillberg C. and Steffenberg S. (1987). Outcome and prognostic factors in infantile autism and similar conditions: a population-based study of 46 cases followed through puberty. *Journal of Autism and Developmental Disorders*, 17, 272–288.

Goode S., Rutter M. and Howlin P. (1994, June). A twenty year follow-up of children with autism. Paper presented at the 13th biennial meeting of the International Society for the Study of Behavioral Development. Amsterdam, The Netherlands.

Goode S., Howlin P. and Rutter M. (in preparation). A cognitive and behavioural study of outcome in young adults with autism.

Gould G. A., Rigg M. and Bignell L. (1991). *The Higashi Experience: The Report of a Visit to the Boston Higashi School*. London. National Autistic Society Publications.

Graham J. (1994). The Interact Centre: An applied communication and vocational skills course for people with autism. Hanwell Community Centre, London.

Grandin T. (1991). Helping high-functioning autistics to succeed. *Asperger's Syndrome Support Network, Newsletter*, 3, Spring. London. N.A.S. Publications.

Grandin T. (1992). An inside view of autism. In E. Schopler and G. B. Mesibov (Eds.), *High-Functioning Individuals with Autism* (pp. 105–125). New York. Plenum Press.

Grandin T. (1995). The learning style of people with autism; An autobiography. In K. A. Quill (Ed), *Teaching Children with Autism*: *Strategies to Enhance Communication and Socialization*. (pp. 33–52). New York. Delmar.

Grandin T. and Scariano M. (1986). *Emergence Labelled Autistic*. Novato, Calif. Arena Press.

Gray C. A. (1995). Teaching children with autism to 'read' social situations. In A. Quill (Ed.), *Teaching Children with Autism*: *Strategies to Enhance Communication and Socialization*. (pp. 219–242). New York. Delmar.

Haddock G. and Slade P. D. (Eds.) (1995). *Cognitive-Behavioural Interventions with Psychiatric Disorders*. London: Routledge.

Hadwin J., Baron-Cohen S., Howlin P. and Hill K. (1996) Can we teach children with autism to understand emotions, belief and pretence? *Developmental Psychopathology*, 8(2).

Happé F. G. E. (1994). Current psychological theories of autism: the 'Theory of Mind' account and rival theories. *Journal of Child Psychology and Psychiatry*, 35, 215–230.

Happé F. G. E. and Frith U. (1995). Theory of mind in autism. In E. Schopler and G. B. Mesibov (eds), *Learning and Cognition in Autism*. New York. Plenum Press.

Haynes C. and Naidoo S. (1991). *Children with Specific Speech and Language Impairment. Clinics in Developmental Medicine*, 19. Oxford. Blackwell.

Hobson P. (1993). *Autism and the Development of Mind*. London. Erlbaum.

Hollins S. (1994). *Going to Court*. London. The Sovereign Series.

Hollins S. and Hutchinson D. (1993). *Peter's New Home/A New Home in the Community*. London. The Sovereign Series.

Hollins S. and Roth T. (1994). *Hug Me – Touch Me*. London. The Sovereign Series.

Hollins S. and Sireling L. (1994). *When Mum Died/When Dad Died*. London. The Sovereign Series.

Hollins S., Murphy G. and Clare I. (1996). *When You're Accused*. London. The Sovereign Series.

Howlin P. (1989). Changing approaches to communication training with autistic children. *British Journal of Disorders of Communication*, 24, 151–168.

Howlin, P. (1991). Supported employment schemes for people with autism. Lecture presented to the National Autistic Society. Annual Conference, London, October 1991.

Howlin P. (1994a). Special educational treatment. In M. Rutter, E. Taylor, and B. Hersov (Eds.), *Child and Adolescent Psychiatry: Modern Approaches*, 3rd edn. Oxford. Blackwell.

Howlin P. (1994b). Facilitated communication and autism: Are the claims for success justified? *Communication*, 28, 2, 10–12.

Howlin P. and Clements J. (1995). Is it possible to assess the impact of abuse on children with pervasive developmental disorders? *Journal of Autism and Developmental Disorders*, 25, 1–17.

Howlin P. and Peacock G. (1994). Supported employment. *Communication*, 28, 2, 3–4.

Howlin P. and Rutter M. (1987). *Treatment of Autistic Children*. Chichester. Wiley.

Howlin P. and Yates P. (1996) Increasing social communication skills in young adults with autism attending a social group. (Submitted for publication).

Irlen H. (1995). Viewing the world through rose tinted glasses. *Communication*, 29, 1, 8–9.

Jolliffe T., Lansdown R. and Robinson T. (1992). *Autism: A Personal Account*. London. The National Autistic Society.

Jones G. and Newson E. (1992). Summary report on the provision for children and adults with autism in England and Wales. Unpublished report: Child Development Research Unit, Nottingham University.

Jordan R. and Powell S. (1995). *Understanding and Teaching Children with Autism*. Chichester. Wiley.

Kanner L. (1943). Autistic disturbances of affective contact. *Nervous Child*, 2, 217–250.

Kanner L. (1949). Problems of nosology and psychodynamics of early infantile autism. *American Journal of Orthopsychiatry*, 19, 416–426.

Kanner L. (1973). *Childhood Psychosis: Initial Studies and New Insights*. New York. Winston/Wiley.

Kanner L. and Eisenberg L. (1956). Early infantile autism 1943–1955. *American Journal of Orthopsychiatry*, 26, 55–65.

Kaufman B. (1981). *A Miracle to Believe in*. New York. Doubleday.

Kerbeshian J. and Burd L. (1987). Are schizophreniform symptoms present in attenuated form in children with Tourette's disorder and other developmental disorders? *Canadian Journal of Psychiatry*, 32, 123–135.

Kerbeshian J., Burd L., Randall T., Martsolf J. and Jalal S. (1990). Autism, profound mental retardation and atypical bipolar disorder in a 33-year-old female with a deletion of 15q12. *Journal of Mental Deficiency Research*, 34, 205–210.

Kitahara K. (1983). *Daily Life Therapy* (Vol 1, Tokyo). Musashino Higashi Gakuen School.

Kobayashi R., Murata T. and Yashinaga K. (1992). A follow-up study of 201 children with autism in Kyushu and Yamguchia, Japan. *Journal of Autism and Developmental Disorders*, 22, 395–411.

Komoto J., Usui S. and Hirata J. (1984). Infantile autism and affective disorder. *Journal of Autism and Developmental Disorders*, 14, 81–84.

Krantz P. J. and McClannahan L. E. (1993) Teaching children with autism to initiate to peers: Effects of a script-fading procedure. *Journal of Applied Behavior Analysis*, 26, 121–132.

Kurita H. and Nakayasu N. (1994). Brief report: An autistic male presenting seasonal affective disorder (SAD) and trichotillomania. *Journal of Autism and Developmental Disorders*, 24, 687–692.

Lainhart J. E. and Folstein S. E. (1994). Affective disorders in people with autism: A review of published cases. *Journal of Autism and Developmental Disorders*, 24, 587–601.

Lalli J. S., Pinter-Lalli E., Mace F. C. and Murphy D. M. (1991). Training interactional behaviours of adults with developmental disabilities: A systematic replication and extension. *Journal of Applied Behavior Analysis*, 24, 167–174.

Langdell T. (1978). Recognition of faces: An approach to the study of autism. *Journal of Child Psychology and Psychiatry*, 19, 255–268.

Layton T. L. and Watson L. R. (1995). Enhancing communication in nonverbal children with autism. In K.A. Quill (ed.), *Teaching Children with Autism: Strategies to Enhance Communication and Socialization* (pp. 73–104). New York. Delmar.

Linter C. M. (1987). Short-cycle manic-depressive psychosis in a mentally handicapped child without family history: A case report. *British Journal of Psychiatry*, 151, 554–555.

Lockyer L. and Rutter M. (1969). A five to fifteen year follow-up study of infantile psychosis: III Psychological aspects. *British Journal of Psychiatry*, 115, 865–882.

Lockyer L. and Rutter M. (1970). A five to fifteen year follow-up study of infantile psychosis: IV Patterns of cognitive abilities. *British Journal of Social and Clinical Psychology*, 9, 152–163.

Lord C. (1984). The development of peer relations in children with autism. *Applied Developmental Psychology*, 1, 165–230.

Lord C. and Rutter M. (1994). Autism and pervasive developmental disorders. In M. Rutter, E. Taylor and L. Hersov (Eds.), *Child and Adolescent Psychiatry: Modern Approaches*, 3rd Edition (pp. 569–593). Oxford. Blackwell.

Lord C. and Schopler E. (1985). Differences in sex ratios in autism as a function of measured intelligence. *Journal of Autism and Development Disorders*, 15, 185–193.

Lord C., Rutter M. and Le Couteur A. (1994). Autism Diagnostic Interview – Revised: A revised version of a diagnostic interview for care-givers of individuals with possible pervasive developmental disorders. *Journal of Autism and Development Disorders*, 24, 659–686.

Lotter B. (1974a). Factors related to outcome in autistic children. *Journal of Autism and Childhood Schizophrenia*, 4, 263–277.

Lotter B. (1974b). Social adjustment and placement of autistic children in Middlesex: A follow-up study. *Journal of Autism and Childhood Schizophrenia*, 4, 11–32.

Lotter, B. (1978). Follow-up studies. In M. Rutter and E. Schopler (eds), *Autism: A Reappraisal of Concepts and Treatment*. New York. Plenum Press.

Lovaas O. I. (1987). Behavioral treatment and normal educational and intellectual functioning in young autistic children. *Journal of Consulting and Clinical Psychology*, 55, 3–9

Lowndes B. (1994). Supported living for people with Asperger's syndrome. *Communication*, 28, 13.

McCaughrin W. B., Ellis W. K., Rusch F. R. and Heal L. W. (1993). Cost-effectiveness of supported employment. *Mental Retardation*, 31, 41–48.

Macdonald H., Rutter M., Howlin P., Rios P., Le Couteur A., Evered C. and

Folstein S. (1989). Recognition and expression of emotional cues by autistic and normal adults. *Journal of Child Psychology and Psychiatry*, 30, 865–878.

MacDuff G. S., Krantz P. J. and McClannahan L. E. (1993). Teaching children with autism to use photographic activity schedules: maintenance and generalisation – a complex response chain. *Journal of Applied Behavior Analysis*, 26, 89–97.

McEachin J. J., Smith T. and Lovaas O.I. (1993). Long-term outcome for children with autism who received early intensive behavioral treatment. *American Journal of Mental Retardation*, 97, 359–372.

Manjiviona J. and Prior M. (1995). Comparison of Asperger Syndrome and high-functioning autistic children on a test of motor impairment. *Journal of Autism and Developmental Disorders*, 25, 23–40.

Matthews A. (1996). Developing a support model within employment for adults with autism and Asperger's syndrome. In H. Morgan, *Adults with Autism*. Cambridge University Press.

Maurice C. (1993). *Let Me Hear Your Voice*. New York. Knopf.

Mawhood L. (1995a). Autism and developmental language disorder: Implications from a follow-up in early adult life. Unpublished PhD thesis. University of London.

Mawhood L., (1995b). A comparative follow-up study of young adults with autism and severe developmental language disorders. Unpublished PhD thesis. University of London.

Mawson D., Grounds A. and Tantam D. (1985). Violence in Asperger's syndrome: A case study. *British Journal of Psychiatry*, 147, 566–569.

Melone M. B. and Lettick A. L. (1983). Sex education at Benhaven. In E. Schopler and G. B. Mesibov (Eds.), *Autism in Adolescents and Adults* (pp. 169–186). New York. Plenum Press.

MENCAP (1989). *A London-wide Directory of Opportunities in Employment for People with a Learning Disability*. MENCAP, London Division, London. (Directories for other areas also available).

MENCAP (1990a). *A London-wide Directory of Opportunities in Adult Education for People with a Learning Disability*. MENCAP, London Division, London. (Directories for other areas also available).

MENCAP (1990b). *A London-wide Directory of Specially Designed Courses in Further Education for People with a Learning Disability*. MENCAP Education, Training and Employment Services, London. (Directories for other areas also available).

Mesibov G. B. (1986). A cognitive program for teaching social behaviors to verbal autistic adolescents and adults. In E. Schopler and E. B. Mesibov (Eds.), *Social Behavior in Autism*, pp. 265–283. New York. Plenum Press.

Mesibov G. B. (1992). Treatment issues with high-functioning adolescents and adults with autism. In E. Schopler and E. B. Mesibov (Eds.), *High-Functioning Individuals with Autism* (pp. 143–156). New York. Plenum Press.

Mesibov G. B. (1993). Treatment outcome is encouraging; Comments on McEachin et al. *American Journal of Mental Retardation*, 97, 379–380.

Mesibov G. B., Schopler E. and Sloan J. L. (1983). Service development for adolescents and adults in North Carolina's TEACCH Program. In

E. Schopler and E. B. Mesibov (Eds.), *Autism in Adolescents and Adults* (pp. 411–432). New York. Plenum Press.

Meyer L. M., Fox A., Schermer A., Ketelsen D., Montan N., Mayer K. and Cole D. (1987). The effects of teaching intrusion on social play interactions between children with autism and their non-handicapped peers. *Journal of Autism and Developmental Disorders*, 17, 315–322.

Miedzianik D. C. (1994). *An Autobiography*. Child Development Centre, Nottingham University.

Mittler P., Gillies S. and Jukes E. (1966). Prognosis in psychotic children: Report of a follow-up study. *Journal of Mental Deficiency Research*, 10, 73–83.

Moon M. S., Inge K. J., Wehman P., Brooke P. and Barcus J. M. (1990). *Helping Persons with Severe Mental Retardation Get and Keep Employment: Supported Employment Strategies and Outcomes*. Baltimore, Maryland. Paul H. Brooks.

Morgan H. (1996). *Adults with Autism*. Cambridge. Cambridge University Press.

Murphy G. and Clare I. (1991). MIETS: A service option for people with mild mental handicaps and challenging behaviour or psychiatric problems. 2: Assessment, treatment, and outcome for service users and service effectiveness. *Mental Handicap Research*, 4, 180–206.

National Autistic Society (1995). *Claiming What's Yours: Guide to benefits for people with autism and their carers*. London. National Autistic Society.

Newson E. and Jones G. E. (1994). An evaluative and comparative study of current interventions for children with autism. Unpublished report. Child Development Research Unit, Nottingham University.

Newson E., Dawson M. and Everard T. (1982). The natural history of able autistic people: their management and functioning in a social context. Unpublished report to the Department of Health and Social Security, London. Summary published in four parts in *Communication*, Vols 19–21 (1984–1985).

Newton J. T. and Sturmey P. (1991). The Motivation Assessment Scale: inter-rater reliability and internal consistency in a British sample. *Journal of Mental Deficiency, Research*, 35, 472–474.

O'Connor M. and Hermelin B. (1984). Idiot savant calendrical calculators: Maths or Memory? *Psychological Medicine*, 14, 801–806.

O'Connor M. and Hermelin B. (1988). Low intelligence and special abilities. *Annotation: Journal of Child Psychology and Psychiatry*, 29, 391–396.

Oliver C. (1995). Self-injurious behaviour in children with learning disabilities: Recent advances in assessment intervention. *Annotation: Journal of Child Psychology and Psychiatry. 36*, 909–928.

Owens R. G. and MacKinnon S. (1993). The functional analysis of challenging behaviours: some conceptual and theoretical problems. In R. S. P. Jones and C. B. Eayrs (Eds.), *Challenging Behaviour and Intellectual Disability: A Psychological Perspective*. Clevedon, Avon. BILD Publications.

Park C. (1992). Autism into art: A handicap transfigured. In E. Schopler and G. B. Mesibov (Eds.), *High-Functioning Individuals with Autism* (pp. 250–258). New York. Plenum Press.

Peterson C. C. and Siegal M. (1995). Deafness, conversation and theory of mind. *Child Psychology and Psychiatry*, 36, 459–474.

Petty L. K., Ornitz E. M., Michelman J. D. and Zimmerman E. G. (1984). Autistic children who become schizophrenic. *Archives of General Psychiatry*, 41, 129–135.

Pozner A. and Hammond J. (1993). *An Evaluation of Supported Employment Initiatives for Disabled People*. Employment Department, Sheffield.

Premack V. (1959). Towards empirical behavior laws: 1: Positive reinforcement. *Psychological Review*, 66, 11–17.

Prizant B. and Schuler A. (1987). Facilitating communication: Language approaches. In D. Cohen and A. Donnellan (Eds.), *Handbook of Autism and Pervasive Developmental Disorders*. New York. Wiley.

Quill K. A. (1995a). *Teaching Children with Autism: Strategies to Enhance Communication and Socialization*. New York. Delmar.

Quill K. A. (1995b). Enhancing children's social-communicative interactions. In *Teaching Children with Autism: Strategies to Enhance Communication and Socialization* (pp. 163–192). New York. Delmar.

Quill K. A., Gurry S. and Larkin A. (1989). Daily life therapy: A Japanese model for educating children with autism. *Journal of Autism and Developmental Disorders*, 19, 637–640.

Quirk-Hodgson L. (1995). Solving social-behavioral problems through the use of visually supported communication. In K. A. Quill (ed.), *Teaching Children with Autism: Strategies to Enhance Communication and Socialization* (pp. 265–286). New York. Delmar.

Reid A. H. (1976) Psychiatric disturbances in the mentally handicapped. *Proceedings of the Royal Society of Medicine*, 69, 509–512.

Richer J. and Zapello M. (1989). Changing social behaviour: The place of holding. *Communication*, 23, 35–39.

Ricks D. M. and Wing D. L. (1975). Language, communication, and the use of symbols in normal and autistic children. *Journal of Autism and Childhood Schizophrenia*, 5, 191–221.

Rimland B. (1994a). Comparative effects of treatment on child's behavior (drugs, therapies, schooling, and several non-treatment events). *Autism Research Review*, Publication 34b.

Rimland B. (1994b). Information pack on drug treatments for autism. *Autism Research Review International*, Information Pack P6.

Rimland B. (1994c). Information pack on vitamins allergies and nutritional treatments for autism. *Autism Research Review International*, Information Pack P24.

Rumsey J. M., Rapoport J. L. and Sceery W. R. (1985). Autistic children as adults: Psychiatric social and behavioural outcomes. *Journal of the American Academy of Child Psychiatry*, 24, 465–473.

Rutter M. (1970). Autistic children: Infancy to adulthood. *Seminars in Psychiatry*, 2, 435–450.

Rutter M. (1972). Childhood schizophrenia reconsidered. *Journal of Autism and Childhood Schizophrenia*, 2, 315–337.

Rutter M. (1983). School effects on pupil progress: Research findings and policy implications. *Child Development*, 54, 1–29.

Rutter M. and Bartak L. (1973). Special educational treatment of autistic children: A comparative study. II Follow-up findings and implications for services. *Journal of Child Psychology and Psychiatry*, 14, 241–270.

Rutter M. and Lockyer L. (1967). A five to fifteen year follow-up study of infantile psychosis: I Description of sample. *British Journal of Psychiatry*, 113, 1169–1182.

Rutter M. and Schopler E. (Eds.) (1978). *Autism: Re-appraisal of concepts and treatments*. New York. Plenum Press.

Rutter M., Greenfield D. and Lockyer L. (1967). A five to fifteen year follow-up study of infantile psychosis: II Social and behavioural outcome. *British Journal of Psychiatry*, 113, 1183–1199.

Rutter M., Mawhood L. and Howlin P. (1992). Language delay and social development. In P. Fletcher and D. Hall (Eds.), *Specific Speech and Language Disorders in Children* (pp. 63–78). London: Whurr.

Rydell P. J. and Mirenda P. (1994). The effects of high and low constraint utterances on the production of immediate and delayed echolalia in young children with autism. *Journal of Autism and Developmental Disorders*, 24, 719–730.

Rydell P. J. and Prizant B. (1995). Assessment and intervention strategies for children who use echolalia. In K. A. Quill (Ed.) *Teaching Children with Autism: Strategies to Enhance Communication and Socialization* (pp. 105–132). New York. Delmar.

Sacks O. (1993). A neurologist's notebook: An anthropologist on Mars. *New Yorker*, 27 December pp. 106–125.

Schopler E. and Mesibov G. B. (1983). *Autism in Adolescents and Adults*. Current Issues in Autism. New York. Plenum Press.

Schopler E. and Mesibov G. B. (1986). *Social Behavior in Autism*. Current Issues in Autism. New York. Plenum Press.

Schopler E. and Mesibov G. B. (1992). *High-Functioning Individuals with Autism*. Current Issues in Autism. New York. Plenum Press.

Schopler E., Short A. and Mesibov G. (1989). Relation of behavioral treatment to 'normal functioning'. Comment on Lovaas. *Journal of Consulting and Clinical Psychology*, 57, 162–164.

Schuler A. L., Peck C. A., Willard C. and Theimer K. (1989). Assessment of communicative means and functions through interview: Assessing the communicative capabilities of individuals with limited language. *Seminars in Speech and Language*, 10, 51–61.

Scragg P. and Shah A. (1994). Prevalence of Asperger's Syndrome in a secure hospital. *British Journal of Psychiatry, 161*, 679–682.

Shafer M. S., Wehman E., Kregel J. and West M. (1990). National supported employment initiative: A preliminary analysis. *American Journal on Mental Retardation*, 95, 316–327.

Shane H. C. (1994). *Facilitated Communication: The Clinical and Social Phenomenon*. San Diego. Singular Press.

Sheldon B. (1995). *Cognitive-behavioural Therapy: Research, Practice and Philosophy*. London. Routledge.

Short A. (1984). Short-term treatment outcome using parents as therapists for their own autistic children. *Journal of Child Psychology and Psychiatry*, 25, 443–485.

Sigafoos J., Kerr M. and Roberts D. (1994). Inter-rater reliability of the

Motivation Assessment Scale: Failure to replicate with aggressive behaviour. *Research in Developmental Disabilities*, 15, 333–342.

Sigman M., Mundy P., Sherman T. and Ungerer J. (1986). Social interactions of autistic, mentally retarded and normal children and their care-givers. *Journal of Child Psychology and Psychiatry*, 27, 647–656.

Sinclair J. (1992). Bridging the gap: An inside out view of autism (Or, do you know what I don't know?). In E. Schopler and G. B. Mesibov (Eds.), *High-Functioning Individuals with Autism* (pp. 294–302). New York. Plenum Press.

Smith M. D. (1990). *Autism and Life in the Community: Successful Interventions for Behavioral Challenges*. Baltimore, Maryland. Paul H. Brooks.

Snow M. E., Hertzig M. E. and Shapiro T. (1987). Expression of emotion in young autistic children. *Journal of the American Academy of Child and Adolescent Psychiatry*, 26, 836–838.

Sovner R. (1988a). Anticonvulsant drug therapy of neuropsychiatric disorders in mentally retarded persons. In S. McElroy and H. G. Pope, Jr (Eds.), *Use of Anticonvulsants in Psychiatry* (pp. 169–181) Clinton, New Jersey. Oxford Health Care.

Sovner R. (1988b). Behavioral psychopharmacology: A new psychiatric subspeciality. In J. Stark, F. J. Menolascino, M. Albarielli *et al.* (Eds.), *Mental Retardation and Mental Health: Classification, Diagnosis, Treatment, Services* (pp. 229–242). New York, Springer Verlag.

Sovner R. (1989). The use of valporate in the treatment of mentally retarded persons with typical and atypical bipolar disorders. *Journal of Clinical Psychiatry*, 50 (Suppl. 3), 40–43.

Spence S. H. (1991). Developments in the assessments of social skills and social competence in children. *Behaviour Change*, 8, 148–166.

Starr E. (1993). Teaching the appearance – reality distinction to children with autism. Paper presented at the British Psychological Society Development Psychology Section Annual Conference. Birmingham.

Steege M. W., Wacker D. P., Berg W. K., Sigrand K. K. and Cooper L. J. (1989). The use of behavioral assessment to prescribe and evaluate treatments for severely handicapped children. *Journal of Applied Behavior Analysis*, 22, 23–33.

Stehli A. (1992). *The Sound of a Miracle: A Child's Triumph over Autism.* Fourth Estate Publications, USA.

Steingard R. and Biederman J. (1987). Lithium responsive manic-like symptoms in two individuals with autism and mental retardation. *Journal of American Academy of Child and Adolescent Psychiatry*, 26, 932–935.

Sugai G. and White W. J. (1986). Effects of using object self-stimulation as a reinforcer on the pre-vocational work rates of an autistic child. *Journal of Autism and Developmental Disorders*, 16, 459–474.

Sverd J., Montero G. and Gurevich N. (1993). Brief report: Cases for an association between Tourette's syndrome, autistic disorder and schizophrenia-like disorder. *Journal of Autism and Developmental Disorders*, 23, 407–414.

Swettenham J. (1996). Can children with autism be taught to understand false beliefs using computers? *Journal of Child Psychology and Psychiatry* 37, 157–166.

Swettenham J., Gomez J. C., Baron-Cohen S. and Walsh S. (1995). What's inside someone's head? Conceiving of the mind as a camera helps children with autism acquire an alternative 'theory of mind'. (Unpublished m.s.)

Szatmari P., Bartolucci G., Finlayson A. and Krames L. (1986). A vote for Asperger's syndrome. *Journal of Autism and Developmental Disorders*, 16, 515–517.

Szatmari P., Bartolucci G. and Bremner R. S. (1989a). Asperger's syndrome and autism: A comparison of early history and outcome. *Developmental Medicine and Child Neurology*, 31, 709–720.

Szatmari P., Bartolucci G., Bremner R. S., Bond S. and Rich S. (1989b). A follow-up study of high-functioning autistic children. *Journal of Autism and Developmental Disorders*, 19, 213–226.

Tantam D. (1991). Asperger's Syndrome in adulthood. In U. Frith (Ed.), *Autism and Asperger Syndrome* (pp. 147–183). Cambridge. Cambridge University Press.

Taylor J. (1990). Adolescents and early adulthood: The needs of the more able young adult. In K. Ellis (Ed.), *Autism: Professional Perspectives and Practice*. London. Chapman and Hall.

Tharinger D., Horton C. V. and Millea S. (1990). Sexual abuse and exploitation of children and adults with mental retardation and other handicaps. *Child Abuse and Neglect*, 14, 301–312.

Tryan G. S. (1979). A review and critique of thought-stopping research. *Journal of Behaviour Therapy and Experimental Psychiatry*, 10, 32–39.

US Bureau of Justice Statistics (1987). In *Adolescents* (Fall 1989) Princeton, New Jersey. The Robert Wood Johnson Foundation.

Van Berckelaer-Onnes. I. (1994). Adult programmes – Paper presented at National Autistic Society International Conference. 'Autism on the Agenda'. Leeds, 8–10 April 1994.

Van Bourgondien M. E. and Mesibov G. B. (1987). Humor in high-functioning autistic adults. *Journal of Autism and Developmental Disorders*, 17, 417–424.

Venter A., Lord C. and Schopler E. (1992). A follow-up study of high-functioning autistic children. *Journal of Child Psychology and Psychiatry*, 33, 489–507.

Volkmar F. R. and Cohen D. J. (1985). The experience of infantile autism: A first-person account by Tony W. *Journal of Autism and Developmental Disorders*, 15, 47–54.

Walker M. (1980). Makaton Vocabulary (revised edition). Surrey. The Makaton Vocabulary Development Project.

Warnock M. (1978). *Special Educational Needs. Report of the Committee of Enquiry into the Education of Handicapped Children and Young People*. London. HMSO.

Watkins J. M., Asarnov R. F. and Tanguay P. (1988). Symptom development in childhood onset schizophrenia. *Journal of Child Psychology and Psychiatry*, 29, 865–878.

Wehman P., Moon M. S., Everson J. M., Wood W. and Barcus J. M. (1988). *Transition from School to Work. New Challenges for Youth with Severe Disabilities*. Baltimore, Maryland. Paul H. Brookes.

Welch M. (1988). *Holding Time*. London. Century Hutchinson.

Werry J. S. (1992). Child and adolescent (early onset) schizophrenia: a review in light of DSM-III R. *Journal of Autism and Developmental Disorders*, 22, 601–624.

Wertheimer A. (1992). *Changing Lives: Supported Employment for People with Learning Disabilities*. National Development Team, Manchester.

Williams D. (1992). *Nobody Nowhere*. London. Corgi Books.

Williams D. (1994). *Somebody Somewhere*. London. Corgi Books.

Williams T. I. (1989). A social skills group for autistic children. *Journal of Autism and Developmental Disorders*, 19, 143–156.

Wiltshire S. (1987). *Drawings*, Selected and with an Introduction by Sir Hugh Cassan. London. Dent.

Wing L. (1981). Asperger's syndrome: A clinical account. *Psychological Medicine*, 11, 115–129.

Wing L. (1986). Clarification on Asperger's syndrome. Letter to the Editor. *Journal of Autism and Developmental Disorders*, 16, 513–515.

Wing L. (1993). The definition and prevalence of autism: A review. *European Child and Adolescent Psychiatry*, 2, 61–74.

Wing L. and Gould J. (1978). Systematic recording of behaviors and skills of retarded and psychotic children. *Journal of Autism and Childhood Schizophrenia*, 8, 79–97.

Wolery M., Kirk K. and Gast D. L. (1985). Stereotypic behavior as a reinforcer: Effects and side-effects. *Journal of Autism and Developmental Disorders*, 15, 149–162.

Wolfberg P. (1995). Enhancing children's play. In K. A. Quill (Ed.) *Teaching Children with Autism: Strategies to Enhance Communication and Socialization* (pp. 193–218). New York. Delmar.

Wolfberg P. J. and Schuler A. L. (1993). Integrated play groups: A model for promoting the social and cognitive dimensions of play. *Journal of Autism and Developmental Disorders*, 23, 1–23.

Wolff S. (1991). Schizoid personality in childhood and adult life. 1: The vagaries of diagnostic labelling. *British Journal of Psychiatry*, 159, 615–620.

Wolff S. and Barlow A. (1979). Schizoid personality in childhood: A comparative study of schizoid, autistic and normal children. *Journal of Child Psychology and Psychiatry*, 20, 29–46.

Wolff S. and Chick J. (1980). Schizoid personality in childhood: A controlled follow-up study. *Psychological Medicine*, 10, 85–100.

Wolff S. and McGuire R. J. (1995). Schizoid personality in girls: A follow-up study. What are the links with Asperger's syndrome? *Journal of Child Psychology and Psychiatry*, 36, 793–818.

World Health Organization (1993). *ICD–10 International Statistical Classification of Diseases and Related Health Problems, 10th review*. Geneva. WHO.

Young R. L. and Nettlebeck C. (1994). The 'intelligence' of calendrical calculators. *American Journal on Mental Retardation*, 99, 186–200.

Zarcone J. R., Rodgers E. A., Iwata B. A., Rourke D. A. and Dorsey M. F. (1991). Reliability analysis of the Motivation Assessment Scale: A failure to replicate. *Research and Developmental Disabilities*, 12, 349–360.

Index